# Break Out
# of
# PR Prison

## Make & Measure Your Own
## News in an Era of Crisis

## Nick Winkler

Nick Winkler

# THE WINKLER GROUP
## STRATEGIC COMMUNICATIONS

**www.thewinklergroup.net**

Copyright © 2012 Nick Winkler
The Winkler Group
Cover art by Shelly Perlman
All rights reserved.
ISBN-10: 0985789107
ISBN-13: 978-0-9857891-0-7

*To Ron Anderson for sowing the seed. Thank you.*
*-NRW*

## Contents

# Introduction

A secret prison exists exclusively for corporate Public Relations staffs. The prison is overcrowded- picture thousands of white-knuckled PR staffers clutching cold prison bars, screaming at the tops of their lungs, and creating a deafening roar so loud no one outside the prison can decipher individual messages.

Outside the prison are the corporation's various publics: customers, media, regulators, elected officials, shareholders, and competitors. They stare at the PR prisoners, who all sound and look alike dressed in their PR prison suits.

None are fully hearing your corporation's key messages.

And none seem to care.

They are having their own conversations about your corporation, interacting with one another, sculpting and massaging your corporation's reputation while your PR staff sits helplessly encased in a tomb of concrete and steel.

It's a prison corporate PR staffs created themselves.

Creativity in regard to innovative narrative steering has been bottled. Any that oozes out is quickly swabbed away by a risk averse corporate culture that would rather be safe than exceptional. A culture that values those who create comfort rather than waves.

Corporate public relations is often a world closed to outsiders. Unfriendly to those with ideas that run counter to conventional wisdom and traditional PR techniques. Corporate PR often walls itself off from the discomfort and uncertainty of change. Change that is ultimately forced upon it.

By then it's too late.

Outside firms are hired to do the heavy lifting corporate PR staffs have been told they cannot. This welfare further robs organizations of the genius they mistake for risky boat rocking.

Corporate PR staffs become fat and sick. As long as they have outside firms to rely on for medicine to cure their ills they'll remain dependent.

There's a better way.

Rather than trying to yell louder to communicate with various publics, organizations with smart PR staffs whisper. Screams are lost in today's digital roar. Whispering forces people to lean in and listen. It forces them to invest in your message.

The cookie cutter, one-size-fits-all PR being practiced today ignores the complexities and transformations inherent in the way content is now disseminated and consumed. Mistaking worn out traditional PR tactics for industry heirlooms worthy of generational passage is a crime that has landed many in the prison.

It's time to break out of PR prison.

Doing so requires organizations to disrupt the way modern media content flows. It requires organizations to begin making and measuring their own premier content in an era of constant crisis.

Assumptions must be shredded.

Traditional PR must be quit cold turkey.

Organizations must reinvent themselves as smart PR staffs.

Rather than continuing to run the gauntlet with average content and outdated distribution methods and hoping the digital guillotine won't hack your reputation to death, smart PR staffs must learn to make the digital guillotine run toward them.

Taunt the guillotine and it'll dull itself.

Becoming a disruptive content generator that upends the flow of media content requires a physical and mental transformation. It's an awkward and public transformation. One that can initially feel humiliating. One that comes with plenty of angst and pain.

Transforming yourself into a smart PR staff requires you to shed the traditional PR smock that has kept you safe and secure for so long.

It requires that you be naked.

People will stare. They'll gawk. They'll wonder whether you've lost your mind.

But don't you want them to stare?

Isn't that the point?

Breaking out will require corporate PR staffs to acknowledge new realities; that corporations are to some degree in a constant state of crisis, that a new group of influencers has emerged from technology and the ashes of traditional media, and that time is no longer a friend.

Corporations unprepared for these realities will not have ample time to respond as they wish.

Most organizations remain selfish, company-centric, and intellectually unwilling to bring about the change necessary to position themselves as exceptional leaders. Reinventing how corporate PR staffs think is one of the greatest challenges an organization faces. Corporations must mentally become media-centric and have a rich understanding of the economic and qualitative changes affecting media dissemination and consumption.

Why?

These changes are threats to your company's reputation and profitability. Intimately understanding these changes, creating content to thrive in a new world, and acquiring the ability to measure results from these efforts against specific objectives will mitigate risk to your company's reputation. It'll also establish your corporation as an industry thought leader, and allow your corporation to leverage its relationships to increase operational efficiencies.

Corporate PR staffs must become innovative idea generators. To disrupt the modern flow of media content, corporations must discard traditional public relations assumptions and clichés. PR staffs must transform themselves into high-tech content generation companies existing solely to support, protect, and enhance the larger company's reputation.

Nick Winkler

What were once critical whispers in a crowded room have now been amplified by technology and further magnified by the push toward increased disclosure. Combine this with a financially and ethically gutted traditional media that is eager to seek out and repeat messages detrimental to a corporation's reputation, and today's corporate communications challenges are formidable.

Embracing the change does not mean submitting to it. In fact, the smartest corporations reset the rules that govern today's media content flow. Right now the rules do not favor corporations. They favor the original rule makers- the media. Creating content and controlling portions of the toll road over which the content travels allows an organization a greater potential to steer a narrative.

To stand out in a world cluttered with messages, corporate PR staffs must begin making and measuring their own news.

The pages that follow will challenge long-held corporate PR beliefs. Some of the strategies and concepts discussed are counterintuitive, controversial, and will likely be voraciously criticized by current public relations practitioners.

I welcome the debate.

The intent is to poke holes in conventional wisdom and become an innovative industry leader by transforming corporate PR staffs and how they communicate. Organizations that resist or refuse change will blend in with other organizations that continue relying on stale and ineffective PR techniques. They'll survive with the status quo. But that's all.

This book is for organizations that want more.

The pages ahead provide an innovative blueprint aimed at triggering intense questioning of accepted PR assumptions. This book will challenge smart PR staffs to place a premium on candor rather than comfort. To embrace unconventionality instead of the status quo.

Optimizing corporate PR staffs in this manner will eliminate the need to hire outside Public Relations agencies for many of the tasks they are currently hired to complete. Transforming corporate PR staffs will increase efficiency, better prepare a company to anticipate crises, and build a relational foundation on which a corporation's reputation can best be protected and enhanced. Corporations that make this uncomfortable transition will also reap financial rewards.

As an Investigative Television News Reporter whose work has been featured on ABC, CNN, FOX News, and network affiliates nationwide, I have routinely uncovered and exposed corruption, waste, and illegal activity. Having designed, engineered, and executed crises targeting corporations, governments, and elected officials, I've seen firsthand how most make matters worse for themselves. The crises I've created have resulted in employment terminations, the filing of criminal charges, and people being imprisoned. Even worse, my investigations have caused entities to lose their most valuable asset- the reputations they have spent lifetimes nurturing.

This book identifies the public relations mistakes made during crises and elsewhere, surrounds them with context and perspective gained from an award-winning career on television, and creates a high-level framework to optimize corporate PR staffs. It also equips corporations with unconventional metrics specifically designed to measure whether transformed PR staffs are successfully achieving objectives.

You'll notice four pivot points scattered along the road ahead. Pivots are simply brief time-outs along the way where we'll pivot away from our overarching goal of becoming premier content creators and examine topics that may initially appear only mildly related to our main objective. In reality though, these pivot points are opportunities to explore topics that'll directly impact how we create premier content during times of stress. We'll investigate these topics from the eyes of a content creator to identify transformative opportunities. Pivot points will illustrate how a state of constant crisis, the birth of new influencers, and continual measurement connect with the content you'll create.

The book will also teach you:

- How to avoid being eaten by idea cannibals
- How to make news like a terrorist
- Why your PR staff is no Nolan Ryan
- Why you're pregnant with ideas
- How to measure fear and character
- Where to find a crystal ball
- Why good ideas are promiscuous
- How to wean yourself from PR welfare
- Why you should practice PR naked
- Why crises are tougher to spot than pornography
- How to avoid being burned by a technological wildfire
- How to starve a crisis
- Why you should learn to box like a banker
- How to divorce fear
- How to find your PR Messiah

# Reinventing PR

*T*he race is on.
*Do not let someone else win the right to steer your narrative.*

# Smart PR

Everything is smarter these days: appliances, farm irrigation systems, predictive analytics programs. Smart innovations boost efficiency, conserve energy, save money, and warn us before something bad happens. At their core, smart innovations deliver content that produce real-time benefits. Public Relations must smarten and sharpen to do the same.

Smart PR disrupts traditional public relations models which are transparently selfish. Smart PR trades immediate gratification for a longer term return. It creates value and is unconventionally delivered to others. For free. Initially, smart PR appears to lack a clear benefit for the benefit creator.

Creating smart PR requires an investment of time and money. Smart PR is given away for free. Organizations must seek out critics, detractors, and others who have the power to hurt the organization. These are the people smart PR is given to. These are the people we are to create value for. These are the people we seek to enhance and create benefits for.

Smart PR is not something a corporation can buy. It must be woven into the culture of an organization. It cannot be faked. It is a mindset. It is principled and flexible and requires those creating it to be so as well. It requires a service minded approach to content generation.

Smart PR is beautiful because of its simplicity; create something valuable and give it away. This beauty will be misidentified initially. That's understandable. Organizations practicing traditional PR for generations will at first view smart PR as running counter to the goal of generating a profit.

To the untrained eye, smart PR will appear unduly risky. Risk averse traditional PR departments will crucify the commandments embedded in smart PR. Smart PR strategies will at first attract criticism, castigation, and little faith.

Believing in smart PR requires faith. Faith that what is invisible at first will become tangible at last. Faith that the fear and discomfort associated with adopting a smart PR mindset will ultimately develop into a quiet confidence. Faith that giving away smart PR will generate a measurable return greater than the returns traditional PR currently earns.

Believe.

Have faith.

Follow me and I'll show you how.

# Creativity Q-tips

Creativity oozes from all of us.

Unconventional thoughts, innovative ideas, and counterintuitive problem solving approaches mingle in our hearts, minds, and souls and combine to create super-ideas with the potential to effect dramatic change within organizations.

However, creativity is an endangered species in many organizations.

Rather than creating environments in which creativity and innovation are merged to make life better for corporations and those they serve, creativity Q-tips are swabbing away much of the ingenuity and individuality we are born with and develop throughout childhood. These Q-tips ambush our creativity and make clear that individual thought and originality are not highly sought after qualities.

Early on we are taught the rules of the game; go to college, find work at an office, and follow orders. Over time our innate curiosity slowly begins to diminish. Each step along the path we trade portions of our creativity for models of acceptance and comfort. Many of us become blind to the ambush; colleges teach rote memorization, office rules require conformity to excel, and rule breakers are isolated or discarded altogether.

Unbridled creativity is out of bounds in today's cowardly game of risk aversion. As soon as a hint of creativity is spotted or creates an itch, it's swabbed. Creativity is scary. It doesn't look like anything we have seen before. It is risky. It is uncomfortable. It's why organizations often perceive creativity as foreign and something deserving of a creativity Q-tip.

Ridding creativity is often rewarded. Those who jam Q-tips into our ears and toss them in the garbage are seen as focused task masters who are doing us a favor by getting rid of the gunk and steering us down the path to job security.

Q-tipping and dumping creativity is safe.

Those who stick out or propose an alternative way of doing something are often perceived as obstructionists or disloyal. Maintaining the status quo and minimizing disruption are the hallmarks of middle managers. Overachievers are often discounted or discredited because their ideas appear foreign or contrary to convention.

Organizations create boxes. And then more boxes to surround the ones they just created. They fill the boxes with cogs and tell the cogs to think outside their box. Thoughts that exceed the boundaries of their individual boxes are simply constrained by the next box.

Cogs that most often think outside their little box but within the confines of the next box are promoted. These are the brainwashed overachievers who are then in charge of making sure ideas fit snuggly within the corporate puzzle. These overachievers understand they must create and nurture ideas that fit nicely within a predetermined paradigm. Those who offer ideas outside the organization's boxing capacity are deemed problematic and discouraged.

Uniformity and conformity are mistaken for efficiency.

Cubicle-bound conformists are chained and bound by sets of expectations and thus produce work that meets those expectations. Mediocrity is often the product of their labor. But it's comfortable. And it's safe.

Our mothers warned us never to put anything in our ears smaller than telephone poles.

Corporations have ignored their mothers.

Creativity Q-tips are swabbing and discarding our best ideas in favor of safety.

# PR Inbreeding

The corporate PR gene pool is relatively shallow.

The inbred world of public relations is often closed to outsiders and those with unorthodox or unconventional messaging strategies. Outliers need not apply. Over the years corporate PR staffs have become deaf and resistant to ideas and strategies not included in traditional PR arsenals.

Corporate PR staffs are often void of anyone not hailing from the PR world. Once anointed into this tight-knit community, PR practitioners abide by sets of rules resistant to change and outsiders. Corporate PR staffs often budge only to accommodate technology forced upon them by their audiences. Once adopted, technology is simply a new way to execute the same old strategies and techniques.

Organizations are often formulaic in the way they conduct messaging efforts. Models are identified and accepted by PR students. They study from the same textbooks and complete group projects without perspectives from non-public relations majors. Students become professionals. They follow the prescribed model: plug in specific inputs and predetermined outputs are sure to follow. It's simple. And it's comfortable. And there's little reason to open up the profession to outsiders who do not understand the model.

Closed communities are unable or unwilling to challenge long-held beliefs and behaviors. Insulating a profession from outside scrutiny allows for the efficient passage of tradition and technique to the next generation. Confirmation that these techniques are effective is gained by observing others practicing the same techniques. Organizations see replication of tactics as assurance they are compliant with the profession's best practices.

It's a protectionist mentality that creates a narrow-minded and often ineffective framework for message dissemination and consumption.

After generations of isolationism, PR staffs have come to think alike, look alike, and behave alike. They are reactionary. They are risk averse. They subscribe to an outdated shotgun approach to messaging. They continue to do so because it is the way they have always done.

Nothing will disrupt their thinking.

This is a world closed to outsiders. Only like-minders need apply. Messaging maladies are passed down and cloaked in the safety of ignorance. Ineffective or outdated techniques are mistaken for tradition and best practices. The comfort that accompanies inbreeding blinds organizations to the perils from which it is born.

# Cookie Cutter PR

Public Relations is now a commodity.

It has become an undifferentiated manufactured product with little or no qualitative differentiation across markets. The same PR product or service that works here is assumed to also work there. Commodity PR ignores culture, class, and caveats. It exists in one form and mistakenly assumes it can thrive across varied contexts.

It's analogous to a subdivision in which all of the homes look the same. While efficient to build and affordably priced, cookie cutter subdivision homes lack the individuality needed to attract more discerning homebuyers. They also magnify mistakes. Return after a night of drinking and enter a home that looks similar to yours and you better hope the homeowner is not armed.

The potential of getting shot has not deterred organizations from treating PR as a commodity though. One-size-fits-all news releases are still king. Pitching stories is still thought to be effective. Impersonal shotgun email blasts are believed to be an investment. These techniques are familiar. They allow PR practitioners to efficiently complete their daily chores.

These techniques are also worn out.

Autopilot appears to be the preferred mode of transport in many organizations. Turn on the autopilot messaging system, sit back, and relax. It is thoughtless and easy. The path of least resistance is taken in regard to message dissemination. Clicks, emails sent, and newswire exposures are mistaken for outcomes. Laziness is rewarded.

Organizations treating PR as a commodity may be forgiven. It has roots in the days when traditional media were still the gatekeepers and agenda setters. Back then corporations had fewer technological variables to be concerned with. Time was on their side. And unidirectional message distribution afforded organizations luxuries they no longer enjoy today.

Remnants of that life remain. The best practices of one era are not the best practices of another. Outdated and worn tactics are ingrained in the cultures of many organizations. Reinvention is not on the radar in many places. Sure, they'll make minor tweaks and label it as innovation. Rethinking habits is not something most PR staffs look forward to. Challenging tradition is uncomfortable. Sticking your neck out is risky. What if you're wrong? What if something new fails? What if you're not sure how to succeed in a new paradigm? Stick with the cookie cutter.

# PR Welfare

Corporate PR staffs are hooked on welfare.

The welfare I'm describing comes in the form of outside public relations firms. These firms are hired to do the heavy lifting corporate staffs either cannot or will not do. These are the firms that are supposed to save reputations during crises. These are the firms with established media contacts. These are the firms that can make it happen.

Or at least that's what they've gotten organizations to believe.

Reliance on outside PR firms has further pushed corporate PR staffs behind the times. Outside firms allow corporate PR staffs to remain lazy and undisciplined. Welfare allows them to continue to be closed minded. Outside PR firms are costly safety nets that allow organizations to continue wallowing in puddles of mediocrity.

The brainwashed zombies mechanically moving about corporate PR departments are more than glad to remain ignorant of their shortcomings. Just like the ineffective techniques they rely on to communicate with stakeholders, they cling to similar unchallenged assumptions about outside PR firms. Outsiders are the experts. Outsiders have the know-how. Outsiders have the contacts.

Corporate staffs have been taught to rely on help from outsiders.

A welfare mentality is created when large organizations come to rely on outside PR firms. Becoming dependent on outside PR firms is not a strategic investment or an efficient allocation of capital. Continually outsourcing PR tasks is often wasteful and even harmful. Corporate PR staffs are underutilized, underperforming, or undervalued.

Welfare often hurts more than it helps. If corporate PR staffs are not capable of performing at a higher level- get rid everyone, save the money, and pay an outside firm to do all of your messaging work.

Caution must be heeded though. Great risk comes with scrapping an underperforming PR staff and is why I will show you how to optimize yours. Not only can a smart, nimble, counterintuitive corporate PR team do it themselves; they can do it quicker and better.

Besides, outside PR firms can be downright disloyal at times.

Just ask Facebook founder Mark Zuckerberg and Secretary of State Hillary Clinton.

They learned this lesson the hard way.

# Burson Betrays Facebook

Facebook founder Mark Zuckerberg likely spent a lot of money to be embarrassed.

He found out the hard way just how loyal outside PR firms can be when faced with a tough choice.

When push comes to shove outside firms will likely sacrifice a client's reputation to spare their own.

Facebook created a public relations fiasco for itself in mid-2011 when it was caught trying to secretly smear Google's reputation in regard to the company's privacy policies. Google and Facebook had been duking it out over the type of information each company would allow the other to have when it comes to each site's users. In a nutshell, Facebook was angry at Google for collecting information people had freely posted on their Facebook pages.

To deflect criticism over its user privacy protection policies, Facebook hired a well known public relations firm, Burson-Marsteller, to pitch stories criticizing Google's privacy policies. The scheme only came to light after a blogger, who was already clearly a Google critic, in essence tattled on Facebook.

The blogger posted emails from a Burson-Marsteller executive who was urging the blogger to write a critical story on Google. The pitch from the Burson-Marsteller executive was misleading if not inaccurate. When the blogger asked the Burson- Marsteller executive to identify his client, the executive refused and the scheme was picked up by the national media.

To make matters worse for Facebook, the heat from the media prompted Burson-Marsteller to betray its client. Burson-Marsteller told the media it had violated its own policies by promising Facebook it would not reveal Facebook had hired it to engage in such practices. Turns out Facebook had hired a hit man and paid for anonymity.

After *The Wall Street Journal* inquired with the Public Relations Society of America about Burson-Marsteller's refusal to disclose Facebook as a client, the public relations disaster ironically spread to the public relations firm at the center of it all, Burson-Marsteller.

The Journal reports that the Public Relations Society of America's Chief Executive Rosanna Fiske characterized Burson-Marsteller's promise of anonymity as violating the organization's ethical standards. The paper quotes Ms. Fiske as saying, "When you are following misleading practices the message is tainted...what else have they done that perhaps I (the consumer) shouldn't trust."

It should also be noted that Burson-Marsteller's story pitches included directives calling on Congress and the Federal Trade Commission to investigate Google's privacy policies. If Burson-Marsteller had just an ounce of foresight, it would have dawned on the PR firm it was also inviting additional government scrutiny for its client, Facebook. *The Wall Street Journal's* L. Gordon Crovitz writes, "It's as if General Motors called for tougher regulations of Ford without stopping to think that any new rules would also apply to it."

Burson treated Hillary Clinton similarly.

Mark Penn, CEO of Burson-Marsteller, was Clinton's top political strategist during the 2008 presidential campaign. Penn also heads his own polling firm, Penn, Schoen, Berland, which Clinton's campaign reportedly paid millions of dollars to for various campaign work.

On the campaign trail, Senator Clinton told supporters she opposed a trade deal with Columbia and would vote against it. The Columbians had been lobbying for Congressional passage of a trade agreement signed years earlier by Columbian President Alvaro Uribe and President George H.W. Bush's administration.

While Clinton was campaigning against the agreement, media reports revealed Penn had been meeting with Columbian officials pushing for passage of the agreement. Further media investigation revealed the Columbians previously paid Penn's firm, Burson-Marsteller, $300,000 to lobby members of Congress with the goal of securing the agreement's passage.

Referring to his meeting with Columbian officials, media outlets quoted Penn as saying, "The meeting was an error in judgment and will not be repeated and I am sorry for it." Penn is later quoted as suggesting Clinton was not aware of his meeting with the Columbians.

If Burson's allegiance to Clinton and Zuckerberg is this thin, what makes you think outside firms would be any more loyal to you?

# Lose Your PR Gut

Organizations with PR guts are unhealthy.

Overindulgence sneaks up on most organizations. An extra pound here. An extra pound there. Years later a mirror makes it clear- your company is fat. No worries, you'll run it off. The diet starts tomorrow. But it never does. Companies with bloated PR departments are undisciplined. They lack self-control. They lack the drive to slim down. They become sluggish and lethargic. Rather than take personal responsibility for being a glutton most organizations place blame. Must be genetics, they say. We were just wired to be this way.

There's some truth to that.

After years of professional inbreeding, companies with overweight PR staffs no longer have the ability or will to engage in critical self-assessment. Uncovering dirty truths can be painful for prideful organizations. The reality is most overweight organizations are to blame for their PR guts. Not only have they created environments where ignorant gluttony is tolerated, in many cases they've also created an environment in which it is expected.

Employees with courage to challenge consensus and the status quo are often punished. They are out of line. They stick out. They are passed over for promotion. They learn quickly; eat what you are being served. Then eat some more. They learn to clean their plates. This is how you climb the ladder. Eat your own cooking. Even if it tastes horrible. Even if it's not healthy.

The consequences often associated with challenging cultural norms within an organization dissuade originality and rigorous debate. It drains creativity. It stifles innovative thinkers. Employees become averse to change. The mindset spreads and eventually becomes ingrained. Entire PR staffs become fearful. Paralysis grips the department and prevents it from working off the fat even if it wants to.

Corporate PR staffs become sick.

When they become too weak to handle their daily responsibilities they reach for the medications outside PR firms are selling. Outsiders promise miracle cures. They push expensive pills. They offer hope where there was none.

Aside from being unhealthy, maintaining a PR gut is costly.

Once a sick corporate PR department comes to rely on the medicine provided by outside PR firms it can go back to its gluttonous ways of operation. No sense in slimming down now. The problem is being solved by the heavy lifters.

It takes brutal honesty to admit this has happened to you.

It takes discipline and will power to reverse course.

Losing a PR gut is a painstaking process. One where progress is initially tough to see. It requires a strong faith. An organization might not initially see visual evidence it's actually losing weight. That's why measuring for progress is key. Jump on a scale each day. Small steps add up. Over time the organization transforms itself.

Not only will corporate PR staffs look and feel better. They'll also perform better. They'll become nimble, quick, and agile. They'll no longer need the addictive pills outside firms are pushing.

They'll save money.

They'll save themselves.

# Disrupting Public Relations

Optimizing corporate public relations staffs requires a singular focus on disrupting the modern flow of media content. Disrupting that flow hinges upon creating premier content and pumping it through a loop the organization partially constructs. A staff that establishes itself as the first to disrupt its industry or sector positions itself as a lone leader among legions of followers. The transformation that must occur to disrupt the normal flow of media content requires cultural, intellectual, and operational shifts in focus.

How does a staff steeped in traditional public relations techniques successfully disrupt the modern flow of media content?

First, it must understand the E-Loop.

# The E-Loop

The E-Loop is a four stage loop illustrating the economic and technological realities responsible for the directional change in the flow of information now impacting corporate reputations and bottom lines. Included in the loop are erosion, empowerment, entitlement, and endangerment. Understanding how content flows through this loop is a prerequisite for disrupting the flow. Below is a more thorough description of the change and potential consequences;

**Erosion** refers to the erosion of influence once held by traditional media. Traditional media were kingmakers in a previous life; information gatekeepers that routinely set agendas determining what information became news and what did not. That influence is eroding quickly as increased competition and a digital shift in advertising spending have negatively impacted traditional media both financially and operationally.

**Empowerment** refers to advances in technology that have disrupted the traditional flow of information dissemination and have given individuals the power to speak to and influence mass audiences. The convergence of social media, affordable audio-video equipment, and the opportunity to publish or upload almost instantaneously have empowered the masses to make and report their own news rather than depend on traditional gatekeepers to set the agenda.

**Entitlement** refers to the sense of entitlement technology-empowered newsmakers often gain after beginning to share content and create audiences willing to receive such content. As the process of gathering and sharing information becomes more transactional, those involved often feel entitled, if not obligated, to routinely share their opinions, judgments, or perceptions as they relate to a specific topic.

**Endangerment** refers to the increased risk to organizational reputations associated with the authority ordinary individuals have to exert outsized influence. Individuals who feel entitled to socially opine on any and all subject matters now carry the potential to harm the reputations of entities they deem as targets.

Individuals who in the past would not enjoy the luxury of traditional media amplifying their viewpoints can now do so on their own. The phenomena is magnified by the fact these individuals have now become agenda setters for the traditional media, feeding content to the very same traditional media outlets by which they were once ignored.

# The E-Loop

**Erosion -> Empowerment -> Entitlement -> Endangerment -> Erosion**

Content flowing through the E-loop gains momentum and strengthens with each pass. Traditional corporate public relations staffs reactively attempting to step in and stop content harmful to their reputations from circulating through the loop have little chance of success. Organizations standing in the way of content accelerating through the loop will likely be run over. To remedy the threat, organizations must become part of the E-Loop. More specifically, organizations that create content and cycle it through a toll road they've created themselves gain the momentum and capability required to steer narratives in this environment.

# PR Reinvented

Accomplishing your messaging goals requires reinvention. Optimized PR staffs must become newsmakers and distribute that news in unorthodox manners to reach intended audiences. The content a transformed PR staff produces must contain substance and quality superior to that produced by competitors. It must become the source from which much, if not all, other like media content is born.

Who are these competitors?

Organizations are competing against new influencers, traditional media, bloggers, and social media purveyors with outsized influence. Many corporate PR staffs have been unwilling participants in this race. Their competitors have bolted from the starting blocks leaving traditional PR staffs in the dust. The race winner is awarded the opportunity to steer the narrative. The loser cedes control of its destiny to someone who may wish to do it harm.

The only option is to win the race and steer the narrative.

An optimized corporate PR staff will report on itself, its competitors, and its industry. It will engage critics, analysts, and third party media reports. It will position itself as the most credible source of content by proactively addressing criticisms, complaints, and concerns even before critics have an opportunity to hurl these verbal jabs themselves.

Transformed corporate PR staffs will distribute this content unconventionally. Simply put, an optimized corporate PR staff will outperform its competitors in the race to become content king.

Instead of initially being the focus of someone else's story, an optimized PR staff becomes the storyteller. It tells its own stories, its competitors' stories, and stories that impact a sector or industry on a much broader basis. An organization that does so positions itself as the dominant storyteller of its domain. Acquiring that status allows a corporation to drive key messages through a variety of distribution channels.

It's helpful to think of media content like electricity.

Electricity seeks the path of least resistance and carries the dual potential to bring both life and death to an entity. Without a circuit breaker, a short or current overload carries the potential to damage components in the circuit. However, a circuit breaker protects components from damage by immediately disconnecting electrical flow when too much or too little electrical current is detected.

Corporate PR staffs are wise to view themselves as breakers in the media content flow circuit.

An optimized PR staff helps to create the circuit by which it continuously pumps premier media content through. Doing so positions the organization as the narrative driver. Likewise, a transformed PR staff also affords itself a greater opportunity to immediately stop undesirable content from continued circulation. When a threat arises, an optimized PR staff simply hits the breaker which has the potential to slow or stop the media content flow.

The objective is to create breakers all along the circuit.

Once the undesirable content is mitigated or more desirable content is created, the organization can again hit the breaker and reopen the content flow. Smart organizations know exactly when to stop the content flow because they are measuring the effectiveness of their content.

Continually measuring public relations efforts provides organizations with the data necessary to routinely tweak message content and message distribution strategy within the loop. Organizations that do so achieve greater efficiencies and key message conveyance rates versus competitors.

The model bloggers and social media kings used to disrupt the content flow once solely controlled by traditional media can be modified for use by corporate PR departments.      However, disruption may only be achieved by becoming a premier content producer. It's this simple: be the premier content creator in your world.

Disrupting traditional public relations behavior will likely draw criticism, be   uncomfortable, and at times seem counterintuitive. Hard work will be required to develop your own portion of the circuit or distribution loop. An even bigger challenge will be creating content that becomes the envy of those with the ability to amplify it.

The race is on though.

Do not let someone else win the right to steer your narrative.

Nick Winkler

# Smart PR Puberty

Transforming into a smart PR staff requires a physical change.

An uncomfortable change.

A change that is both public and at times awkward.

Throw away your business cards.

A staff focused on adopting smart PR strategies must break the hold its business cards have over it. Labeling yourself as a member of a corporation's public relations staff often limits your thinking and creativity. The PR label predetermines how you are supposed to behave and how you interact with your publics.

It's also a turnoff to those who may consume and amplify the premier content you create.

Over the last dozen years I've conducted an informal survey of journalists around the country. I ask a very simple question of the reporters I come across in newsrooms and in the field; what do you think of PR people?

While the answers vary, four commonalities emerge:

1. Reporters are less likely to trust information coming from someone who is a member of a corporate public relations staff.
2. Reporters are less likely to believe a corporate public relations staff member actually has information that meets the criteria that defines something as newsworthy.
3. Reporters are less likely to believe a public relations staff member who fails to acknowledge when something has gone wrong and is always overly promotional.
4. Reporters are more likely to believe corporate public relations staff members are in place to hinder or prevent a reporter from completing a story.

Any wonder why pitching stories to reporters often ends in failure?

By simply including the term "public relations" in job titles, on business cards, or on websites a corporation is stacking the deck against itself. The connotative meaning, or the way reporters feel about the term "public relations", is not positive. In fact it pigeon holes what are often very intelligent people into engaging in work that will likely never be included in a media report.

Generally, reporters have a very short list of PR professionals they actually trust and rely on for story ideas, angles, and information. The PR professionals who develop solid relationships with journalists and whom journalists deem as the better PR professionals were often journalists themselves before becoming PR professionals.

That strikes me as unbelievably sad.

The informal survey I've conducted also reveals four pieces of data that are extremely helpful in understanding why some PR professionals become so successful:

1. Public Relations professionals who fully disclose conflicts of interest, client affiliations, and motives are more likely to be trusted and sought out by reporters asking for information.
2. Public Relations professionals who from time to time proactively engage a reporter with newsworthy information or story ideas unrelated to the PR professional's clients or company are more likely to garner favorable coverage for the client or company at a later date.
3. Public Relations professionals who are willing and able to provide more information than a reporter needs for the current story are perceived by reporters as being honest and transparent and create the potential for positive follow up coverage opportunities.
4. Public Relations professionals who understand what makes something newsworthy, how the news gathering process works, and are conscientious of reporter deadlines are

perceived by reporters not as obstructionists but as credible providers of information who truly want to help.

The survey results can be framed rather simplistically: obstructionist spinmeisters with little or no understanding of what makes something newsworthy are inordinately less successful than their counterparts who partner with journalists to create works from which both can benefit.

This is the beginning of your self-made roadmap.

The "PR" label must go.

It's a label that confines corporations in self-made prisons. Media consumers will occasionally drop by during visitation hours. But by virtue of being in prison, the company will not get a fair shake as the stereotypes associated with someone behind bars color how a reporter or media consumer perceives you inside the PR prison.

Instead, adopt a creative idea mentality.

Hang your hat on the content that flows from these ideas.

Don't allow a label and its preconceptions to define you. Define yourself with the premier content you create.

Breaking out of PR prison is risky. But like any former prisoner with newfound freedom, success will only be achieved if the ex-con finds something productive to do with his or her time.

There's plenty to do though.

# Trashing Assumptions

Corporate PR staffs can only begin to reinvent themselves after they identify the assumptions and clichés that have governed traditional public relations practices. These default tactics and techniques constrain creativity and limit innovation. They allow PR staffers to navigate their day more efficiently but these techniques are simply no longer effective. The problem is PR practitioners are all competing in generally the same way. They use similar methods and strategies. Their content looks alike, blends together, and offers their organization no competitive advantage.

Run these assumptions through a shredder.

Then throw away the shreds.

Rather than pitching a story to a reporter, why not produce it yourself? Instead of wondering which strategy or tactic worked best, why not measure for success and remove all doubt? Instead of hiring an outside firm for its media contacts, why not create something of value and use it to forge a relationship yourself?

Dumping foundational assumptions provides corporate PR staffs the ability to surprise the world. Right now, the world expects companies to spin, obfuscate, and cover up. Ridding an organization of the assumptions it has relied on will enable companies to exceed expectations.

Instead of holing up during a crisis, surprise people with transparent and truthful content that tells a story.

Break bad news yourself.

Create content that teaches an entire industry how to avoid a mistake you made.

Mistakes are opportunities to create narratives designed to enhance your organization's reputation. Doing so will cement the organization as an industry leader that deserves the benefit of the doubt in the future.

Ditching assumptions and reinventing your corporate PR staff is the only way to differentiate your organization in a world crowded with corporate followers. The followers, their messages, and message distribution look alike.

Those who break away from the pack of followers and begin aggressively creating valuable content will stick out as innovative leaders.

Nick Winkler

# Quit Traditional PR Cold Turkey

**D**oes baseball pitching great Nolan Ryan work for your corporation?

I ask this question to prompt a conversation about a generally agreed upon practice in the public relations world: pitching. Pitching is the term used to describe the process of convincing an external source to do a story on a certain topic.

The first newspaper was published in Rome 59 years before Jesus Christ was born. Though Julius Caesar used *Acta Diuma* as a means to announce governmental activities, you can bet the first "pitching" strategy has its roots in Rome as well.

PR professionals allege pitching is part art and part science. The process has been refined, tweaked, and modified to fit technological shifts. Self-proclaimed pitching experts have adopted rules: keep pitches to a certain number of sentences, email a reporter twice and then call, include a date and time your client is available for an interview, win them over with flattery.

Many of these formulaic pitching strategies guarantee a measurable increase in the number of key influencer responses. Many claim they can teach nervous PR staffers the secret to cold calling an influential blogger and successfully garnering glowing media attention.

Corporations have spent millions of dollars trying to get the media to cover their products, services, and charitable efforts.

Much of that money has been wasted.

To be fair, there are sharp PR professionals who have smartly transformed the PR-Media Consumer relationship into a Source-Media Consumer relationship. But the vast majority of PR professionals have not forged relationships with journalists. Organizations often believe relationships with journalists are commodities that can be purchased when outside Public Relations firms are hired.

This is a financially dangerous assumption to make.

Organizations often have little understanding of what is actually occurring after an outside PR firm is hired. Executives and managers at some large outside PR firms view the practice of pitching as beneath them; therefore, pitching is often assigned to junior level staffers. These staffers lack the contacts for which organizations are paying a steep price.

These staffers are often right out of college and have rarely, if ever, had meaningful conversations with journalists. They certainly do not have rolodexes full of cell phone numbers for bloggers and key influencers.

Unfortunately, this lack of dedication on the part of some outside PR firms can cost corporations tens of thousands of dollars a month.

Removing the PR cloak many corporations wrap themselves in not only requires a physical transformation, but also a fundamental shift in thinking as well. The shotgun approach to news releases is an expensive path to failure. Reporters, with all their faults, are sophisticated enough to see through the practice.

Traditional pitching is insincere and impersonal. Those promising instant results are not being truthful. Those who deliver on their promises are simply leveraging existing relationships. Relationships your corporation can learn to build on its own.

Corporations can no longer employ traditional PR techniques as conduits for routine message dissemination. Technology has democratized content creation and dissemination. Many organizations fear this. That fear is misplaced.

Those who embrace it will lead.

They will take hold of their fate.

They'll steer the narrative they create.

Corporations can and should reduce their expenditures and reliance on outside Public Relations firms. However, dependence must be replaced by an optimized smart PR staff. Staffs already

35

contain many of the skill sets necessary to transform. Most of the skill sets they lack are teachable.

There are only a handful of great pitchers like Nolan Ryan, baseball's all-time strikeout leader. There are even fewer great PR pitchers despite what you might here. Unless you are lucky enough to have a Nolan Ryan already working on your PR staff, it's time to change course.

It's time to stop pitching.

It's time to start producing.

# The PR Messiah

Has your corporate PR staff been born again?
Organizations that recognize and accept content creation as their PR savoir will be reborn with renewed purpose. Accepting content as your savior washes away the sins of traditional PR and grants you entry into the heavenly kingdom of narrative control.

Corporate PR staffs that are born again also stop believing in devils like conventional wisdom. Conventional wisdom poisons organizations with fallacies, groupthink, and illogic that stifle innovation. Conventional wisdom is relied upon, repeated, and ultimately goes unquestioned until it becomes generally accepted.

Accepting conventional wisdom is lazy.

Challenge the conventional wisdom of traditional public relations.

The idea that companies have less control over their messages in today's technology-driven environment is one I see repeated often. With so many new voices contributing to increasingly public conversations, companies are often told their power to control a narrative has diminished immensely. This nugget of conventional wisdom is repeated by PR consultants and not often questioned by corporate PR staffs.

Conventional wisdom is wrong.

Organizations have never had a better opportunity to control a narrative's destiny. Never have corporations enjoyed such an opportunity to cost-effectively create and distribute their own narratives. The opportunity is amplified by the fact traditional media outlets are starving for content.

Feed them.

Conventional wisdom apparently assumes the same tools responsible for diluting an organization's narrative-steering authority are not available to the organization. The same tools are accompanied by built-in audiences: customers, shareholders, regulators etc. These audiences are captive. In some cases they must listen to what you say. These audiences are not only paying close attention to what you say but also how you say it.

So say it more creatively than someone else would.

Accepting creative content as your PR Messiah means the world is a blank slate awaiting your organization's trailblazing content inventions. Create your own corporate reality show and deliver it to the world. Broadcast your own satellite radio station or a company specific newscast. Publish your own book or magazine specifically aimed at critics and detractors. Develop a website dedicated to critiquing media reports involving your industry.

The objective is to flip conventional wisdom on its head.

Lobbying lawmakers at the Capitol is a dirty job, right? No one wants to see how their sausage or laws are made. So surprise people with your lobbying efforts. Create content outlining your legislative goals and how they'll make the world a better place for people. Don't keep it secret. Show people how your lobbyists interact with lawmakers. Record it. Document it. Produce content that is both unconventional and truthful.

Identify negative conventional wisdom people hold in relation to your organization. Then go out and produce content designed to expose flaws in that wisdom. Doing so positions the organization as an industry leader.

It differentiates your company.

It also has the power to turn critics into customers and customers into mouthpieces willing to amplify your message.

Organizations that accept content creation as their savior afford themselves the opportunity to control the narratives that define their reputations. Companies that worship valuable content are blessed with forgiveness during times of crisis. Corporations living a public relations life in accordance with the PR Messiah will enjoy favor not afforded nonbelievers.

# DIY Smart PR

D o-it-yourself Smart PR is the new model. Creativity Q-tips should be dumped in the trash. Wean your organization off PR welfare. And lose the PR gut. Create an environment where messaging risk is embraced. Create a culture in which being wrong is seen as being one step closer to right. Rediscover the creativity that has been stolen. Reignite the innovation that's lying dormant.

The rest of this book is dedicated to convincing you all of this is possible.

Unlearning public relations will be challenging. Doing it yourself will be uncomfortable and at times frightening. You won't always be certain which direction to go, where to pivot, or when to change course. There isn't a map to point you in the right direction. You'll make wrong turns. You'll make mistakes. And you'll be better off for it.

Doing PR yourself and doing it successfully will yield financial and operational benefits. While outside PR firms will always have their place, relying on them less will cut costs and force corporate PR departments to increase efficiency and productivity. Doing it yourself also gives organizations a greater degree of control over their narratives. Best of all, doing it yourself creates independence.

The independence that comes with charting your own way enables a corporation to move much more quickly than its competitors. Quickness wins races. Quickness gives companies flexibility. Flexibility gives companies the ability to adapt to change more quickly. Adapting to change quicker than competitors positions an organization to be a leader. Leaders steer narratives. Followers chase them.

Organizations adopting the new do-it-yourself model will discover there are many paths to success. Identifying the most effective and efficient is what's important. The rest of this book aims to equip organizations with the tools needed to find the right path. These paths will not always exist. So the tools and strategies outlined here allow organizations to create their own paths.

You are the snow plow.

Not the vehicles blindly following.

# Taunt the Guillotine

The digital guillotine is relentless.

Getting caught in today's digital guillotine is far more painful than being decapitated by an 18th century guillotine.

Decapitation by an old time guillotine is a luxury. It is quick. After the initial shock- it's over. You're dead. An original French guillotine is a preferred means of death versus the guillotines of today.

The digital guillotine catalogues your every word. It saves each of your ideas. It tucks away each of your mistakes. Every infraction is saved on a server in Silicon Valley and backed up by two others in Romania. All of it is immediately retrievable with a quick Google search.

Break a promise, miss expectations, or get caught with your hand in someone else's cookie jar and you can expect the digital guillotine to hack your reputation to shreds. What's worse is you'll be alive as it happens. It will not be quick. It's a slow death characterized by futile defenses and false hope.

Run arrogantly through today's digital guillotine and your reputation will die a slow death. A public death. One that your customers will have a front row seat to. The digital guillotine will even invite them to participate. You're helpless once the hacking starts. You'll know you're dying. You'll feel the pain. But there'll be little you can do to stop it.

What to do about a digital guillotine so detrimental to your organization's reputation?

Taunt it.

Rather than aggressively forcing your creations through the gauntlet, let the gauntlet come to you. Become so exceptional, members of the digital guillotine seek out your creations. Create such an aura of anticipation for your next creation that the digital guillotine loses its edge.

Let it dull itself.

Stop running the gauntlet hoping you might sneak past with something average before someone notices your frailties or weaknesses.

Once new influencers label you as an aggressive giver they'll no longer hide out waiting to take from you. The treacherous world your reputation must navigate will no longer be as hostile or intimidating once you reverse the flow of media content. Once you give.

Taunting the digital guillotine with premier content not only blunts the guillotine's power but also prompts others to ride to your rescue in times of need. While you'll never be able to satisfy every facet of the digital guillotine, cultivating a loyal following of new influencers who'll shield your organization's reputation from the digital guillotine is crucial to survival.

Stop running the same old gauntlet with the same old content and distribution methods. At the very least you'll go unnoticed. That's if you're lucky. And what good will that do? At worst, your subpar content and means of delivery will be hacked to death by an unforgiving digital mob intent on decapitating your reputation.

Instead, change the flow.

Make them run toward you. Toward the gifts you are making for them. Toward something exceptional they can share and take partial ownership in as well.

Become so exceptional they'll run to you. So great they'll arrive early. So magnificent they'll wait in line in advance of the gift just so they can be one of the first to pass it along to those they influence. So they'll feel like the gift is partly theirs to redistribute.

When you create and give in such a manner the guillotine loses much of its power. Those with the power to hack and hurt will be too preoccupied with getting. With consuming. With becoming a part of the spread of something special.

Taunt the digital guillotine.

Invite it over.

Keep it close.

# Rule Reset

You've been playing by someone else's rules.

The rules do not favor the players who must follow them. In fact, they are designed to create disadvantages for those trying to follow them. It's why creativity and innovative thinking have been detriments to employees in large organizations. Companies must follow the rules or face consequences. So the external rules are imparted on those within the corporation. Rules trickle down. They handcuff and hamstring organizations.

Rule makers are winners. Those who make the rules create a competitive advantage for themselves. They win more often. They set boundaries and parameters that must be observed. Self-interest inspires rules. Rules are not in place to protect participants. They are created to control and direct.

The PR rules companies have abided by for generations were not established by PR practitioners. From the outset, those practicing public relations were at a disadvantage. They were reacting to a set of rules constructed by traditional media. Traditional media used the advantage to create an unequal playing field. The rules forced PR practitioners to be reactive. The rules imposed arbitrary deadlines. The rules put the burden of proof on those targeted by the media.

Today's rules are much different. They are fluid. They are soft. So why not grab hold and mold them yourself? The rule makers are much more numerous. The rules change more frequently. PR practitioners are even more reactive. The time a PR practitioner has to react is even smaller. The deadlines are even tighter. A judgment of guilt in the court of public opinion may be handed down simply for being late. Truth may not trump a social media tidal wave of criticism.

Organizations that try to follow the new rules soon learn the deck is stacked against them. They play the game because they are told they have to. Conventional wisdom says they must join the conversation. But joining a conversation assumes you are already late to the conversation. It assumes you'll play a reactionary role. Joining a conversation that has already begun without you forces you to play by the rules of the conversation starters.

Don't join the conversation.

Start your own.

The smartest most nimble organizations start conversations prior to those started by others. Doing so allows you to make the rules. It allows you to create advantages none of the other participants can enjoy. Rule creators position themselves in a manner that makes it difficult for participants to hijack the narrative.

Becoming a rule creator is not an activity in which everyone can engage. Only those who are committed to hustling harder than competitors and critics can do so. Only those who are committed to creating premier content enjoy the luxuries that come with making the rules. Starting a conversation is scary for corporations used to following sets of rules created by others. Starting a conversation may be perceived as risky. It can be. But setting the agenda and steering a narrative at its outset creates a competitive advantage that none of the conversation participants will enjoy. That advantage is reserved for the conversation pioneer.

Organizations can reset the rules by observing the following themes:

- Become deadline creators versus deadline observers
- Produce versus pitch
- Tell on yourself versus being caught
- Set expectations versus meeting them
- Create media instead of consuming media
- Be divisive rather than unifying
- Violate boundaries instead of observing them
- Measure rather than guess
- Become self-critical versus self-defensive
- Become aggressive givers instead of passive takers

Resetting the rules creates the single greatest advantage an organization enjoys in terms of protecting and enhancing its reputation. It requires great courage. It requires a trailblazer mentality. It requires the ability to overcome the fear of being first. It requires initiative. It demands the creation of a conversation in which critics and detractors are not only invited but encouraged to join.

Those who test the water with their toes will be passed by.

Those who jump into the conversational waters all at once return to the surface first. They soak up the oxygen and regain their breath while the others slowly wade into the conversation. Embrace the initial shock of jumping in. Allow it to invigorate you. Enjoy creating.

Be first.

# Divorce Fear

Resetting the rules is not enough to create something beautiful.

A rule reset simply gives you an advantage. A competitive edge. But simply acquiring an edge will not in and of itself produce victory. It's not valuable by itself.

Rules favor the rule maker. But even rule makers must still play the game. And they must play it better than their opponents. Rule resets only come in handy when the game is close. When a last minute outcome hangs in the balance. Rule makers get the benefit of the doubt. They'll be called safe when non-rule makers are called out.

This advantage is realized only after a hard fought battle. Advantages catapult those who are on the verge of victory. Those who sweat. Those who bleed. Those who have given it their all. Only after all of this can a self-created edge separate your company from the rest.

The key is to exploit that edge.

Exploiting a self-created edge requires creating valuable content. Creating valuable content demands unconventional ideas. The problem is many of the great ideas that come from within are invisible to us.

If one bubbles to the surface it's blocked just as pop-up advertisements are by web browsers.

If a great idea slips past our internal pop-up blocker creativity q-tips quickly swab it away.

Ideas like these are suppressed by our emotions. These emotions are triggered by risk averse compliance. If we're wrong we won't be promoted. No reason to take a risk. No need to rock the boat. Go along to get along. This mindset provides safety. It provides comfort.

We learn to live in a cage. In self-created prisons. We rationalize our confinement and somehow convince ourselves we're okay with it. It works. The paychecks keep coming. And we reward ourselves with material things. This is the trade we make. Things rather than freedom.

When innovative ideas outside our circle of comfortable compliance are born, fear is triggered. That fear tells us to put the idea away. Block it. Bury it. Whatever you do don't act on it. It could be wrong. Or unaccepted.

All of these scenarios create risk and uncertainty. Risk and uncertainty circle back and amplify the fear triggered by smart ideas. Snap decisions are made. These decisions are based on emotion rather than logic.

Dramatic drops in stock markets are the most tangible proofs of this behavior. Most investors perceive plunging stock prices as increasing risk and uncertainty. Instead of rigorous research it's easier to sell on the way down. It's perceived as safer. Get out now. No reason to be a hero.

You sell on the way down.

You buy on the way back up.

Rather than buying stocks when they're on sale our emotions prompt us to buy after the sale is over and the prices have increased.

We follow the herd.

The good news and the bad is that these emotions are learned. Unfortunately, seeds of fear were planted in us as children. They're sculpted and grow with time. They are reinforced in the workplace.

These emotions and our reactions to them become social norms.

When we see them adopted by others, especially those who are perceived as successful, we tell ourselves we are on the right track. We continue to suppress. We become even more compliant.

In the beginning we had to consciously ignore ideas. Over time and with reinforcement it becomes much easier. We don't acknowledge them. We become apathetic toward them. With time we stop seeing them altogether. They become invisible.

There is a silver lining.

Since this fear we have of not being accepted is learned, it can be unlearned. We must unwind years of risk averse compliance. We must rid ourselves of an entire mindset. We must shed the comforts associated with this mindset.

We must divorce these emotions.

# Thinking about Thoughts

Divorcing a spouse isn't generally quick or easy.
Divorcing your emotions is even dirtier.
Remember, over time the smart thoughts you create have become invisible. Idea apathy has tricked you into believing you don't have smart thoughts. You're taught these thoughts can get you into trouble.

In reality, they're the key to freedom.

But picking the jail door lock to this fear requires discipline. It demands concentration. It requires you to become a high self-monitor.

Academics define high self-monitors in a variety of ways that have no bearing on divorcing your emotions. Becoming a high self-monitor simply means you begin to think about the things you are thinking about. High self-monitors recognize when a thought enters their mind and triggers the fear of falling out of compliance.

It is only by recognizing the mental entry of these thoughts that we can begin the process of countering them. This is the first step in stripping the invisibility from our smart ideas. We must first see them to do something about them.

Once we are consciously aware of these thoughts we can begin assessing the risk associated with our thoughts. However, accurately assessing risk is extremely difficult for most. People are notoriously bad at assessing risk. For instance, gamblers with money on a horse routinely overestimate their horse's chance of winning versus people without money on that particular horse.

Assessing idea risk is starkly different.

Defining the downside to an idea can be determined individually. It can be determined from within. But it must be determined with honesty and humility.

As long as we are willing to be honest with ourselves when an idea is not a Nobel Prize winner, we can begin to accurately assess idea risk. The sooner we become willing to emotionally part with lesser ideas the sooner we will find those that are keepers.

Rather than initially perceiving ideas as risky begin seeing them as investments. Start seeing them as opportunities. They are byproducts in the creation of value.

Most ideas are not great. The majority will fail. You must be okay with this. You must accept this. You must be willing to continue sticking your neck out knowing that the digital guillotine is waiting with an axe.

When you learn to thrive under these conditions you'll be free. The axes will be blunted. Idea apathy is replaced with idea courage. Repetitive acts of courage will turn into confidence. The confidence to be wrong. The confidence to handle rejection. The confidence to get back up and try again.

Successful door to door salesmen adopt this mindset quickly. They understand in advance they'll be rejected 99 times before making a sale on the 100th attempt. They're okay with the uncertainty that comes with not knowing when that next sale will come.

They hustle through rejection. Each door that slams in their face is brushed off. It means they are one step closer to a sale. One step closer to creating value. They have divorced their fear of rejection. They have embraced it as a natural and inevitable phenomenon along the path to success.

Divorce your fear and you'll become free to fail.

And free to create.

# Pivot Point #1

It's time for our first pivot.

Before I show you how to give birth to your great ideas and turn them into magnificent content, we must acknowledge a current reality; businesses are stressed.

Economic growth is weaker than business would like. Regulatory scrutiny is growing stronger than business would like.

Economic headwinds are aplenty.

And technology gives almost everyone the ability to ratchet up the pressure.

Creating premier content becomes even more important once your organization acknowledges crises are omnipresent.

So let's pivot.

It's time to examine crises and identify smart PR techniques to mitigate them.

# Constant Crisis

*K*eeping quiet, even when information is lacking, is akin to wrapping the organization's fragile reputation in a blanket, leaving it on a doorstep in the middle of the night, and hoping whoever finds it raises it with kindness and love.

# Constant Crisis

Corporations are in a state of constant crisis.

Most crisis consultants recite the same old tired line regarding crises, "It's not if but when and how bad." However, it's worthwhile to question whether that type of logic is wholly accurate anymore. In fact, this type of ration is dated and no longer pertinent in a business climate now governed by increased regulation, legislation, and litigation. Combine those threats with heightened activism, overzealous prosecutors, and a less than skeptical traditional media and corporations subscribing to an outdated notion of crisis management will be caught flat-footed.

It's why corporate crises are constant and now simply a matter of degree.

Technology, in essence, allows everyone to buy ink by the barrel now. Traditionally, crisis consultants have advised corporations not to argue or pick fights with entities flush with ink.

This strategy is no longer effective either.

Crises are more robust, dynamic, and complicated than ever before. Therefore, a corporation's crisis communications strategy must evolve with even greater efficacy. Today's crises are multi-layered and are being fought on multiple fronts which require tailored micro-strategies simultaneously targeted at each individual or stakeholder audience.

We'll let academics and consultants debate the differences between "issues management" and "crisis management" and how the former is often dictated by a proactive approach and the later a reactive approach. Philosophical feuds are outside the scope of this book.

The current business environment requires that corporations fundamentally change the way they think about crises. Corporations must become ferociously aggressive in terms of protecting their reputations. Many believe they have already adopted a more aggressive approach as they have taken proactive measures such as creating dark websites that can be activated in the event of a crisis. Others that have considered various crisis scenarios and developed mitigation plans possess a false sense of preparedness as well. While these steps are proactive and potentially helpful they are not, in and of themselves, adequate anymore.

Corporate crisis strategy must be injected with steroids.

Pumping up a company's aggressiveness toward emerging threats is vital in an environment where anyone with a smartphone is capable of launching a multimedia attack. An unsatisfied customer with a Twitter account or the desire to post an unflattering review online poses a threat that did not exist a short time ago. The same holds true for a lone blogger with an axe to grind or a reporter looking for the story that'll catapult him or her to their next job. Non-governmental organizations (NGOs) have it down to a science; create incendiary content or claims, use various media to magnify the claims, use the headlines generated to increase membership and fundraising, then use the money to target and tarnish the next corporation on the hit list.

This is why crises are a matter of degree not of existence.

An aggressive sprint toward emerging threats to your reputation is in order. If you are not moving as fast or faster than those attempting to create a crisis, you'll no doubt lose the race to protect your reputation. Corporations must outfit themselves with the protective gear necessary to run into burning buildings to rescue their reputations. Storm in unprepared and you are sure to be burned.

Embracing chaos and learning to thrive in it is, in part, what will set your corporation apart from competitors. Engaging adversaries in this manner is what will allow you to steer the narrative. Exerting this type of aggressiveness is essential when attempting to galvanize your corporation as the primary source of information during a crisis. Ceding or failing to immediately take hold of the steering wheel during the birth of a crisis will likely result in failure. What's more, time is not on your side.

Don't be burned by a technology wildfire.

Even that which appears to be of minimal risk to a corporation's reputation can virally morph almost instantly into a crisis of a much greater degree. Technology is capable of spreading reputation damaging content almost instantaneously. As telecommunications providers build out their 4G networks and the Federal Government considers allowing additional spectrum for use, expect even higher speeds and hotter fires.

The threat of crisis is further amplified when you compound technology with the current economic and ethical conditions present in today's media. Police reports, search warrants, and regulatory reports are considered by many of today's reporters as having the same veracity as the words written in red in the Bible. Accusations often equal guilt in the court of public opinion. Often, those without the means to hire an attorney to resolve a dispute turn to a local television station. It's a good bet the station will gladly do the complainant's bidding in return for a promotable sound bite patting the station on its back. Corporations are often the victims in these circumstances rather than the complainant.

"Muffingate" is an example of what can happen when technology and irresponsibility collide. Toward the end of 2011 the Office of the Inspector General released a report detailing the amount of money U.S. Attorneys spent on food at various conferences between 2007-2009. The total was nearly a half-million dollars. But that's not what the media keyed in on. *The Washington Post, New York Times, USA Today* and a host of others focused their reports on one meeting where the Department of Justice supposedly paid $16 per muffin.

Reporters and government watchdogs poured on the criticism, hurled accusations, and demanded change in regard to conference spending.

Problem is there were no $16 dollar muffins.

# Break Out of PR Prison

As the media pounced on the alleged wasted tax dollars it came to light that the $16 bill was for the entire breakfast lawyers were treated to, which included a muffin. The story was localized and repeated in markets around the country for days until a few sparse corrections began appearing in reports.

In a *Wall Street Journal* opinion piece James Q. Wilson, a Pepperdine University professor, argues that "gotcha" news must end but concedes that may not be possible because, "In the current news climate..newspapers losing circulation, television programs locked in bitter conflict with their rivals, and bloggers searching eagerly for some way to call attention to themselves does not lend itself to careful reporting and thoughtful analysis."

The round-the-clock aggressive reputation defense now required of corporations may seem overwhelming at first. But elected officials, litigants, and regulators are increasingly abandoning personal responsibility in favor of a sense of entitlement. That has prompted them to behave much more aggressively toward corporations which are routinely singled out as culprits. Matters that could once be settled with little fanfare are now magnified and used to polarize a population. Moreover, entities now exist to capitalize on the risks of doing business in this environment.

AIG, the insurance giant that needed a $182 billion dollar federal bailout to survive the 2008 financial collapse, is now offering crisis insurance. It's called ReputationGuard, and for a fee, the product is designed to offset the costs associated with hiring outside PR firms during a crisis. The product is allegedly marketed to smaller or mid-sized companies lacking PR departments that might be willing to pay a $10,000 yearly premium or more.

If a crisis triggers the insurance, a policyholder is eligible to receive consulting services from a public relations firm such as Burson-Marsteller. Please excuse taxpayers if they wince at this next piece of information. Burson-Marsteller is the same firm AIG hired after it received its multi-billion dollar bailout.

The good news is this: even smaller companies have the ability to create their own crisis insurance policy. By transforming the prism through which your organization perceives risk, aggressively pursuing threats the moment they're born, and implementing counterintuitive crisis communications strategies, a corporation can insure its own reputation without having to pay a hefty premium.

In your favor is the fact that the bar as to how corporations respond to crises is relatively low. The public expects corporations to underperform and underwhelm during times of disaster. In the midst of turmoil corporations often default into a defensive, faceless entity that proceeds to delay, obfuscate, bullshit, or even lie and cover up the crisis at hand. All of which, unless the corporation has been unduly negligent or malicious, generally worsen the crisis.

Fortunately, corporations can perform at a level much higher than the expected norm. Exceeding expectations may actually prove easier than you might think after executives overcome the anxiety associated with embracing counterintuitive strategies and techniques designed to neuter crisis creators. Some of the techniques laid out in the following pages will likely run counter to those often employed in the past. Adopting them will likely be uncomfortable at first. Creating a culture that lives and breathes some degree of constant crisis may be perceived as exhausting and insurmountable. It may even be perceived as overkill.

If so, stop reading right now.

But for those whose livelihoods are built on their reputation- the following pages are for you.

# Crises & Pornography

If only crises were as easy to spot as pornography.

Regrettably, former Supreme Court Justice Potter Stewart is most often remembered for the concurring opinion he wrote in a 1964 obscenity case in which he acknowledged pornography was hard to define but that, "I know it when I see it." Years later Stewart retracted his view on the ability to define pornography, but his original statement resonates with many and has been applied to other subjects and contexts.

Too bad Stewart's words do not often ring true for corporations and crises.

Corporations often do not know a crisis when they see one. Crises clearly define themselves but only after it's too late for organizations to prevent them from developing into larger threats to their reputations. They're akin to stock market bubbles. Most are invisible until they pop.

The goal is to make crises as easy to spot as pornography. Crisis books and consultants often include a laundry list of crises a corporation might face. I happen to believe organizations are likely already aware of these and need little help identifying obvious crises. Planes crash, oil spills, and foods and medicines are recalled. However, it's worthwhile to study the characteristics inherent in crises so corporations can better respond to the not so obvious risks to their reputations. Crisis characteristics include:

- risk starts small
- risk appears unchanged over period of time
- risk suddenly and quickly grows
- risk is amplified by technology
- risk appears on multiple stakeholder fronts and requires individually tailored mitigation strategies
- risk multiplies and leads to litigation, regulation, legislation
- risk results in loss of customer, potential customer, profitability
- risk results in damaged reputation

While individual crises masquerade or conceal themselves differently based on industry, space, and context, it's important to be familiar with the common characteristics crises often possess. Some often unforeseen threats companies should adapt their radars to spot include:

- how company success may be linked with controversy
- how required disclosures may be used against you in court of public opinion
- how lobbying efforts may be linked with the behaviors and voting records of elected officials
- how corporate travel and expenditures may be framed by critics
- how proactively addressing and solving a problem or concern may not be something that garners a positive reaction
- how overall industry turmoil or controversy can overshadow or mar individual accomplishments
- how attracting top workforce talent could also attract controversy
- how rewarding shareholders can cause pain for the corporation

While this list of often unforeseen threats is not all-inclusive, it is meant to spark boardroom conversations regarding assumptions. What might at first blush appear to be positive may in fact expose an organization to unwanted or potentially unflattering attention. Even the most noble of intentions must be scrutinized in the context of a crisis culture. An organization that fails to identify potential repercussions, with at least the same amount of rigor as a crisis creator, will be unprepared in the event of a crisis.

By the time a crisis clearly defines itself a corporation does not have time to engage in the activities outlined above. Should it attempt to do so, it will simply fall further behind.

The impact a crisis can have on a company should make clear why an ultra-aggressive and continuous mitigation strategy is required in most instances. Crisis consultants often frame the matter in thirds: pre-crisis, crisis, and post-crisis. Again, this is an outdated model that will ultimately prove far less effective than the transformative approach I'm proposing.

Dividing crisis mitigation strategy into thirds assumes there are times of non-crisis which is simply no longer valid. Additionally, there is no operational benefit to receiving information that your corporation has moved from one stage to another. An executive who is made aware his or her organization has just entered one of the three stages is going to act swiftly to end the crisis as soon as he or she is made aware a crisis exists. As a threat mounts, nothing positive can happen waiting on the next update to see if the organization has moved into a different stage.

Instead, the mitigation strategies in the pages ahead will make clear that crises are transactional by nature and are not easily categorized into thirds. Modern threats may emerge, dissipate, re-emerge or take any number of paths to becoming high-degree crises. Crises are wall clouds. At any moment they can spit out deadly tornadoes. Wall clouds also have the power to recall tornadoes. And the power to spit them out again.

Rather than adopting a set of rules and activities based on what stage a crisis has allegedly entered, successful corporations will learn to simultaneously deploy threat mitigating tools aimed at quelling threats before they can be classified as entering any stage at all.

Once a corporation becomes familiar with the characteristics associated with crises and identifies the often unforeseen consequences of seemingly good intentions, it may then engage in the five step analysis below:

1. Determine whether the threat is real or perceived

2. Determine the maturity of the threat, or its growth trajectory
3. Identify the consequences of not addressing or waiting to address the threat
4. Identify ingredients needed for threat to become crisis
5. Tailor mitigation strategy to starve threat of needed ingredients

Real-time analysis is complex and difficult. However it requires corporations to begin looking inward as a crisis creator might. In doing so, an organization might encounter incongruities with company strategy and norms. Looking inward critically may cause discomfort in regard to standard operating procedures or strategies that were approved and thought to be smartly conceived.

Organizations that opt not to become aggressively self-critical can be assured a crisis creator will.

For instance, an organization may be rolling along without a crisis in sight, but become the focus of a targeted attack by simply being successful. An organization does not even have to make an error or do anything wrong to become a magnet for negative publicity. If being targeted for being successful is not a concern of yours because your organization is a good corporate citizen and the facts are on your side, your organization is a bit naïve.

In March of 2012, gun manufacturer Sturm, Ruger & Company, Inc. announced it was no longer accepting new orders for firearms. Demand had become so great the company was no longer able to keep up with the one million gun backlog that had piled up. While the company tried to catch up with its success, antagonists pounced. Anti-gun activists complained to me and lobbied the media to run stories on how Ruger's success is dangerous.

The activists attempted to link Ruger's success with the Trayvon Martin shooting death incident. Martin was the unarmed 17-year-old shot and killed by a community watchman in Sanford, FL a month earlier. Florida's "stand your ground" self-defense law kept police from arresting the shooter immediately, which prompted questions of racism. Martin was black and the shooter is white. Protests and demonstrations were staged nationwide.

Anti-gun activists suggested companies like Ruger are partially responsible for gun violence like that in the Martin case. At a Martin rally in the upper Midwest activists went so far as to say corporate greed killed Martin. When asked, none of the activists I challenged could tell me what type of gun was used in the Martin shooting.

It was a Kel-Tec 9mm, not a Ruger.

I'm aware of no one protesting outside Kel-Tec's headquarters or negatively linking it with the Martin controversy. So why was Ruger targeted? As illogical as it is, Ruger's announcement touting its success was made at an inopportune time and used by anti-gun activists as a bridge to controversy.

Ruger did not foresee how voluntarily stepping into the spotlight with terrific company news could be used against it by activists and left-leaning media outlets. The company made its announcement five weeks prior to releasing its first quarter earnings results. It could have waited and mentioned the information during the conference call. Or since wholesale gun dealers obviously knew Ruger had stopped taking orders, maybe the company felt compelled to disclose to investors what amounted to material information.

Either way, the company likely never foresaw how news that took shares of Ruger up 10 percent the morning following the announcement could be manipulated and used against it. No amount of logic will ever defeat an activist incapable or unwilling to behave rationally. Even when the facts are on your side, a threat can evolve into a reputation damaging crisis.

Success hinges upon how an organization prepares and behaves prior to a crisis and often dictates the duration and damage a crisis causes.

Nick Winkler

# Secrets of a Crisis Creator

I took a deep breath, grabbed the television microphone, and told my photographer, "Let's do this."

As an Investigative News Reporter I had been doing surveillance on a small town City Manager for several weeks. He was gambling at a casino instead of going to work and it was time to confront him on camera.

The risk level for us was high. The casino was on tribal land which means we would not enjoy the same rights we were entitled to on non-tribal land. If we were caught entering the casino with a camera we would likely be detained, our video confiscated, and our cover blown. All of which would ruin the story we had spent so much time on.

However, thorough surveillance allowed us to dramatically reduce our risk. We noticed each of the casino security guards would step outside at the same time for a smoke break every day. After confirming the pattern we timed the smoke break. On the day we were assigned to confront the target of our investigation, we knew exactly when and for how long the casino would be without security guards.

We stormed the casino, found the City Manager sitting at a slot machine, and launched a barrage of questions which were answered with painful to watch stuttering lies, inaccuracies, and half-truths. By the time security was made aware of what had occurred, we were already gone and had hidden the video of the encounter just in case we were later pulled over by tribal authorities.

As an Investigative News Reporter I've created crises and public relations nightmares, for those deserving of them, nationwide. I've targeted greedy corporations, scoundrels, narcissists void of morals and ethics, and even girl scouts and church pastors.

So who better than a professional crisis creator to help you prevent and mitigate those crises?

# Break Out of PR Prison

Contrary to what some managers are accustomed to believing the majority of crises are not random or unforeseeable. Aside from natural disasters, acts of God, or once in a lifetime occurrences, there are generally two types of crises:

1. Those that an organization creates itself.
2. Those that are conceived, hatched, and executed by a crisis creator.

We'll address self-created crises later. The focus here is on crises created by reporters, activists, competitors, adversaries and the like. Corporations practicing smart PR techniques will be tipped off to emerging threats quicker than those practicing traditional PR. However, until an organization better understands the mechanics behind these well orchestrated schemes, there is little else a company can do to stop them.

It is important to first understand the objectives underlying a crisis created by investigative reporters, new influencers, and activist bloggers. Simply put, media producers are using the crisis to make money. It is no more complex than that. Remember the two most important criteria for newsworthiness:

- A story must be teasable or promotable
- A story must be deemed more likely than others to generate ratings or increase viewership

An important matter of public health, safety, or finance may be ignored by media producers despite its unquestionable news value if it lacks sizzle or sexiness. Conversely, a story of very little news value may be teased, promoted, and stretched out over a matter of days if a media producer believes viewers or readers will gravitate toward it.

Like it or not, these are the rules by which those who are targeted are forced to play.

Therefore, the only way to successfully mitigate an attack is to immerse oneself in that environment and learn the rules of the game prior to resetting them. Additionally, organizations must investigate the methodologies and techniques used to execute the attacks. Finally, an organization can then use that intelligence to create smart and often counterintuitive strategies designed to ultimately starve the crisis.

Listed below are key objectives investigative media producers have identified and attempt to execute. They are not likely written down anywhere. They are not likely communicated directly to subordinates either. But they guide strategy and execution efforts.

- Expose wrongdoing
- Reveal waste
- Uncover corruption
- Identify ethical lapses
- Highlight errors in judgment
- Find and close legal loopholes
- Prompt legislative hearings
- Change laws
- Alter public policy
- Shift the focus of a debate
- Prompt a lawsuit
- Remove someone from a position of authority
- Coin a new term
- Identify and name a phenomena
- Prompt a recall
- Expose inefficiencies
- Follow up to see if problems have actually been corrected

In and of themselves there may not be anything inherently wrong or unethical about these objectives. Plenty of good could result from accomplishing these objectives. And sometimes it does. However, corners are being cut at cash starved traditional mediums. The threat compounds when the limited mental capacities of some of the crisis creators are taken into account.

Awards and recognition are byproducts of these goals. Both are extremely important to media producers. Fights have erupted over which staffers are entitled to trophies after being recognized for their work. Even smaller media outlets spend thousands of dollars submitting awards entries. It is pay to play. Those who win then quickly promote the fact in hopes of boosting ratings, circulation, or page views.

But let's not forget, these micro-goals as I call them, are all designed to do one thing and are housed under one umbrella objective: to increase revenue for the media producer. In an effort to avoid hypocrisy, taking on risk in a business endeavor with the goal of profiting is not wrong. However, it is unseemly when corporations with the same overriding goal are targeted unfairly.

The conflict at hand becomes even more transparent when the objectives of a crisis creator are compared with those of an organization embroiled in crisis:

- Minimize crisis duration
- Minimize damage to reputation
- Minimize mitigation costs
- Minimize liabilities
- Minimize customer loss
- Minimize profit decline
- Minimize share price decline
- Minimize employee turnover
- Minimize regulatory impact
- Minimize continued media attention
- Minimize loss of stakeholder trust & support
- Minimize chance of repeating crisis

Clearly, the objectives of the two rivals outlined above are not congruent. In fact, one could make a case they are diametrically opposed. However, there is one objective the rivals share- to fix the crisis at hand. Each of the parties would of course prefer to fix the crisis at hand on their own time and in their own way. Each at least would prefer to play a role in steering the other toward a fix beneficial to their reputation. The party that succeeds in steering this segment of the crisis is the one that can count themselves as a winner.

But how does an organization wrest control of the wheel and begin steering it in a more favorable direction? It's worthwhile to examine the methodology underpinning the manner in which crises are executed. Earlier, we briefly outlined four broad tenets characteristic of crisis creation game plans used by many NGOs:

1. Create incendiary content or claims
2. Magnify the content using technology and the media
3. Leverage attention to boost membership and fundraising efforts
4. Pour money raised into next target

Breaking down this framework even further reveals the following 15 methodologies and strategies on which many crises are modeled:

- Target that which is vulnerable
- Build & train a base prior to going public
- Gather intelligence
- Infiltrate entity and collect video & pictures
- Engage entity with written communications or pleas to provoke private response
- Identify and reinforce stereotypes regarding entity
- Magnify misconceptions
- Position entity as counter to cultural or legal norms
- Localize conflict
- Bridge or link entity to conflict
- Alert media to event or display

- Confront entity publicly
- Highlight entity's delayed or incomplete response
- Feed media follow ups
- Make public an entity's private written communications and highlight inconsistencies

Crises are often well-planned, well-organized, and executed while organizations are preoccupied with managing day to day business operations. An organization that has not devoted time and resources to detecting and mitigating threats to its reputation will be no match when months of crisis planning rain down unexpectedly. If an organization is surprised when confronted with crisis, it's too late.

Reverse engineering a crisis is one strategy investigative reporters may use to conceptualize a story after receiving a tip or database. More specifically, an investigative reporter might sketch out a framework of the story in advance of actually gathering additional information or first discussing the piece with the target. An argument can be made this ensures completeness; if a reporter only has one shot at confronting a target he or she is ethically bound to give the target an opportunity to respond to each of the allegations to be mentioned in the report. The bigger issue for an organization is the amount of preparation a crisis creator has usually undertaken versus that of the target.

The preparation imbalance can determine the severity of the damage to a reputation. For instance, after intense preparation I would often finally confront a target when he or she was unable to immediately extract themselves from the confrontation. This allowed for plenty of harsh questioning and plenty of opportunity for a target to react inappropriately. It's human nature to become angry, flustered, and nervous when unexpectedly trapped in a high pressure situation.

A crisis creator can rehearse, role play, and refine their strategy in advance of the confrontation. A target gets only one shot. Most are unprepared. And most perform poorly whether they are guilty or not.

It's horribly unfair.

But it's also preventable for those who deem their reputation as an asset worthy of a small protective investment.

# Suicide by Crisis

Putting a crisis gun to an organization's head and pulling the trigger happens all too frequently.

This section addresses a common but largely avoidable mistake; self-created crises.

The external threats to an organization's reputation are often easier to spot than those that may be right under a corporation's nose. Far too often though, corporations overlook, underestimate, or are simply blind to internal threats that can be equally or even more devastating than those originating outside the organization.

Self-created crises distract corporations from their goals, reduce operational efficiency, and open the door for additional probing by outside threats. The irony is self-created crises are far more common than those created by external threats. Identifying behaviors and activities that may internally spark a crisis is necessary for corporations eager to avoid suicidal crisis tendencies.

Grocery chain Kroger learned this lesson quickly.

As part of the company's marketing plan it sponsored a contest in which a participant could win $10,000 by sinking a half-court shot during halftime of a University of Kentucky basketball game. UK freshman Vincent Swope was chosen to take the shot. Swope heaved the basketball from half-court, sank the shot, and was reportedly running a victory lap when contest organizers approached.

A video replay of the shot suggested Swope may have launched the shot an inch past the half-court line. Swope was an inch too close to the basket. It meant Swope had violated the contest rules and that Kroger was no longer required to dole out the prize money. However, it did not take Kroger long to see the error of its ways.

By the second half of the game, a radio program was rallying behind Swope and against Kroger. A protest was launched via Twitter and at least two students reportedly took handmade signs and protested outside a Kroger store.

Kroger bowed to the pressure. The grocer wound up paying Swope the $10,000 it had advertised for sinking the shot.

It's not likely that anyone decided not to shop at Kroger over the incident but it is not helpful for a company in a competitive, low-margin business to raise doubts about its integrity. Why give anyone a reason not to like you? The lesson here is that Kroger's self-created crisis prompted negative publicity on the radio, online, and on social media.

Kroger took what was clearly an opportunity and turned it into a crisis.

The grocer could have easily pointed out that while Swope was technically across the line the company was still going to award Swope the prize because Kroger is an organization that values people and their accomplishments. It would have earned the company a customer for life. Instead, the company earned a PR headache that cost much more than the $10,000 prize money.

As an Investigative News Reporter, I've seen the self-created crisis mistake made routinely. After a self-created crisis I often found myself listening closely to discussions among reporters covering the crisis. Reporters are often shocked by how tone deaf or blind a corporation is in regard to anticipating consequences. Common reporter refrains include, "Had the company not done X, I never would have thought to look at Y." Reporters view self-created crises as gifts.

Stop giving reporters gifts.

A self-created crisis puts an organization on defense and opens the corporation to further probing from the media. A self-created crisis is often reason enough for reporters to begin digging further. Self-created crises are often preludes to externally created crises that inflict even greater damage on an organization's reputation.

Below are 10 common origins of self-created crises:

- Accounting errors and restatements
- Compliance issues
- Promotion
- Speculation
- Careless use of email
- Greed
- Failure to identify reporter agendas
- Lobbying efforts exposed
- Executive speeches
- Travel and perks
- Questionable personal/professional relationships

The idea here is not to list each and every origin from which a self-created crisis may be born but rather to make clear the importance of identifying the avoidable internal risks to an organization's reputation. Steering a narrative is a challenge in and of itself. It is inefficient and costly to create additional problems. Below are the five most common avoidable self-created crisis mistakes:

1. Failure to recognize a threat
2. Failure to accurately gauge the impact of a threat
3. Failure to prioritize threat
4. Allowing another entity to define an issue or your organization
5. Lacking or possessing weak relationships to mitigate threats

Suicide by crisis is entirely avoidable. Identifying where self-created crises originate and avoiding the mistakes most common in these types of crises allows an organization to more aggressively pursue external threats and steer narratives.

However, corporations often do just the opposite and make matters worse.

# Making the Crisis Kitchen Even Hotter

I've won bets with other reporters by correctly predicting a corporation's next PR blunder.

It's rather easy to do.

While the specific details embedded in a crisis will vary, corporate responses to common mistakes and crises often do not. Organizations in the midst of crisis routinely make the same errors when responding. For instance, corporations repeat clichés because they are deemed as safe. And much like a deer caught in a vehicle's headlights, corporations often freeze and allow themselves to be run over.

Toyota Motor Corp. is a prime example.

The company has built its reputation around making vehicles of a higher quality than competitors. However, in 2010 the carmaker was forced to recall millions of vehicles because of sticky gas pedals that some say caused vehicles to suddenly accelerate. Rather than delivering the bad news itself and all at once, the company engaged in what I call the **slow bleed**.

Slow bleeds are costly.

The National Traffic Highway Administration fined Toyota more than $16 million dollars for purposefully withholding safety information from the federal government. Even Toyota now admits it did not communicate well throughout the ordeal. Here we have a company that ultimately threw away much of the goodwill it had built with a forgiving public.

Instead of ripping the bandage off all at once to immediately begin the healing process, Toyota opted for an approach favored by many suicidal organizations: the slow bleed. The organization did not respond promptly and was perceived as being forced to do the right thing rather than choosing to do so. Pieces of bloody news dripped out of Toyota's wounds almost daily over the course of months.

During a slow bleed, a corporation becomes a piñata that is repeatedly beaten by competitors, politicians, and the media. By making this common mistake, a wound often becomes infected and leads to other health problems for an organization's reputation. When a company prolongs a crisis and simultaneously erodes its credibility, it neuters its PR department. Below are 10 common mistakes organizations make that worsen crises:

1. Lie
2. Cover Up
3. Bullshit
4. Slow bleed
5. Hide
6. Speculate
7. Unnecessary document creation
8. Document destruction
9. Total deference to legal counsel
10. Total deference to outside PR firm

Embedded in each of these common crisis-enhancing mistakes is the element of time. More specifically, each of these mistakes increases an organization's crisis response time to some degree.

Showing up late to the crisis party puts an organization at a disadvantage from which most are unable to fully recover. It makes no difference whether you are unaware of the party or simply were not invited. Corporations unprepared to aggressively and immediately respond to a crisis often belatedly determine it's time to barge through the door, crash the crisis party, and turn the lights out on those hurting the organization's reputation. However, doing so causes damage to the organization's image.

It's much like crashing a wedding.

Picture a guy barging into a church just as the couple is ready to say "I do" and announcing he's in love with the bride and that the bride loves him. Even if the guy is right, he's still an asshole for crashing the wedding and hurting so many people emotionally and financially. The guy should have spoken up sooner. As a result, no one leaves the church a winner.

Arriving late to a crisis only increases the number of losers.

Don't be a loser.

Organizations mired in crisis also often fail to segment audiences and stakeholders. A one size fits all approach is not a recipe for success, especially when a corporation is being attacked on multiple fronts.

I call it a **failure to tailor**.

Corporations must be mindful to tailor crisis communications by medium, by reporter, and across all stakeholder groups. For instance, if a PR staff headquartered in the Northwest fails to understand cultural nuances of a stakeholder in the Southeast, then crisis communications will not be as potent. Regional, cultural, and religious differences must be considered when developing a crisis communications strategy. If not, the organization risks alienating a potential source of support during times of crisis.

Breaking the insane but repetitive cycle of common crisis-worsening mistakes outlined in this section is a fate only the organization itself may dictate. Most only learn the hard way.

A smarter way exists.

Nick Winkler

# Early Recognition

The bases are loaded.

The ballgame is tied.

Now picture 50-thousand fans screaming belligerently as their beloved hometown slugger comes to the plate in the bottom of the ninth inning with no outs and the chance to win the game in hero-like style.

If you're the team with its back up against the wall, who do you want on the mound? Who do you hand the ball to who has the confidence and ability to pitch his way out of this jam? Many would turn to their ace with the best fastball. Or an intimidating pitcher with a knee-buckling curveball.

Greg Maddux had neither of those.

But as one of Major League Baseball's all-time best, team managers repeatedly turned to Maddux over parts of three decades during times of crisis and strife. Barely six feet tall wearing spikes, Maddux's fastball was underwhelming, rarely topping the upper-80s in speed. You might even mistake a bespectacled Maddux for a school teacher or professor when not on the pitching mound.

However, Maddux was the picture of calm amid chaos.

An unrelenting competitor, Maddux used finesse, pitch location, and ball movement to outclass more athletically gifted competitors. When the chips were stacked against Maddux, he bore down and focused even harder. He was stubborn too. In fact, Maddux once said he'd rather walk in the winning run than cave to the pressure and give a batter a pitch he could hit.

So how does an undersized Texan with an underwhelming fastball go on to win 355 games and four Cy Young awards?

One reason is Maddux actively sought out crisis scenarios prior to an actual crisis. He envisioned strategies to successfully overcome crises. All of it simultaneously helped him become more confident and comfortable in crisis situations.

Maddux accomplished all of this without even setting foot on a baseball field.

I was a young sports reporter working my way through school when I snuck into a locker room prior to a game to learn the secret of Maddux's success. Maddux was kind enough to tell me how he often visualized succeeding against talented hitters in stressful situations. Mental visualization was an important component of Maddux's training model.

By the time Maddux actually found himself on the mound facing a tough hitter, he had already visualized how he wanted to pitch to that hitter. He had already seen himself locating pitches exactly where he wanted. He had already seen himself performing at a high level under difficult circumstances. So when it was time to actually throw a pitch Maddux was supremely confident in the outcome because he had already seen himself successfully handling the situation time and time again.

If the bases were loaded with no outs and a slugger coming to the plate to win the game, Maddux wasn't shaken. He had already been in that exact scenario dozens of times before in his mind. He already knew what it would take to escape the crisis with a win and had pictured himself doing it repeatedly. Maddux was already a winner without even throwing a pitch.

Similar preparation can help organizations avoid a common yet grievous error: not recognizing a crisis or the potential for one.

Historically, large corporate PR departments are often late in recognizing or detecting emerging threats. The oversight is compounded by the fact that time is not on your side during a crisis. Corporations that fail to envision crisis scenarios are less likely to recognize them when they actually begin to emerge.

Crises are not invisible.

Early detection is possible but you must know where to look and what to look for.

Well prepared corporations actively seek out and prepare for potential threats or crises they may encounter. Doing so gives an organization the head start it needs if it is going to aggressively confront an emerging threat and stop it from becoming a crisis.

Initially, organizations are well served by conducting a thorough risk assessment. Prior to learning how to spot an external emerging threat, a corporation will benefit from identifying where it is weak or most vulnerable. In other words, identify the low-hanging fruit by which a reporter, critic, or activist might first be enticed. Several areas for potential investigation are listed below:

- Balance sheet weaknesses
- Debt load or covenants
- Accounting practices
- Environmental policies
- Workplace harassment
- Executive personal behavior
- Questionable or unconventional business strategies
- Potential to be acquired
- Shareholder friendliness
- Minority employment

The idea here is to prepare by attacking yourself. Taking an honest look at your vulnerabilities or perceived vulnerabilities will remove the gun from the hand of a lazy reporter or activist. However, being self-critical internally is a practice some organizations find uncomfortable. I'd argue it'll be much more uncomfortable if someone else finds and uses these vulnerabilities against you.

An exercise like this will do more than simply identify potential areas critics may easily exploit. Critical self-examination will also position a corporation to identify blind spots, or areas of vulnerability of which it is not immediately familiar. Ultimately, the goal is to avoid being surprised by the media, critics, and activists. Self-evaluation is an internal check and balance designed to avoid groupthink and middle management's proclivity for being overly deferential to executives.

Identifying blind spots may be done in a variety of creative ways but is based on the following five tenets:

- Constantly question assumptions
- Continually seek out data contradictory to your strategy
- Constantly evaluate whether the facts your strategy is based on are still facts
- Aggressively evaluate strategy for errors in logical thinking
- Continually evaluate the efficacy of alternative strategies

Put more bluntly; an organization that blindly accepts its own business strategy, marketing, or public relations as superior to all others without continuous rigorous testing and comparison is arrogantly and ignorantly traveling down the pathway toward self-destruction. Identifying blind spots is a precursor that allows corporations to transition from internal threat detection to external.

A corporation that takes an outward-in approach to these areas of concern can begin to view itself the way a critic might. Identifying issues that may be easily plucked by critics and used to harm the organization's reputation may be mitigated or eliminated altogether using this approach. Doing so enables organizations to focus more time and attention recognizing external emerging threats.

The key to successfully identifying external emerging threats hinges upon a single skill: active listening. Arguably, becoming an active listener is the key behavior around which nearly all business should be focused. Often, the best reporters, sales people, and managers possess active listening skills. The information gathered by using active listening skills is the foundation on which strategy, directives, and communications is based.

For our purpose, the textbook definition of active listening is irrelevant. Here, active listening means tenaciously seeking out and listening to what is being said about your organization, industry, competitors and then using the information gathered to anticipate and prepare communications that simultaneously mitigate risk and bolster reputation. In essence, active listening is akin to gathering intelligence. It is not a time for communications or shared understanding. It is solely an exercise in intelligence gathering that will ultimately dictate strategy.

Organizations that aim to successfully extract intelligence must leverage existing relationships for a full and accurate picture. For instance, it is not enough to map and build relationships with reporters. It is not enough to continuously monitor media and social networking content. Organizations must also gather intelligence from sources that often feed or prompt news reports and activism. Five of the most common crisis ignition sources are listed below:

- District Attorneys
- US Attorneys
- Trial Attorneys
- Attorneys General
- Auditors and Inspectors

These crisis ignition sources often enjoy a distinct advantage over the targets of the crisis. By virtue of the authority each possess these sources often strike first in the media and court of public opinion. Entities targeted by any of these ignition sources are often immediately put on the defensive. Later, I'll outline strategies to mitigate the advantage these ignition sources hold over their targets.

Additionally, corporate PR staffs must become voracious media consumers as part of their active listening routines. An organization that actively hunts for emerging threats positions itself to eliminate the threat early with a fire extinguisher rather than later when a fire truck hose will be needed. Below is a list of places organizations should visit frequently for active listening sessions:

- Industry gossip rags & websites
- Complaint boards
- Social review sites
- Unflattering websites containing organization's name
- Local legal blogs
- Guest newspaper opinion columns
- Comment sections beneath online media stories
- Union newsletters
- Shareholder newsletters & websites
- NGO (Non-governmental organization) newsletters & websites
- Political campaign contribution disclosure filings

CIA spooks will tell you the best type of intelligence is HUMINT, or human intelligence. This is the type of data gathered by people who have infiltrated a group or organization. Since NGOs, unions, and political foes are not likely to openly welcome you into their strategy planning sessions, organizations are well served when they spend time and money smartly gathering HUMINT.

Organizations or their liaisons must join these groups. Keeping enemies closer than friends will likely require a counterintuitive approach. Organizations will likely have to donate money to causes potentially detrimental to the organization. Doing so allows for access to strategy planning meetings and newsletters. However, a small donation or yearly membership dues entitles the organization to a valuable behind the scenes look at the threat. Gathering intelligence in this manner may also require organizations to personally join protests or rallies held by NGOs.

Extracting HUMINT in this manner arms an organization with the information it needs to accurately determine the impact of a potential risk. Without the proper intelligence a corporation is less likely to correctly forecast impact. When attempting to gauge the impact of an emerging threat it is essential to determine the following:

- Validity of threat
- Potential for threat to spread or develop widespread support
- Potential for threat to garner media attention
- Potential for threat to prompt legislation, regulation, or litigation
- Potential for threat to impact profitability
- Potential for threat to impact share price
- Potential for threat to impact customer loyalty
- Potential for threat to impact reputation
- Potential organization has of reducing threat

Crisis consultants often advise organizations engaged in this type of analysis to also determine the urgency of an emerging risk. However, I'd argue that urgency is irrelevant if a threat meets several of the above criteria. If a threat has the potential to negatively impact a company it should be mitigated or eliminated immediately or as soon as resources are available to do so. Urgency should be high for any threat that meets the criteria above. There is little or no advantage to assigning a degree of urgency to a threat. If a threat can adversely affect a corporation it should be eliminated as quickly as possible not ranked on an urgency continuum.

That said, urgency should not be confused with prioritization. When an organization is confronted by multiple emerging threats deemed as having the potential to adversely impact the organization, the goal remains the same; mitigate or eliminate the threats as soon as possible. However, that may not be possible on all fronts.

While it's preferential to attack threats simultaneously an organization may lack the needed resources to eliminate multiple threats all at once. If this is the case, organizations must prioritize the threats. Prioritizing threats is done by determining which has the greatest impact on the corporation. Organizations must attack those first. However, further prioritization may be achieved by determining the maturity of a threat. Threats with the greatest level of maturity have the greatest potential for impact and will become priorities versus those possessing less maturity and potential for impact.

If the potential for harm is low then it may be in an organization's interest not to address the threat. If an emerging threat is deemed not to be valid it might very well dissipate due to lack of support. However, the threat should continue to be monitored in case the organization's analysis is incorrect. Or if the emerging threat catches a second wind and materializes. Or if the threat merges with a similar threat with a greater potential for impact.

None of this is possible without first recognizing the existence of a threat. An organization is powerless to mitigate a threat it does not first recognize. If a threat is not detected early, the organization will likely be caught flat-footed, unprepared, and on the defensive. Catching up to a threat is extremely difficult. But actively seeking out and anticipating potential threats, visualizing how to overcome those threats, and executing a tailored strategy when it's time to do so for real are the secrets of preparedness.

It made Greg Maddux one of baseball's best.

It can do the same for your organization.

# Hire a Headache

Headaches hurt.
Getting rid of them quickly often prevents them from getting worse.

However, masking the pain of a public relations headache is not optimal.

Organizations aiming to safeguard themselves from public relations headaches should think counterintuitively. Instead of reaching for aspirin at the first sign of discomfort, smart organizations probe deeper in search of the headache's root cause. Instead of bombarding a migraine with prescription medication, successful corporations embrace the pain associated with the unflattering discovery.

In fact, the sharpest corporations actually seek out headaches and pain.

Seeking out pain prolongs the suffering internally. But identifying the root cause of the pain is much more beneficial to corporations that would prefer to heal themselves privately rather than allowing symptoms of the pain to be made public.

Organizations need a CETO, or Chief Emerging Threat Officer.

A CETO is a person who digs up a corporation's dirty laundry long before it can be found and aired publicly by a reporter or regulator. A CETO is constantly searching internally and externally for emerging threats. He or she is on the prowl for wrongdoing, inefficiency, and corruption. It's analogous to inviting Mike Wallace of *60 Minutes* into your company's inner workings and telling the adversarial newsman to run amuck. The difference here is that Wallace would be reporting his findings to top executives, not the public.

The need for a CETO, or something similar, became clear to me early on as a reporter. I am constantly surprised at how surprised crisis targets are when confronted. An executive unprepared for an ambush interview or congressional hearing is one whose team has let him or her down.

Especially in an age where executives are expected to be what I call hyper-accountable.

The expectation was born out of the Enron scandal in 2001. The Sarbanes-Oxley Act resulted, requiring costly additional accounting and regulatory measures. Seven years later, the financial collapse of 2008 prompted additional financial regulation in the form of the Dodd-Frank Act. In this context the cost of compliance has risen dramatically and so too has the accountability expected of today's corporate executives.

Fair or not, this is a time when executives are being held accountable for the behavior of each and every employee scattered across the globe. It is no longer excusable for an executive not to know about wrongdoing at his or her corporation, despite multiple layers of management between the executive and a wrongdoer. Combine this with auditors possibly being required to pass judgment on an organization's accounting strategies and SEC filings along with a whistleblower act that creates financial incentives for employees to contact authorities prior to notifying management, and more has never been expected of senior managers.

It's why senior managers need their own bulldog reporter unearthing threats before others do.

Think of a Chief Emerging Threat Officer as an investigative reporter, regulatory compliance officer, and newspaper ombudsman all rolled into one. A CETO's job is to uncover anything and everything that may be unflattering to an organization and its executives. A CETO is expected to tenaciously follow leads, instigate investigations, and follow the money wherever it might lead.

A CETO is purposefully expected be a thorn in managements' side. He or she is expected to create headaches. A CETO is required to speak truth to power. He or she must be given the range to move inconspicuously throughout the organization with the sole intent of finding dirt. Executives should cringe when they receive a CETO's verbal report (reports will not be made in writing). However, most executives would agree it is much better to face and deal with bitter truths internally.

Tenaciously seeking out faults prevents emerging threats from growing into crises. The labor a CETO can save a corporate PR department is substantial. An effective CETO allows a corporate PR staff to proactively focus on key message conveyance rather than crisis mitigation.

Each organization employing some version of a CETO will determine the means by which a CETO gathers intelligence. A corporation lacking the resources to hire a full-time CETO may choose to periodically bring in an outside CETO to conduct a threat assessment. To compete with the Securities and Exchange Commission, an organization may find it beneficial to construct financial incentives for employees to first pass along information to a CETO rather than regulators. The CETO will obviously monitor employee communications, aid in identifying unintended media leaks, and determine responsibility for unresolved customer complaints.

While a CETO will be aggressively proactive in his or her queries, the CETO will also find work from tips received just as a reporter would. After communicating internally about the role of a CETO, an organization might include a "Contact Me" button on its intranet site or provide anonymous means for contact.

Determining the proper authority and role for a Chief Emerging Threat Officer is a discussion to be held within each organization that deems the idea valuable. Effort must also be taken to ensure employees view the concept as a proactive approach to becoming a better company rather than a distrustful spying scheme. Concerns aside, there is little debate over the value derived from ruthless self-examination in terms of reputation management.

The underlying goal is simple; find that which is wrong before a reporter, regulator, or litigator does.

After identifying emerging threats the next logical step is to determine how to eliminate or mitigate the threat. Often, consultants advise corporations they must form crisis teams or committees to deal with such matters. Corporations have spent tremendous sums of money on consultants who outline crisis teams and plans. However, the advice often provided to corporations is cookie cutter in nature- a template that is used across industries and contexts and lacks the specificity an individual organization deserves.

In other words hiring outsiders to identify who should be on your crisis team is a waste of time and money.

Executive teams and middle management are already in place. Shuffling or selecting certain individuals to form a crisis team is actually a disservice to the organization's reputation. Publicly identifying a crisis specialty team tells those not selected for the team they do not have to be concerned with emerging threats. Doing so signals they are not key components in protecting the organization and its reputation. Each and every employee has a stake in the corporation. And everyone should be accountable and included in the proactive defense of the organization's reputation.

All hands should be on deck.

Crisis and emergency preparedness consultants have made livings creating teams and selecting groups within organizations based on the idea that specially selected groups are better equipped to handle a crisis. However, it has been my experience creating additional groups that must then hold additional meetings simply adds layers of bureaucracy and slows an organization's response. Specialty crisis teams will simply delegate much of the heavy lifting to employees anyway. Those employees that lack a crisis mentality or who were not privy to the crisis team meetings will likely not be trained to respond with the swiftness required of a crisis.

What should be clear by now is that everyone within an organization should be on the crisis team.

If an organization employs the strategies outlined thus far and prepares rigorously for emerging threats, dedicated crisis teams are not needed. When an organization embraces the concept of actively hunting emerging threats and crises it positions itself as an entity not needing a special team of all-stars to extinguish fires. When identifying and eliminating threats becomes second nature to an organization, it will no longer be hampered by time wasting meetings and bureaucracy that hobbles and slows organizations that are surprised and unprepared.

Obviously, unforeseen crises will arise in the form of natural disasters and acts of God that will require an organization to activate a plan or a predetermined series of actions. And if a corporation feels more comfortable preselecting a specialty crisis team then it should do so. However, I'd argue a corporation that instills emerging threat detection in its DNA arms each and every employee with the mindset needed to quickly spot and extinguish threats. This strategy multiplies an organization's eyes and ears and dramatically increases the chance for early mitigation.

Instilling a crisis mentality in each employee rather than relying on a select few to handle a crisis after it has grown also allows corporations to avoid blind spots and group think. The greater the number of radars an organization has increases the odds it will identify a thunderstorm. Nimble corporations should use each and every set of eyes and ears at their disposal to spot a wall cloud before it spits out a tornado. Doing so allows management to be notified and educated early. Then it is simply a matter of executing the most efficient and effective mitigation strategy.

By now many organizations already have in place plans for a number of crisis scenarios specific to their industry. Many have dark sites, or non-published websites into which specific crisis details may be plugged and brought online immediately after a crisis. Ultimately, the goal of this type of preparedness is to position the organization as the primary source of information during a crisis. Becoming the primary narrator affords an organization more control than it would have otherwise. Creating redundancies in terms of technology, manpower, and narrative control is commonplace as well.

However, I routinely observe organizations that thought they were prepared for crises stumble. Missteps and mistakes are easy to make during crises. The fact of the matter is an organization's reputation will be bruised if an organization is not perfect during a crisis. It's analogous to preventing a terror attack; a terrorist must only be right once whereas the U.S. Department of Homeland Security must be correct each and every time to be successful.

Before outlining the framework on which any successful crisis plan may be based, keep in mind that creativity, ingenuity, and a fix-it-yourself mentality are the safety nets onto which you fall if and when a crisis spirals outside the limitations of a mitigation plan. While the framework outlined below is listed in a methodical order readers should not view the behaviors as actions to be taken only after the prior step is completed. Instead, the steps outlined below should be executed simultaneously and used in tandem to achieve the goal of establishing the organization as the primary narrator during times of crisis. Be the first to do the following:

- Announce the crisis
- Contact victims' families
- Get to physical location of crisis
- Ensure response is visible
- Bring dedicated crisis website public
- Establish and cater rest area for first responders & victims
- Seek out critics
- Seek out third party advocates
- Establish and cater media staging area
- Supply backup power and cellular phone infrastructure
- Reassure vendors, suppliers, customers, regulators, elected officials

- Provide pictures and video of response not visible to media
- Rank the crisis
- Identify media deadlines and potential for maximum influence
- Steer daily narrative beginning with morning newscasts
- Publish own news around the clock
- Publicly declare daily goals
- Continuously show progress or attainment of goals
- Visibly solve crisis access or communications issues for first responders

This framework aims to outline steps that may be taken in the event of a major crisis. Many, if not all of these steps, are avoidable if emerging threats are detected early. Some of the strategies mentioned here will be expanded upon in greater detail in the pages to come.

# Starve the Crisis

A crisis dies if it is not able to eat.
Therefore, an organization's job in defending its reputation against a crisis is to spark a crisis famine. However, an organization can only position itself to starve a crisis after it identifies the nutrients a crisis needs to grow. While these nutrients will vary depending on where and how a crisis originates, several of the more common crisis ingredients are listed below:

- Grassroots activism
- Financial contributions
- Political agendas
- Media sympathy & amplification
- Undercover video footage

- Product safety concerns
- Claims of negligence or recklessness
- Business practices that run counter to cultural norms
- Inequality concerns
- Plaintiff's attorney sponsorship

An organization's degree of control over each of these crisis nutrients varies but ultimately the goal is to cut off as quickly as possible the access a crisis has to each of these ingredients. While mitigation strategies will vary depending on the specific circumstances of a crisis, the overall key to starving a crisis is to become an **Empathetic Aggressor.**

An empathetic aggressor is defined as a subject who can inconspicuously package the organization's tenacious effort to stem a crisis within a framework that, when applicable, is capable of publicly acknowledging, sympathizing, or complimenting the tenets or characteristics of a crisis or its creator. An empathetic aggressor is, when applicable, capable of subtly displaying respect for a crisis, its creator, or the universally felt emotions that permeate a crisis.

Put more bluntly, an empathetic aggressor is the guy who smiles politely after being punched in the nose and caringly asks the attacker if his fist is okay. The empathetic aggressor engages in this manner in an effort to disarm the attacker. An attacker's strategy is often based on rote memorization. If you respond like most, then the attacker can continue down his or her choreographed path.

However, organizations that immediately respond with a combination of empathy and aggression are more likely to startle an attacker. An attacker who is startled often retreats. Knocking an attacker off course is a sure way to limit a movement's ability to gain momentum and fundraise.

Characteristics of empathetic aggressors include:

- Conveys organization's willingness to listen
- Conveys organization's appreciation for critical viewpoints
- Conveys organization's desire to be good corporate citizen
- Acknowledges difficult or tough choices on which critics are seizing
- Conveys appreciation for critic's contribution to dialogue
- Acknowledges critic's intense feelings
- Conveys appreciation for the effort put forth by critics
- Identifies emotions or skills organization shares with critics

Exhibiting empathy toward a crisis or its creator removes some of the venom from its bite. Doing so immediately removes four of the more common unifiers that underpin a crisis:

1. The organization doesn't listen
2. The organization doesn't care
3. The organization is out of touch
4. The organization is not willing to change

Crisis creators often exploit these four widely held beliefs toward corporations in an effort to build support that otherwise would not exist. Immediately diffusing these beliefs prevents a movement from gaining momentum from those possessing these four beliefs but who otherwise lack a strong emotional connection to the actual movement or cause. Fringe support for a movement is likely to wane when the target of a movement exhibits empathy.

Once fringe support for a crisis is eliminated, an organization gains additional visibility to the core of a crisis. The core of a crisis is comprised of advocates no amount of empathy or reason will convince or deter. For this reason the savviest of organizations leverage the paradoxical advantage of becoming an empathetic aggressor. The outward engagement displayed by an empathetic aggressor is only equaled by the tenacity with which he or she pursues the elimination of the crisis core. Specific tactics aimed at aggressively diffusing crises will be outlined later.

Before an organization goes on the offensive it must first gather intelligence on those who comprise the core of a crisis.

Investigating an organization's accusers is a prerequisite to developing a sound mitigation strategy. Remember, in the court of public opinion, an entity is only as good as its worst perceived attribute. The same goes for an accuser and it's the job of the targeted organization to find and exploit an accuser's weakest perceived attribute. An organization cannot accurately define the issue, identify what's at stake, or develop a mitigation strategy without thoroughly researching the crisis creator.

Besides examining previous crises the accuser has orchestrated, it is critical to determine who is funding the crisis. Starving the crisis of funding may be the single most important key in ending the crisis quickly. Often though, a large financial backer of a crisis will likely believe fervently in the crisis and not easily be dissuaded. This is why a rigorous background check is important. If one cannot cut off the funding of a crisis one must focus on cutting the credibility of the crisis.

Acquiring intelligence on a crisis creator is done most efficiently by leveraging an organization's network of contacts. Well prepared organizations may already rely on developed relationships to determine which media producers may be more likely to amplify a crisis. Likewise, an organization's lobbyists can mine elected officials for data regarding the crisis creator.

Crisis creators are often veterans of the trade and leave an ample track record to examine. A thorough examination will reveal past missteps and strategies other targets employed that proved both successful and not. Learn from these. Activists often follow a strategy template much like the one described earlier in the book. Their tactics can always change. However, amassing a database of past behavior and combining it with personal, financial, and behavioral intelligence will provide an organization the ammunition needed to go on the offensive.

Below is what I call the **Offensive Crisis Communications Playbook**. It includes five strategies, in no particular order, aimed at using the intelligence an organization has gathered to reduce the duration of a crisis or increase an organization's ability to steer the narrative during a crisis:

1. **Blitz the Accuser-** This is where an organization's intelligence gathering pays dividends. When attacking an accuser's credibility, organizations will use a crisis creator's contradictions, errors in logical thinking, unethical practices, inconsistencies, intentional omissions, and context-lacking assertions to reduce the crisis creator's credibility. Doing so will also reveal hidden agendas, uncover unsavory motives, paint the accuser as a hypocrite, or prompt stakeholders to perceive the accuser as indecent. Blitzing the accuser is not the same as blaming a victim. Blaming a victim is not a tactic that often yields success. *Note: Organizations are always well served to leave a bullet in the chamber in regard to intelligence gathering. More specifically, always keep a piece of inflammatory or embarrassing intelligence in your back pocket and make sure the accuser knows you have it. It's similar to possessing a nuclear weapon, a great deterrent that is better left unused.*

2. **Tell on Yourself-** The savviest organizations strike first during a crisis and are the first to alert the media to an organizational crisis. This tactic runs counter to the way many organizations handle a crisis and that is why it is so effective. The media expects corporations to cover up or minimize bad news. Striking first might be impossible in the event of a natural disaster or act of God, but an organization can make a similar impact by alerting new influencers and journalists to a crisis. Engaging the media

in this manner tilts the balance of credibility in the organization's favor. It'll be early in the crisis. The organization will have few if any details. None of that matters though. By calling reporters and telling them a crisis has occurred, you are on the way to the scene, and you'll meet them there with an update, an organization positions itself as the primary narrator, unafraid to address bad news, and already working toward a solution. Notifying the media of a crisis may be the most effective means of building instantaneous credibility. Doing so often dictates how the media cover your corporation for the duration of the crisis. A reward often goes to those who come in first. Be first and reap the rewards.

3. **Hold a Cattle Drive**- Prior to a crisis, smart corporations already have strategies in place to drive the media to the organization for crisis information. Think of it like a cattle drive; the organization's goal is to surround the herd of media producers and lead it safely to a predetermined location most beneficial to the organization. This establishes the organization as the primary narrator and will dictate how initial media coverage is shaped. Without a reporter cattle drive, members of the media herd will scatter in a number of directions and begin gathering information not provided or verified by the company. Eventually, this is likely to happen anyway. But at least initially, in the moments following the birth of a crisis, the organization must establish itself as the primary source of crisis information. If not, there is little hope of steering stray reporters back into the herd for direction from the corporation.

4. **Ride a Cutting Horse**- Cowboys use cutting horses to "cut" or remove individual calves from a herd. A similar

strategy should be employed when a corporation identifies problem media producers during a crisis. Problem reporters are defined as those who are reporting inaccurately on the crisis or those who are well-sourced and reporting accurate but unflattering information before their colleagues. As soon as a scoop is reported an organization will be inundated with requests for confirmation. This is where organizations are often caught flat-footed, become reactionary, and fall behind in the sprint to the crisis finish line. By cutting out problem reporters from the herd, an organization can provide special attention not afforded to the rest of the herd. There are several benefits to doing so. First, pulling a reporter aside for a private conversation can be flattering and exploit the narcissism inherent in many reporters. Often, a reporter receiving special attention will do what is necessary to continue receiving attention above and beyond his or her colleagues. Second, cutting a reporter from the herd and explaining how reporting a scoop could actually harm the crisis response or make the crisis worse will resonate with a reasonable reporter. Be prepared though to give the reporter something exclusive in the future if he or she agrees to hold a scoop. Cutting a reporter from the media herd will require time and savvy. But doing so can prevent the organization from being overrun by the entire media herd.

5. **Run For President**- Organizations in the midst of crisis are well-served to pattern themselves after politicians running for the Presidency. Common among most successful politicians is their ability to crystallize an issue, or themselves, before their opponents. In other words, the first to successfully define themselves or an issue often wins the contest or debate. The same is true for organizations that find themselves in crises. Corporations

that allow a critic or the media to define a crisis and its consequences are not likely to recover or ultimately win the public relations battle. Organizations must be first to define the crisis they find themselves in. They must anticipate the rebuttal that is to follow. And they must include content contrary to that rebuttal in their initial definition of the crisis. Not only does striking first allow a corporation to crystallize the crisis at hand, it simultaneously neutralizes an opponent's first attack on the organization's definition of the crisis.

The benefits of being aggressive before, during, and after a crisis are clear. Striking first in a public relations war is a strategy some organizations are either hesitant or unprepared to employ. Going on the offensive will prove fruitful across contexts. After all, the fighter who strikes his opponent first often goes on to become the victor.

There is one exception, though.

An organization that finds itself embroiled in a crisis with regulators or elected officials must initially replace its offensive tendencies with deference. Run-ins with politicians or entities with regulatory oversight in many cases must be handled with a touch more finesse. Rather than immediately going on the offensive, organizations are best served by first identifying any hidden agendas behind congressional inquiries or allegations made by regulators.

Obviously, if a regulatory body appears open to cooperation and settling differences privately, it makes little sense to begin lobbing bombs at the first sign of attack. In cases like this, the organization often has little or no choice in terms of allowing the attacker to strike first. If the attacker is willing to work with the organization then a mutually beneficial conclusion can be created together.

In cases where politicians have unfairly demonized a corporation in the media it is often in the organization's interest to show restraint. Politicians must often be treated the same way executives treat business acquaintances in Asia, where the concept of "face" is all-important. Allowing an entity to save face is one of the greatest generosities one can afford a business partner in Asia. Applying the same rationale to politicians in the U.S. can be advantageous for organizations as well.

The day after a politician is elected, he or she begins running for the next election. They often say things they shouldn't and organizations that aggressively corner them on such mistakes often make matters worse for themselves. Politicians always appreciate a way out. Showing a politician a backdoor exit often leads to a better outcome for a corporation in crisis than starting a war.

Organizations that find themselves in conflict with Attorneys General, congressional oversight committees, or regulators must first use tact rather than brawn. Quickly determine whether the attacking entity is open to cooperation. Identify what is truly motivating the attacking entity's behavior.

Only after an organization determines an Attorney General or politically motivated regulatory body is using the corporation as a means to a political end should the corporation aggressively and publicly dismantle the attacker. Granted, the organization will begin its fight at a disadvantage. However, it is well worth the risk when dealing with entities that possess the ability to levy fines or charges against an organization.

These are the only instances in which an initial lack of aggression may be beneficial to an organization.

# What to Say, How to Say it, & in What Order

Reputations are both ruined and solidified beneath the crisis spotlight.

The time to speak during a crisis is a time at which an organization is simultaneously most vulnerable and afforded the biggest opportunity. Unfortunately, the relationships built, intelligence gathered, and rigorous preparation in which an organization has engaged will provide little help when it is time to actually speak during a crisis.

The only things that matter here are your words. Hanging on each of your words is a host of people ready and willing to make snap judgments: the media, customers, law enforcement, regulators, prosecutors, victims, and your own employees. Your words must be strong enough and possess the stamina to withstand the pressure and weight from those who are hanging on them. Your words must have the courage to address scrutiny and uncertainty.

Your words will be judged immediately.

And you'll get just one shot.

Immediately after a crisis the media will ask your organization for comment. The organization will not have many, if any, facts. You may not know what caused the crisis, how many victims there are, or how long it'll take to end the crisis. You may even know less about the crisis than the media does.

A lack of information is not a reason to remain quiet.

I can already hear corporate attorneys protesting loudly. In-house counsel will likely advise CEOs not to speak about crises of which they know little about. Counsel will likely advise doing so increases the liabilities and risks associated with dynamic situations.

Legal counsel would likely advise executives to remain mum until more is learned. However, under this logic a CEO would only be permitted to speak after the crisis has concluded, after congressional hearings, and after the subsequent prosecutorial investigations. By then the narrative has already been dictated by others. Keeping quiet, even when information is lacking, is akin to wrapping the organization's fragile reputation in a blanket, leaving it on a doorstep in the middle of the night, and hoping whoever finds it raises it with kindness and love.

If that's a risk you are willing to take, there is no need to read any further.

If not, learning what to say and how to say it when you know very little about a crisis are worthwhile investments.

The key to successful crisis communications during times when information is lacking is to build bridges. **Bridges** simply connect the unknown with the known. For example, while you might not know why the explosion occurred, you do know how you feel about the explosion. So under that hypothetical scenario building a bridge might look like this, "We're as eager to find out what happened as anyone, right now we're just hoping those involved are okay."

When you know little or nothing in the way of facts, your job is to take the media by its hands and walk it across a bridge from the unknown to the known. Below are subjects or "crutches" on which an executive can lean when information is lacking:

- Express emotion
- Describe how you feel
- Express your hopes
- Empathize with victims
- Compliment first responders
- Acknowledge devastation
- Reassure better days are ahead

Use these as crutches to fall back on when faced with a question you have no answer for after the birth of a crisis. The media actually wants to know how a Chief Executive feels immediately following a crisis. This is an opportunity to humanize the organization and connect with stakeholders on an emotional level.

The list of "crutches" may be further expanded by thinking about what an organization wants to be during a crisis and what it does not want to be. The difference is stark and may be reflected in media interviews immediately following a disaster:

| Be | Do Not Be |
|---|---|
| a problem solver | absent |
| an idea company | a blamer |
| a fixer | reliant on government |
| a giver | afraid to apologize |
| compassionate | afraid to get dirty |
| trusted | opaque in behavior |
| a leader | an obfuscator |
| responsible | a taker |

Taking time to be the things on the good list is an investment in the organization's reputation. Exhibiting the characteristics included on the bad list reinforces stereotypes and has the potential to worsen or elongate a crisis.

Ironically, the job of a crisis communicator becomes more difficult as more information becomes available. When facts begin to emerge, feelings take a back seat. This does not mean empathy is no longer important; it simply changes the rules in terms of how an executive must speak.

Everyone knows a reporter's job is to get it right. However, I've always contended getting it in the right order is just as important. Accurate facts put together in the wrong order do not make for a strong news piece. The same holds true for anyone speaking to the media during a crisis after factual information begins to emerge. The job is to get it right and get it in the right order.

The subjects to be addressed as facts emerge during a crisis must follow the order outlined here:

1. Victims and people
2. Damage to environment or animals
3. Damage to property
4. Impact on profit and money

Making statements and addressing crises in this order immediately conveys an organization's priorities. Speaking first about a matter other than the impact a crisis has had on people is reputational suicide. An organization may have perfect responses for every question asked. But if it does not correctly order its responses, the organization may be perceived as insensitive or placing a greater emphasis on profits than people.

How an executive communicates is also important. Besides being mindful of an executive's nonverbal communications, an organization must follow a strict set of rules when determining how to say something during a crisis.

Breaking the 14 rules below will likely lead to less than optimal media mentions:

**<u>Do Not</u>**
- Phrase a statement negatively
- Repeat a reporter's question
- Speculate
- Discuss liabilities
- Estimate damage or loss of life
- Discuss what could've been done to prevent crisis
- Answer closed ended questions with a single word

**<u>Do</u>**
- Phrase statements positively
- Speak in complete sentences
- Repeat key messages and facts

- Acknowledge impact on people
- Usher reporters to those who have answers you do not
- Answer closed ended questions with statements
- Be brief

The media and much of the public expect corporations to take the low road during a crisis. Skeptics immediately assume large organizations are simply trying to reduce liabilities, loss of revenue, and impact on share price. Again, the bar is pretty low here. But often, organizations meet those lowly expectations.

Understand that a language barrier is part of the problem. Corporations often speak their own language. Abbreviations, acronyms, and industry terminology do not always lend themselves to easy translation. The problem is compounded when the reporters covering the crisis are young or unfamiliar with the industry. Accurately translating and conveying industry jargon is a challenge in and of itself. However, corporations often make matters worse by relying on clichés or ineffective language.

Therefore, it's important to identify these language pitfalls. It's even more illuminating to translate them for tone deaf organizations. Below is a translation guide illustrating some of the things organizations say and what the media actually hear:

| **Corporation Says**: | **Media Hears**: |
|---|---|
| No comment… | Guilty |
| This is not a story… | This is definitely a story |
| It's old news… | They're hiding something |
| The media is partially to blame… | They're guilty of more |
| I don't recall… | Liar |
| I'll be honest... | Liar |
| It appears as if… | They're ignorant |
| Haven't yet reviewed lawsuit… | Allegations in suit are true |
| We're not releasing details… | It's worse than expected |
| On the advice of my attorney… | Guilty |

An organization that chooses to use one of the phrases above may do so based on sound reasoning and advice from legal counsel. But all the logic in the world will not prevent the media from instantly translating what is said. Organizations that use these types of phrases can expect key message conveyance to plummet as the media will likely be busy translating your words rather than actively listening.

Get rid of legalese and tired clichés.

Adopt a more conversational approach. Creatively choose your words and smartly deliver them. Tailor them to the crisis and to the individual media producer. Doing so will go a long way in breaking down the language barrier that exists between corporations and much of the media. Besides increasing key message conveyance, ridding your organization's vocabulary of legalese will also reduce a reporter's skepticism. Nothing more quickly alerts a reporter you've already lawyered up than legalese that obviously came from an attorney.

Speaking more conversationally also further humanizes large corporations. It puts the reporter at ease. I cannot begin to tell you the number of times I've heard reporters look at each other following a news conference and say, "Oh, he seemed normal." The media expects you to speak like you dress. Violate this assumption. If an executive in business attire suddenly begins speaking conversationally, avoids industry jargon, and speaks as a "normal" person would, he or she instantly builds credibility with the media and will be cut slack not afforded to someone a bit more stiff or buttoned up.

# Apologies & Attorneys

Saying you're sorry is tough. But people apologize to one another all the time. Corporations do so less frequently. Why?

The fact that your organization's legal counsel may be trying to pry this book from your hands right now gives you a clue. Lawyers argue apologies are often admissions of guilt or public declarations of liability. In some cases the attorneys are correct. However, it is possible to apologize without accepting liability for a crisis. I'm sorry I didn't write this book sooner but I'm not liable for your organization's public relations blunders prior to publication!

Apologizing is definitely an art form. But there is a growing body of science on which executives can rely for guidance. What might the effect of an apology be? A group of academics studied the matter and reported its findings in the February 2004 issue of the *Journal of Applied Psychology*.

Peter Kim, Donald Ferrin, Cecily Cooper, and Kurt Dirks examined how trust might be repaired after it is broken and the implications of apologies. The researchers found that, "...trust was repaired more successfully when mistrusted parties: 1) apologized for violations concerning matters of competence but denied culpability for violations concerning matters of integrity, and 2) had apologized for violations when there was subsequent evidence of guilt, but had denied culpability for violations when there was subsequent evidence of innocence."

The research seems to indicate something we all likely learned prior to kindergarten; say you're sorry if you owe someone an apology. While some attorneys may be in denial, it is possible to express regret without admitting guilt. An executive can express regret, remorse, and sorrow without accepting liability for the crisis at hand.

However, there does appear to be a line that, if crossed, will render an apology useless and potentially even harmful. If an organization's behavior crosses the line from negligence to maliciousness then even a perfect apology will lack sincerity and further hollow the organization's reputation. In cases where malice is present, it's best just to keep quiet and wait for the jury's verdict.

When an organization is unquestionably liable for a crisis it has a difficult decision to make. One attorney tells me it's like picking your poison; you can place your reputation in the hands of a jury or in the hands of a generally forgiving public. Trusting the public will forgive you is a difficult choice for most corporations to make. It often requires executives to ignore advice provided by legal counsel. It also requires an executive to give up some of the control he or she might retain in a courtroom.

However, I would argue the choice is actually an easy one to make for organizations that are unquestionably liable for a disaster. Corporations clearly at fault should have no inhibitions about publicly apologizing. They already know there will be legal and financial consequences to their behavior. The only question still lingering is how large the penalty will ultimately be.

An apology, if done correctly, will not negatively impact the size of the penalty. In fact, apologizing when an organization knows it is liable actually stimulates the healing process. Rather than waiting to repair the organization's reputation following the conclusion of legal proceedings, apologizing as soon as you know you are liable gives the organization a much needed head start.

A crisis for which an organization is liable will undoubtedly cost the organization money.

It should not also cost the organization its reputation.

In fact, research even suggests an apology can be used to positively impact an apologizing organization's legal defense strategy. Ameeta Patel and Lamar Reinsch published a piece in the March 2003 issue of *Business Communication Quarterly* outlining how complex and difficult it is to legally define an apology. This can benefit an apologist in court.

More importantly, the piece references research that suggests victims often accept lower settlement offers when they are accompanied by an apology. While it is clear that a plaintiff can use an apology against an organization in court, the article also points out how an apologist can use it as well. For instance, research indicates organizations can use apologies to protect themselves against, "...having to pay punitive (but not actual) damages."

The article correctly points out that apologies have no effect on actual damages. However, in cases where a judge or jury may be looking to make an example of the organization by way of hefty punitive damages, the authors write, "...an apology can provide a reason to limit or even to forego punitive damages." The article goes on to compare outcomes accompanied by apologies and those that did not and finds, "...both judges and juries tend to appreciate apologies and look upon them favorably."

The article concludes by illustrating several states that have amended their laws to, "...exempt expressions of sympathy or remorse from being used against a party as an admission of guilt."

Is your state one of them?

The line between expressing sorrow and admitting fault is fine. But smart corporations clearly identify that line and create opportunities to apologize while simultaneously protecting themselves from legal repercussions. Look at the examples below Patel and Rainsch provide:

"I'm sorry for hurting you."

"I'm sorry you were hurt."

The legal consequences inherent in the first apology are immense and potentially haunting. However, making a minor change linguistically, as was done in the second example, dramatically reduces the potential legal consequences. The second apology shows the organization as empathetic but does not admit fault like the first example does.

Investing the time and effort necessary in crafting an effective apology can immediately rescue an organization's reputation without increasing the legal consequences the organization may face. Below you'll find **Six Rules for a Perfect Apology**:

1. Apologize quickly
2. Word apologies in passive voice
3. Make ultra-specific apologies
4. Construct partial apologies
5. Exclude excuses and explanations
6. Include how you plan to fix the problem

# Expect an Ambush

Crises have at least one thing in common with war: ambushes.

Being ambushed and taking verbal shots from an aggressive reporter can feel like you're stuck in a war zone with no way out. In reality, there is no exit or backdoor during an ambush. An executive must address the reporter or risk being perceived as hiding something.

Reporter ambushes are often pre-engineered and executed at a purposefully inopportune time for the target. Unless you are fortunate enough to have secret service-like security, reporter ambushes are largely unavoidable.

Even with a security entourage a target is still susceptible to an ambush. Former Georgia Governor Sonny Perdue knows this well.

Years ago, Perdue was lying low in Atlanta as the state legislature negotiated a controversial budget bill on the final day of the legislative session. Like dozens of other reporters, I was looking for Governor Perdue when word leaked that the budget bill contained an item the Governor had promised would result in a veto.

That meant no budget.

The stakes were high.

The Governor had been hiding from reporters the entire day. He did not want to be confronted or answer questions about the hurried last minute deal making characteristic of the final hours of a legislative session.

However, I got a tip that evening (from a barber) the Governor would be leaving an office building and walking to the Capitol for a final face to face negotiation with Democrats.

My photographer and I camped outside the building but did not wait long. When the Governor emerged I politely asked if he'd be willing to speak with us about the current budget bill and whether he still planned to veto it. But the Governor was not interested in talking with us and his security detail was less than polite as it moved us away.

The security officers were large men. They were state troopers. They carried weapons. And we were greatly outnumbered. However, as soon as my photographer turned on his camera and top light those security officers became powerless. No amount of security can protect a politician from a camera.

The Governor was in a tough spot. It was a 150 yard walk to the Capitol. And there was nowhere he could hide from a reporter and photographer who had just been roughed up by security.

Rather than stopping to simply tell us he was on his way to negotiate and assure us he'd update us when he knew more the Governor tried to avoid us. We pushed our way back through security which could no longer touch us now that the camera was rolling. I put the microphone in front of the Governor and hit him with a barrage of tough questions.

He was clearly frustrated and angry.

The Governor would need to appear strong, confident, and in control when negotiating with Democrats awaiting him at the

Capitol. However, he was exhibiting none of those qualities moments before the big meeting. On camera and under pressure the Governor appeared as if he had lost his composure. He was simply unable to control the situation prior to one of the biggest negotiations of his political career.

The Governor's handlers understood how badly he had mishandled the situation. After the confrontation had ended and the Governor was safely inside the Capitol his communications staff called my news boss. The Governor was asking us not to broadcast the confrontation on television. In return, the Governor promised an exclusive interview after the negotiations had concluded.

We declined the Governor's offer.

The self-inflicted damage had been done. And it made for great television.

The Governor could have easily avoided all of it. But he lacked the savvy and preparedness one might expect from a person with his authority.

Besides continuously preparing for an ambush, executives can take steps to reduce the chances of an ambush during crises or delicate times. Routinely producing content and updating media producers is one way to minimize risk, especially if it's the executive who is speaking. Ambushing an executive who is routinely available to the media reflects poorly on the reporter and the outlet employing the reporter. Therefore, making executives available to media producers at news conferences reduces the risk of ambush and allows the executive to retain a degree of control lacking in an ambush situation.

Executives will never be available as frequently as the media would like though. And there will always be a reporter looking to make a name for himself or trump his competitors by being the first or only one to corner an executive during a crisis.

# Break Out of PR Prison

Below are strategies designed to minimize the risk of an ambush:

- Have someone else answer your phone and door
- Reduce the length you must walk to get from location to location
- Vary routines
- Vary entrances and exits used
- Become aware of less often used exits
- Avoid eating out
- Limit attendance of extracurricular events

These behavioral changes may appear extreme or even overly paranoid. But the strategies listed above are simply results of the ambushes or "unscheduled interviews" I executed as an Investigative Reporter. Most people who are being followed have no idea they are being followed. They are completely unaware of the exits that exist around them. And most targets make ambushes easy for reporters to execute by routinely creating too much distance between points of safety.

The only true tonic for an ambush interview is preparedness. Rigorous preparation and a clear understanding of the dynamics inherent in ambush interviews are required to survive and thrive. Not understanding the rules is why most executives do so poorly when surprised by a television news crew.

Joyce Gilchrist knows the rules.

Gilchrist is a former Oklahoma City police chemist and is accused of maliciously helping to send innocent men to prison-even death row. Gilchrist maintains she has never lied in court. But judges, prosecutors, and investigators believe she fabricated evidence or falsely testified in at least a dozen cases which resulted in innocent people serving nearly 100 years in prison.

However, Gilchrist has never been prosecuted.

That's why Investigative Reporter Britten Follett and photojournalist Billy Dry tracked Gilchrist to her home in

Houston several years ago. It was time to ask Gilchrist the questions prosecutors had refused to ask.

After tedious surveillance, thorough crossing of public records, and a bit of luck the crew caught Gilchrist outside her home with no place to hide.

However, Gilchrist did not make the same mistake Georgia's Governor did.

Gilchrist stopped when the crew approached her with camera rolling. She smiled and did not run from them. She was polite and answered many of the crew's questions. Gilchrist even took responsibility for her actions and told the crew she acted alone and was not coerced or pressured to falsely testify.

Gilchrist's reaction to the ambush was not what the crew had expected.

She surprised them.

The result was that the ambush interview was over in just a few minutes. Being polite to the news crew stripped any reason it would have to chase her. Answering questions allowed Gilchrist to steer the narrative and avoid the barrage of questions that would have surely come had she run.

Gilchrist was dealt a bad hand.

But she played it well.

Executives are used to making the rules others must follow. They bark orders and expect others to follow those orders. Executives exert control over how a business operates. All of which makes ambush interviews so problematic for executives who are used to being in charge.

Below are the rules present in an ambush interview:

- Confrontation is unexpected
- Control is lacking
- Answers will be demanded immediately
- Questions will be biased or unfair
- Time will not be given to gain composure
- Interruptions are common

- Answer time will be limited
- Mistakes will be exploited

Not only is the executive at a great disadvantage by virtue of the rules, he or she is also disadvantaged by the evident role reversal. Executives who fail to appreciate and respect the role reversal will fare far worse than those who embrace it. While the executive may feel like a helpless hostage, there are strategies available to reduce the disadvantage.

Remember the goal of the reporter is to surprise the executive. It's also important to realize that the reporter executing the ambush is likely loosely following a script. Embedded in that script, which has been rehearsed to some degree, are assumptions and expectations the reporter has in regard to how the target will respond. Therefore, a target's goal must be to respond unconventionally.

If an executive surprises a reporter with his or her initial response to the ambush, then the script on which the reporter is relying is no longer useful. Take away the reporter's script and you also take away part of the advantage they hold. Once again, the low expectations the media have in terms of an organization's response to an ambush can be used to your advantage.

Reporters expect ambush targets to run, hide, become angry, and obfuscate. When a target behaves counter to those expectations he or she begins to shift the balance of power. Upending this balance often creates opportunities not afforded to executives who behave in accordance with reporter expectations.

Envision the following two ambush examples:

**Reporter**: "Mr. Executive, Nick Winkler with Winkler News, we'd like to speak with you briefly..."
**Executive**: "Not now, I told you we had no comment on the phone..." as the executive simultaneously attempts to cover the camera lens with his hand.

The reporter then launches into a rehearsed barrage of questions designed to embarrass, exploit, and convict as the executive is shown retreating. But what would happen if an executive quickly recognized the situation as an ambush and instead behaved like this...

**Reporter**: "Mr. Executive, Nick Winkler with Winkler News, we'd like to speak with you briefly..."
**Executive**: "Hi Nick, I'm sure you're interested in (fill in the specific crisis) and I'd be happy to tell you everything I can..."

A response like this immediately and dramatically alters the dynamics of the ambush. Instead of being perceived as a fearful nonparticipant, responding in such a manner positions the ambush target as a willing participant interested in being transparent and helpful. An executive behaving in this fashion is using a velvet hammer to hit back. Doing so eliminates the element of surprise the reporter intended to use as a weapon.

Remember, the key is to recognize the ambush, acknowledge you do not make the rules anymore, and behave in a manner that will knock the reporter off his or her script. Doing so will tip the balance of power and reduce the advantage the reporter holds. It also resets some of the rules and expectations.

Below are two sets of rules an ambush target may use to counter an ambush and **Turn a Gotcha Moment into a Win**:

<u>**Do Not**</u>:
- Run away
- Get angry
- Answer defensively
- Discuss what should've happened
- Criticize the reporter for interrupting
- Repeat the reporter's question in your answer
- Look at the camera

- Ask to schedule an interview at a later time
- Speculate
- Use contractions

**<u>Do</u>:**

- Smile
- Greet reporter
- Offer to address crisis
- Speak in complete sentences
- People first
- Active voice
- Compliment the question
- Suggest an even better question
- Bridge when needed
- Look at the reporter
- Display gratitude for reporter interest
- Use the word "not" rather than a contraction
- Rank crisis
- Highlight what you are doing to fix problem
- Reassure better times are ahead

An ambush is simply an opportunity disguised as a threat. Uncomfortable as it might be, the greatest rewards often stem from the greatest challenges. Count an ambush as one of those challenges. Being sincere and genuine will bleed through the hidden agenda often possessed by the reporter executing the ambush. Often, the goal of an ambush is not to extract information or facts. The goal is to embarrass the target under the pretense that the journalist is holding the powerful accountable.

Prepare for the worst and anything less will be a walk in the PR park.

Nick Winkler

# Litigation Communications

A s a young reporter, I was startled by the hurried voice on the newsroom intercom, "Winkler, the District Attorney just called. Drop what you're doing and go. The perp walk is in twenty minutes."

The prosecutor's office had called my television station so we'd have time to pre-position for what's known as a "perp walk". A perp walk, short for perpetrator, occurs when authorities parade a handcuffed, often disheveled criminal suspect in front of the media for pictures and a barrage of shouted reporter questions.

I remember driving to my first perp walk wondering, "This is going to make great television but why would the D.A. call us in advance and how does he know precisely when police will be hauling the suspect through the jail doors?" I was able to quickly answer my own questions as we pulled into the jail parking lot.

To my dismay and surprise, I was not the only reporter standing outside the jail waiting for the suspect to arrive. I wasn't special. I wasn't chosen exclusively. I was simply one of many the prosecutor had lined up on his side to verbally assault the suspect and sway public opinion.

In the years that followed, I've attended dozens of perp walks all over the country and all of them have been orchestrated similarly by prosecutors who routinely manipulate the media for their own benefit.

Pictures and video have a much greater impact on an audience than words. Prosecutors know this and frequently orchestrate perp walks to steer the narrative. If a television news viewer were to mute his or her television and only see a handcuffed suspect being led into jail or police headquarters it's reasonable to assume the suspect is guilty of something, despite having not been convicted of a crime or even charged with one. The same is true for a newspaper reader seeing a photograph of the alleged perpetrator. The initial thought upon seeing only the picture is one of wrongdoing.

This is the advantage prosecutors and those in similar positions enjoy. The advantage of striking first in the media is a challenge that, at least initially, is difficult to overcome. Combine this first-to-strike advantage with the fact that prosecutors, attorneys general, and trial attorneys are often trusted media sources and the communications challenges for a defendant can appear daunting.

The advantages people in positions of legal authority hold are listed below:

1. They strike first
2. They establish the initial set of facts on which media reports are based
3. They are often perceived by the media as having more credibility than the accused or the defense attorney
4. Their statements often receive less media scrutiny than those of the accused

Defense Attorneys often make matters worse when they attempt to shield their clients from the barrage of reporter questions that accompany perp walks. Rather than attempting to stop the media from asking questions or trying to speak for the client during a perp walk, the most media savvy defense attorneys understand a perp walk is not a battle they are likely to win against a media in attack mode.

A chance to strike back will not likely come until damage has already been done at a news conference, at trial, or during a hearing. However, a robust litigation communications strategy can effectively halt the impact a litigator has on public opinion. Aligning litigation communications with courtroom strategy will also lessen the advantage the plaintiffs' bar enjoys.

The secrets to minimizing the first-mover advantage may appear initially as unconventional. However, savvy defense attorneys understand the importance of a thorough and aggressive litigation communications strategy. Simply winning in court is of little consolation to a corporation whose reputation has been decimated in the media. Choosing to only defend an organization's reputation in a courtroom and not the court of public opinion may at times be more devastating than losing in court. What good is a win in court if customers no longer see the organization as reputable?

Courtroom strategy and media strategy are not mutually exclusive. With the exception of a judge's order, savvy defense attorneys and PR staffs execute both simultaneously and consistent with one another. Choosing to ignore the media during litigation can be just as costly as a loss in the courtroom.

While strategies must be tailored to the type of litigation (securities, class action, product liability, antitrust, bankruptcy) a collection of techniques on which to base a tailored strategy exists. Below are five strategies designed to counter the first-mover advantage the plaintiffs' bar and prosecutors enjoy:

1. **Do Not Ignore Elephants & Gorillas**- Counsel must not ignore the elephant or 800-pound gorilla in the courtroom. If an organization is defending itself against loss of life, that loss must be acknowledged. When an organization finds itself up against a sympathetic victim it must become an Empathetic Aggressor. Remember, an apology worded passively can dramatically reverse negative public sentiment without creating liability for the organization. Acknowledge, bridge, and counter.

2. **Humanize the Organization**- Corporations must shed the faceless, impersonal, or greed-ridden perceptions much of the public hold. An attorney or spokesperson who can quickly build rapport with reporters, convey sincerity, and

illustrate the organization is comprised of people with children, feelings, and hopes immediately levels the playing field. The best feature reporters use personification to humanize buildings or inanimate objects. Doing so forces people to associate a desired emotion with the inanimate object. A similar technique may be used for corporations during litigation.

3. **Compliment Frequently-** Reassuring the media that a better judge could not have been selected to oversee a proceeding and expressing confidence in the outcome is a technique that often has a greater impact on the media than it does the judge. Complimenting a judge or even a plaintiff's attorney or prosecutor can remove some of the hyperbole or vitriol associated with high profile litigation. It is especially useful when an organization's defense is superior, steering the media away from personal confrontation and toward the key tenets to be argued in the case. This technique often reverses how an organization is treated in a newspaper headline. Rather than being the object in a subject-verb-object structured headline, an organization can position itself as the subject that acts upon the object or litigator in the case.

4. **Attack Attorney Credibility-** This strategy is most effective in class action suits. Pointing out the attorney stands to reap millions of dollars while his or her individual clients stand to gain far less reinforces existing stereotypes. While doing so is not advised in other types of suits in which a sympathetic victim is present, positioning a class action attorney as selfish and greedy can unflatteringly shift the narrative and put the plaintiffs' bar on the defensive.

5. **Expose Hidden Agendas-** Publicly revealing a trial attorney or prosecutor's hidden agenda or unseemly motives shifts the media's focus and puts a litigator on defense. Doing so forces he or she to defend their integrity rather than convey key messages. Raising conflicts of interest and the like plants seeds in the media that trusted sources like prosecutors may not be as trustworthy as previously thought. Hidden political and financial agendas brought to light during the course of litigation have clear benefits in and out of the courtroom.

An organization involved in litigation will take into account the judge selected to oversee the matter before settling on a litigation communications strategy. The proper course of action must include the judge's preferences as they relate to speaking to media. Executing a strategy that does not offend the judge may be avoided by specifically tailoring the strategy to satisfy the needs of both parties.

In the event that a judge is highly sensitive to seeing attorneys quoted in the newspaper an organization may determine it's in its best interest to say no more after its initial reaction to the allegations levied against it. Initially, an organization may view this decision as one that formally ends the litigation communications strategy. However, the opposite is actually true. Organizations must simply become more creative when making their case in the media.

When an organization decides to stop speaking to the media so as not to offend a judge the organization, by default, may alienate or offend the media in the process. This can be especially problematic when the plaintiff's attorney or prosecutor continues to routinely speak to the media. While the organization may not be able to speak to the media for attribution it can still covertly and creatively execute a litigation communications strategy.

Savvy legal counsel will meet with a reporter and prepare the reporter to effectively question the prosecutor or plaintiff's attorney the next time an opportunity arises. In essence, the reporter is being trained to cross examine the other side. The reporter or reporters will have to be chosen carefully. But this is a strategy that can actually reap greater rewards than if the organization spoke to the media for attribution.

I learned this technique firsthand as a reporter.

I routinely met with defense attorneys, identified weaknesses in the prosecution's case, and then publicly asked prosecutors about those weaknesses at news conferences and outside courtrooms. Not only did doing so often make for good television but the defense enjoyed a great benefit as well.

The public will often be skeptical of whatever the defense says publicly. But when the public perceives the reporter as independently poking holes in the prosecution's case, the defendant attains a level of credibility it is not capable of attaining on its own. When a reporter is armed with the ability to damage a litigator the defense enjoys an advantage not available to organizations that speak to the media for attribution. In essence, an organization is recruiting members of the media to cross examine and reduce the credibility of the litigators.

The strategy involves some degree of risk. Sharp reporters are aware they are being used. But more often than not, if an organization can factually show a reporter why a litigator's argument or allegation is flawed, the reporter will be inclined to use the information against a litigator. After all, it is a reporter's job to talk with all sides. If the ammunition you provide them is sound and based on fact, they're likely to use it.

This strategy, or a derivative of it, will be useful when a much larger challenge arises: what to say when it is in the organization's interest to say nothing at all. Or even worse, when a judge orders the organization to be silent. In cases in which a judge orders attorneys not to speak to the media at all, organizations must become more creative in defending their reputations.

Imposing a gag order amplifies the advantage a plaintiff's attorney or prosecutor already enjoys. Here again, an organization involved in litigation may view a gag order as the end of its litigation communications strategy.

That's not the case though.

Even with a gag order an organization can still use the media to mitigate damage to its reputation. Organizations that find themselves in this predicament must rely on third party advocates like satisfied customers, elected officials, and other stakeholders to make the organization's case in the media. A proactive smart PR staff employing the strategies discussed throughout the book will have already identified these third party advocates and have established relationships with them.

An often forgotten component of a complete litigation communications strategy is listening actively. Smart corporations listen closely to the reporters with whom they talk. You might think of it like a second discovery period. Savvy legal counsel will mine reporters for information that may be clues or tip-offs to prosecutorial strategy.

You're aware that reporters will spend time discussing legal matters with prosecutors and plaintiff's attorneys. You also know that often these will be "off the record" conversations. Often, with a little finesse, organizations can tease out these golden nuggets and gain a better understanding of the opposition's strategy.

Reporters are takers. But organizations that see them only as takers are forfeiting an opportunity that may provide them an edge in the courtroom or during settlement negotiations. Reporters also have something to give. This information will not likely be offered voluntarily. But corporations that take the time to mine for it will often find a diamond.

# Lawyers vs. Public Relations

Often during crises an internal struggle erupts between legal counsel and public relations chiefs. Disagreement often results in wasted time, tarnished reputations, and allows crisis creators a head start in manipulating the media. The turmoil is rooted in each of the party's respective disciplines.

In-house counsel may view PR chiefs who want to immediately address the media following a crisis as reckless or legally irresponsible. Conversely, PR chiefs may perceive in-house counsel as overly cautious or tone deaf in regard to their company's reputation. Neither party is entirely wrong. And neither is entirely correct.

Often, the problem is that the parties fail to realize they share the same goals during a crisis: limiting liability and damages. What makes realizing the objectives such a challenge are the starkly different means by which each of the parties use to achieve the objectives. Lawyers immediately begin gathering facts. PR staffers immediately begin attempting to steer the narrative.

The two means by which the objectives might be achieved must not be diametrically opposed to one another. Below are several common disputes in-house counsel have with PR chiefs during times of crisis:

- Whether to address media
- Whether to apologize
- Whether to admit any responsibility
- Whether to address the issue of victim compensation
- Whether to specifically detail steps employed to mitigate disaster

An organization addressing these matters for the first time during a crisis will not likely fare well. The disputes common between attorneys and PR practitioners should and must be addressed prior to disaster.

Corporate attorneys must be made to realize their futures are tied to preserving the corporation's reputation during a crisis. Alternatively, public relations chiefs must be made to realize their futures hinge upon limiting liabilities and damages caused by a corporation during a crisis.

A company that survives a crisis legally and financially must also survive a crisis with its reputation intact. The sooner corporate counsel and corporate PR staffs realize they are dependent upon one another during a crisis, the sooner they'll sit down and hash out evident differences prior to a crisis.

Identifying common ground on which the parties can create mutually acceptable crisis communications strategies will free each to perform optimally. Conversely, identifying disputes over strategy that cannot be resolved among the parties affords executives time to determine the best course of action. Having these strategy sessions before the strategies are needed is the key to performing optimally during a crisis. It also affords an organization time to determine who should deliver messages to the media during times of crisis.

Identifying the public face or faces of an organization will be dictated by the specific crisis. Chief executives are the preferred choice and will undoubtedly have to speak publicly at some point during a crisis. However, an executive who lacks presence or public speaking skills may not be the best choice for regularly scheduled news conferences or targeted interview requests.

Corporate attorneys are often not the answer either. Intuitively, selecting legal counsel to speak with reporters appears logical on the surface. But an attorney who has achieved success in the courtroom may not always achieve success in the court of public opinion. It's analogous to forcing a baseball pitcher to quarterback the football team; success on the mound doesn't necessarily translate into success in the pocket.

It is preferable to have the company attorney speaking to the media but not always advantageous. If legal counsel is not able to condense and abbreviate complex legal and strategic messages he or she is probably not the optimal choice for a spokesperson. Below are common reasons why attorneys do not always make the best corporate spokespersons:

- Speak in legal terms
- Underestimate media influence
- Stiff and unconvincing
- Lack ability to crystallize complex matters simplistically
- Focus on legal issues rather than people
- Lack charisma and relationships with journalists
- Focus on legal precedent rather than crisis at hand
- Display bias toward fact rather than emotion

Conversely, some of the most effective orators are attorneys. The problem is they tend to be trial attorneys and politicians instead of in-house counsel. If an organization is blessed to have legal counsel who also doubles as a gifted orator, turn them loose on the media. If not, counsel is best used to educate and prepare spokespersons. In cases like this, corporate attorneys are better off teaching a charismatic, well-liked spokesperson how to immediately identify legal traps laid by the media. Equipping non-lawyer spokespersons with the skill set to step around those legal minefields is one of the most underappreciated tasks corporate legal counsel can undertake.

Identifying crisis communications strategies and spokespersons prior to when they are actually needed are the keys in reducing tensions between lawyers and PR staffs. The push-pull dichotomy between the parties is not one to be avoided but rather embraced. Both parties have the company's best interest in mind. They simply go about protecting that interest in manners that appear contradictory on the surface.

The objective of any organization should be to penetrate that surface prior to a crisis. Know in advance of a crisis the framework that'll map out what is to be said, how it is to be said, and by whom. Establishing boundaries, protocol, and rules prior to a disaster allows organizations to bypass the internal fight that distracts and dooms many corporations embroiled in crisis.

# Crisis Mitigation Weapons

Think of the strategies outlined here as weapons.

During a military offensive, armed forces identify an enemy's weaknesses and choose weaponry that best exploits those weaknesses. Doing so ensures the most efficient path to victory and limits casualties.

The same mentality may be adopted during a crisis.

Once an organization has identified a crisis creator, how the crisis is funded, and how the crisis is being amplified, it can then develop a strategy designed to reduce the duration of the crisis. Reducing crisis duration and reputational damage are most efficiently achieved by selecting the proper set of weapons.

Weapons that prove effective in one crisis may not be as effective in another crisis. Careful consideration must be paid to the nuances of a specific crisis, the consequences of using a particular weapon, and whether the use of a weapon has the potential to backfire.

The ten weapons below have the potential to salvage reputations, reduce costs associated with crises, and ensure brand survival.

Choose wisely and good luck!

1. **Crisis Vaccination-** The idea of injecting small amounts of really bad stuff into a person's body to better protect the person against much greater amounts of that really bad stuff may also be applied in the context of a crisis. Injecting a target audience with a bit of the crisis that is soon to be

unleashed can protect an organization from becoming terminally ill when the crisis explodes publicly. Proactively telling the media about a crisis before the crisis is evident or explodes publicly prepares reporters for what is to come. It sets expectations while simultaneously building credibility. It shows you are transparent. Doing so eliminates the first-mover advantage many crisis creators enjoy. It allows an organization a greater degree of control over the narrative and prevents the organization from being reactionary. Vaccinating the media, shareholders, or potential jurors reduces the impact a crisis has once it becomes evident. Vaccinations eliminate the shock and surprise that initially feeds a crisis. For instance, prosecutors have used crisis vaccines ahead of controversial charging decisions. The day before Oklahoma County District Attorney David Prater charged a pharmacist with shooting and killing a teenager who attempted to rob the pharmacist, Prater laid the groundwork for favorable treatment in the media. Prater knew the charging decision would be controversial. The pharmacist, Jerome Ersland, 60, would argue he was simply defending himself. Two teens, one with a gun, entered the pharmacy to rob Ersland in May 2009. Ersland shot the unarmed 16-year-old in the head then chased the 14-year-old gunman out of the pharmacy. When Ersland returned he grabbed a second gun and fired five more rounds into the 16-year-old who had been lying on the floor since being shot the first time. Prater would argue Ersland had gone too far and the threat to his life had been mitigated following the first shot. Still, Prater knew it'd be a tough sell in Oklahoma's gun-friendly court of public opinion. So the day before he announced the charge against Ersland, Prater sought out a reporter and said, "Hey, I need you at the news conference tomorrow because I know you'll be fair..." Prater was vaccinating the reporter against the sea of criticism he would soon be inundated by. He was preparing the reporter for the worst. The reporter would not be surprised by anything the critics would say. Prater had already prepared the reporter. He had gotten to the reporter first. Prater was steering the narrative before the competition knew there was even a narrative to steer. Ultimately, Prater won the case. Ersland was convicted of murder and sentenced to life in prison. Vaccinating reporters prior to a storm allows the prosecutor to set expectations. When the criticism starts, it's nothing new to the reporters covering the story. The media is trained to focus on what's new. Vaccinating the media ensures the crisis to come is not new to them. Injecting targets with crisis vaccines is an offensive strategy that runs counter to the way many organizations operate. Crisis vaccinations do not guarantee a target will not become infected with a crisis. Vaccinations do however increase the chances for survival and reduce the time it takes to heal.

2. **Crisis Landfill**- One of the most effective ways to reduce the duration of a crisis is to make one trip to the landfill rather than many. What I mean is dump all of the bad at once. Don't fall victim to slow leaks of bad news day after day. Slow bleeds are reputation killers. Unfortunately, organizations make this mistake frequently and elongate the crisis they are enduring. Rather than making a major one-time crisis dump, some organizations believe they can keep the most embarrassing portions of a crisis private. Sometimes they can. But often those organizations wind up prolonging the suffering as they are confronted with new details of a crisis day after day. Dumping the entire crisis at the outset remedies this issue. After an entire crisis is hauled away to the landfill there is nothing left for

reporters, regulators, or activists to use to prolong the crisis. It is old news. Don't be mistaken, a one-time crisis dump will be extremely painful. But once the details are known reporters will move on to something fresh and new. And the organization will be able to begin healing much sooner than others that continue to make trip after trip to the crisis landfill.

3. **Create Straw Men**- When a crisis lends itself to placing third party blame it is smart to identify or create a straw man. Straw men are prone to blow away or wilt under scrutiny but that's not the point. Straw men buy an organization time to gather facts and develop strategy. Straw men offer a partial solution to a crisis while a solution with a much stronger foundation is created. Straw men work well when sympathetic victims are involved in a crisis. Organizations fearful of accusing a victim of being somewhat responsible for their own demise can initially cast blame on a straw man. Straw men may be intangible or otherwise hard to conceptualize. They are impersonal and reinforce stereotypes. For instance, blame may be placed on bureaucracy, the system, or patchwork regulations. Straw men may be only partially to blame. But until an organization can gather additional facts, determine liability, and to what extent a victim's actions may have caused the harm they are experiencing, straw men provide additional time. They don't have feelings and can't talk back. No one gets hurt blaming a straw man.

4. **Rank the Crisis**- Ranking a crisis is a more subtle way of influencing the media. It should replace the act of telling a reporter that a topic is not newsworthy. Ranking a crisis adds perspective and gives context. It places a crisis in a hierarchy that minimizes the importance of the crisis. I've

used the tactic in editorial meetings when arguing with managers over which story I would be assigned. For instance, "You want me to do a story on a puppy that was tossed from a truck on a day when the legislature is considering a bill that would increase taxes for anyone who eats food?" Ranking a crisis is a subtle way organizations can help the media prioritize the world. It is an effective way of helping the media discover the crisis at hand pales in comparison to others.

5. **Dig Crisis Graves**- Organizations no longer even need shovels to dig graves for unflattering news items created during a crisis. A search engine optimization (SEO) team should be working to bury reputation damaging headlines. Reporters in a hurry often never see past the first page of a Google search. Moving unflattering news pieces from the first page to those that follow is a task that should be executed during and after a crisis. Organizations creating premier content will be more successful burying bad news in light of Google's recent tweak to its search ranking algorithm. The tweak enables more recent information to rank higher. Therefore, a public relations staff continually creating new content during a crisis creates an advantage for itself in terms of search rankings. Combine that advantage with an SEO team working to bury negative news items and an organization can exert considerable authority over what appears on the first page of a Google search. If you need some help digging a crisis grave Michael David at TastyPlacement in Austin, TX wields a big shovel. The promise on his web site (tastyplacement.com) says it all, "...if we don't increase your business- fire us."

6. **Paint Crisis Black & White**- This strategy is used to create an either/or fallacy. It compartmentalizes all behavior as right or wrong, black or white. The strategy does not allow for a third option. It simplifies a crisis and removes any potential areas of gray. The strategy is most effective in the case of a sympathetic victim or someone whose behavior may have contributed to the harm they endured at the hands of your organization. Removing gray areas means the accuser's behavior is either right or wrong. Doing so broadens the area of behavior in which an accuser may be wrong. Defining an accuser's questionable behavior as wrong can limit an organization's perceived liability in a crisis. Examples might include people who take medicine for purposes other than its intended use or people who become injured after sneaking onto a carnival ride they were not permitted to be on. Organizations that paint this behavior as black or white create the parameters by which the accuser will be judged.

7. **Convert Bombs to Boomerangs**- The strategy involves taking the accuser's most potent accusation against the organization and using it against the accuser. The goal is to convert the bomb the accuser tosses at an organization into a boomerang that returns to explode on the accuser. This strategy works best with accusers who have engaged in questionable behavior in the past or whom intelligence gathering identifies as hypocritical. If an accuser is critical of an organization's accounting practices he or she is deserving of a boomerang bomb if they've been late with the rent or have a lien filed against their vehicle. The strategy is designed to reduce an accuser's credibility.

8. **Top the Crisis**- Topping the crisis simply means finding a better story on which the media can focus. Organizations

executing this strategy have a lot of leeway. Whether the story becomes the accuser, a systemic oversight failure, or how the crisis the organization is experiencing actually happens frequently in the industry, the goal is to shift the media's focus away from the organization. It matters little where that focus is shifted. Only that it is shifted. It doesn't cause the crisis to disappear. But it does lessen your organization's presence within the crisis. While difficult to do in a crisis involving major loss of life, creating an alternative story on which the media would rather feast is one of the quicker ways to shorten the duration of a crisis.

9. **Expose Crisis Funding**- Exposing how a crisis is funded is a method that often proves successful in discrediting crisis creators. Outside of charities, fundraising is often associated with underhandedness. Money is literally dirty. The means by which it is raised are often viewed as even dirtier. Exposing how an activist raises money can often eliminate a specific source of funding. For instance, a group that often celebrates the deaths of U.S. service members and protests outside their funerals received a lot of attention until its fundraising efforts were exposed. The group would intentionally provoke confrontations with the hope of being assaulted by someone offended by its inflammatory statements. After an assault the group would file suit. Money received from the suit funded the next protest. After the group's fundraising mechanism was exposed it became much more difficult for the group to raise money.

10. **Guarantee Failure**- Organizations that indicate they're doing all they can to avoid similar crises in the future are best served by acknowledging that despite best efforts a reoccurrence is possible. This strategy humanizes corporations and lowers expectations. Organizations in the

midst of crisis are often quick to promise horrible events will never happen again. This is foolish. After apologizing and clearly illustrating the steps that have been taken to fix the problems, organizations often make the fatal error of over promising without a guarantee they can deliver. Organizations that show good faith in addressing and fixing a crisis doom themselves by setting the bar too high in regard to reoffending. This strategy is not likely to be effective after a crisis defined by major loss of life. But setting realistic expectations that an organization is sure it can exceed positions the organization to overachieve. Establishing proper expectations is a prerequisite to steering the narrative.

# Pivot Point #2

It's time to pivot again.

On our way toward learning how to engineer smart ideas and premier content, it's useful to investigate why corporate crises have become constant to some degree.

The E-Loop shows us what has changed. Technology not only empowers individuals but is also stimulating a generation that feels entitled. Entitlement is a double-edged sword. On one hand it equips do-gooders with an achievement mentality. On the other, it provides those with ill intentions the ability to do more harm than they once could.

These are what I call the new influencers.

New influencers are the writers, watchdogs, and publishers in an always connected world. There are no longer a small set of agendas being set by a handful of traditional media outlets. Instead, billions of micro-agendas are being created by anyone with an Internet connection and an opinion.

The new influencers are the new gatekeepers.

They are creating original content.

They are out-producing traditional media in terms of quality and quantity.

Increased competition has created a new dynamic. New influencers are feeding a weakened traditional media. Smart PR staffs will identify this new pecking order and prioritize premier content around it. The new influencers matter. Many matter more than traditional media.

But traditional media will not go down without a fight.

Traditional media finds itself with its back against the economic wall. It is cornered. It is scared. It is desperate. It is fighting to survive.

The pages ahead illustrate why it poses such a danger to your organization.

# Corporations in the Crosshairs

*F*inding the courage to create is a choice.
*It's too late to begin searching for your courage after your skeleton is made public.*

Nick Winkler

# Corporations in the Crosshairs

The newspaper industry took a verbal punch to the nose in February 2012.

That's when Wall Street banking titan James Dimon, Chief Executive at J.P. Morgan Chase, highlighted the hypocrisy inherent in so many newspapers. At the bank's investor day, Dimon took the opportunity to address the voracious criticism the media have heaped upon Wall Street's compensation practices.

Especially since the financial crisis of 2008, much of the media have become fascinated with the compensation-to-revenue ratio at Wall Street banks. The compensation-to-revenue ratio is the percentage of revenue a firm pays its employees. An exceedingly high ratio suggests these big banks are greedy and egregiously sinful, especially as they continue to foreclose on would-be homeowners whose tax dollars were used to save many of these same financial institutions.

"Just for fun," Dimon told investors, he calculated the compensation-to-revenue ratio for the newspaper industry. Low and behold, Dimon told the group the newspaper industry, at 42%, actually has a higher compensation-to-revenue ratio than his so called greedy bank. Dimon then landed a knockout blow telling reporters, "We pay 35% and we make a lot of money…worse than that you (the newspaper industry) don't even make any money."

Dimon's approach is certainly not a public relations strategy most corporations will likely adopt. However, Dimon bloodied a bully's nose because he knows the bully is damn near broke, on life support, but still hypocritically lobbing bombs made of ink that damage corporate reputations in an attempt to hang on.

As corporate media profitability erodes in the face of digital competition and a historic shift in how and where advertising dollars are spent, newsrooms across the country are cutting or forcing out experienced journalists which is dramatically degrading the quality of the news product you see in print, on television, and online.

In place of the well-trained senior journalists who often no longer have places in the margin-compressed realities of corporate media, younger poorly trained narcissists are taking hold of microphones, cameras, and keyboards and are being tasked with creating an ever increasing quantity of content to be spread across multiple platforms.

Put another way, the reporters being hired today are often young, inexpensive, and ill-equipped to grasp and accurately convey the intricacies and complexities of the corporations in their communities.

The pepper haired, detail-oriented, truth seekers who once filled newsrooms across the country are no longer economically viable in many of today's newsrooms. Often, experienced journalists have been replaced by hedonistic social media addicts who recently graduated from college and are more concerned with how many "friends" or "followers" they have than understanding and portraying your company accurately.

In some instances, reporters are even being replaced by puppets.

A Cleveland television station, WOIO, has elected to cover one of the biggest federal corruption trials in the state's history with puppets. Television cameras were not allowed in federal court so the station re-enacts the proceedings in segments called "The Puppet's Court". At issue is a racketeering trial that could land the defendant, former county commissioner Jimmy Dimora, in prison for up to 500 years for allegedly taking bribes in return for county contracts.

Media critics, journalism professors, and some elected officials have criticized the station's use of puppets as "absurd", "circus-like", and destructive "to the dignity" of local television news. While critics argue the station has crossed the line, it's not likely that News Director Dan Salamone cares much. *The Wall Street*

*Journal* reports that "The Puppet's Court" has, "...led a ratings surge for the station's late news show...".

Expect Muppet-like puppets to appear in a newscast near you.

Substantive investigative reporting is financially and labor intensive. However, it is the only type of work that genuinely differentiates a news outlet from its competitors while simultaneously increasing viewer ratings, readership, and profitability. Despite the economic hardships corporate media outlets are facing, a growing number believe they can do investigative journalism on the cheap.

By cutting corners or taking shortcuts, many of today's corporate media outlets believe they can still enjoy the financial rewards associated with thorough investigative reporting. Many of these entities deem corporations as low-hanging fruit, able to be quickly plucked for revenue generating investigations.

Reporters are being trained to target corporations in what can only be described as pseudo journalistic investigations in which minimal time is spent linking corporations with some type of wrongdoing or controversy for the sole purpose of boosting the media outlet's viewer ratings, circulation numbers, or web page views.

This reality has been prompted, in part, by the media's tardiness in recognizing and adapting its business model to the digital shift in advertising dollars and the dramatic change in the way people consume media. *The Wall Street Journal* estimates U.S. online video advertisement spending at $3 billion in 2012, nearly triple that of 2010.

Advertisers have good reason to move ad dollars online. Recently, online measurement firm comScore released data revealing that online video sites such as YouTube have much larger audiences than traditional television networks. In January 2012 alone, comScore says more than 151 million unique visitors watched video on sites Google operates.

Corporate media executives, who had a decades-long head start in regard to infrastructure, business modeling, and audience creation, ceded substantial portions of those advantages to online digital startups that in many cases were not even a decade old.

Many of these same executives, forced to change only in the face of double digit margin compression, thought a sustainable business model included digitizing their only product and giving it away online. Since letting the journalistic genie out of the bottle newspapers are now trying to stuff it back in by erecting pay walls. The *New York Times* is attempting to wean readers away from free content by first limiting readers to 20 free articles a month and then 10 per month in March of 2012.

Television news is dying as well. However television news is dying at a slower rate than the newspaper industry. It's still hemorrhaging viewers though. The *Columbia Journalism Review* calculates 28.9 million fewer people were watching network news in 2010 than in 1980.

Consider too how online media outlets like Google are encroaching on territory that once belonged only to the television networks. Each year in May, television network executives gather and meet with potential advertisers to brag about new programs. It's called "upfront" week. The goal is to hook advertisers on these new shows and get them to buy television commercials months in advance. Now outfits like Google, Yahoo, and AOL are holding their own online versions of "upfront" week. While the online advertising spend pales in comparison to television, online is growing at a much faster pace. Further splintering the traditional upfront advertising mechanism is Facebook, which just months before its initial public offering, held its own advertising event. Increased competition for advertising revenue is another factor directly impacting television news.

The tangible decline of both newspapers and television newscasts diverges starkly at the local level. Think of television news stations as being on life support, lingering on much longer than they should when judged by their qualitative decline.

Conversely, newspapers do not have similar cash hoards and simply die.

Statistics bear out the failures plaguing the newspaper industry. The *Columbia Journalism Review* reports there were 1,761 daily newspapers in the U.S. in 1961. As of 2009, the *Review* reports just 1,387 daily papers.

Contrast this with the state of television news in a report published by the Federal Communications Commission in May 2011. The FCC acknowledges the decline in newscast ratings; at the time of publication, television news audiences and revenues remained about 10% below their 2007 levels. However, the FCC study says, "...local television news remains the most popular news medium, with a sizable majority of Americans (78%) stating they get at least some of their news from a local television station in a typical day."

So just as the quality in local television news craters, we also see the medium as being the most popular among general news consumers. It means a corporate PR staff cannot afford to ignore or blow off local television news reporters.

Declining traditional media are passing judgment on your company's business acumen. Often, they'll use young reporters concerned more about their makeup and meteoric rise to superstardom than the executives, products, and services at your company.

There is a malicious effort underway to identify and publicly demonize corporations that, when featured online, on air, or in print, will theoretically increase a media entity's ability to charge advertisers more money.

While disturbing, it makes sense.

Media companies that did not anticipate change, new technologies, or shifts in consumer behavior are now clearly targeting the leaders. The innovators. The corporations that have created, transformed, and thrived. Those left behind in business are now trying to trip up those running ahead.

The creation of journalism schools, training conferences, and a mechanized system designed to churn out reporters to target Corporate America on the cheap combined with new technology have made protecting your company's reputation, image, and profitability more complicated than ever.

It's your reputation they're after.

They're hunting it.

They'll stuff it and hang it on the wall if they can kill it.

# A Secret Shared

The seed was planted in a hotel ballroom full of journalists. They had gathered for a weeklong conference aimed at training them to become better investigative reporters.

That's when one of the training session leaders shared a secret.

He told the crowd a journalist can immediately measure the impact of his or her work by watching how the stock price of a company reacts after news reports are printed or broadcast.

The session was focused on for-profit colleges and featured several investigative reporters who had uncovered data critical of the schools' business practices. In essence, the reports painted a picture of an industry using the Federal Student Loan program as its personal piggy bank.

Attendees were taught how reporters uncovered details about the industry's marketing strategies, the degree to which the industry allegedly intentionally inflates its graduation and job placement statistics, and how the industry fought against increased governmental scrutiny by making large political donations.

One of the session leaders told the group immediately after his investigation was published he checked the stock prices of the companies targeted in his investigation.

Share prices had plummeted.

The reporter appeared to be proud his work had a negative impact on the companies' share prices and told the crowd this was a metric they too could use to measure the success of their corporate investigations.

But that's not the end of the attack on the industry.

In fact, it may just be the beginning.

After disapprovingly noting that the share prices of for-profit colleges had staged a dramatic rebound after the Department of Education had laid out new industry regulations far less stringent than investors had expected, a third member of the session panel took the microphone.

This session leader is a former investigative reporter who now works for a consumer law firm which is suing for-profit colleges on behalf of former students who allege, among other things, their degrees are in essence worthless and that for-profit schools provide few, if any, real job prospects.

This panelist passes out business cards and urges conference attendees to do similar reports on the for-profit college industry in their hometowns. She offers to help reporters by checking her law firm's database for student victims in markets where these reporters work.

Corporations with well known executives or that do business in environmentally sensitive geographies have always been ripe for media criticism. But the for-profit college example is just one of many that suggest there is now an increased focus on investigating corporations. Combine that with the fact law firms are in essence recruiting journalists to adversely influence public opinion about corporations and the job of protecting your company's reputation has never been more challenging.

If the seeds planted in that hotel ballroom are watered and fertilized with the help of lawyers and agendas aimed at impacting a company's share price, the crop that ultimately grows will yield nothing positive for companies targeted.

# An Industry Deteriorating

The increased risk to corporate reputations and bottom lines directly correlates with the news industry's financial decline. For instance, Gannett Co., which publishes 80 daily newspapers including *USA Today* and owns 23 local television stations, has been reducing its headcount for years. The company finished 2010 with more than 32,000 employees, about 17,000 fewer than just four years earlier.

Reduced headcount is only part of the story.

Besides Gannett's decision to furlough higher paid employees to reduce costs and avoid additional layoffs recently, the company is using its television stations to subsidize its print business. Gannett is home to several television stations that at one time were considered the best in the country when measured by journalistic integrity. However, Gannett has begun the process of staffing those stations with what the company calls "multimedia journalists". (**Note:** *Mid-way through Gannett's experiment with multimedia journalists, several sources say it has been suspended at some affiliates, at least temporarily).*

The designation "multimedia journalist" is meant to describe a television journalist who is trained and equipped to disseminate content through multiple channels; on air, online, in print, and socially. In reality though, "multimedia journalist" is industry code for "one man band". A "one man band" is a person who must do it all: shoot, write, edit, and deliver the content on air. One man bands work without the help of photographers, sound equipment operators, and field producers.

Rather than focusing solely on accumulating content and articulating it accurately as a reporter should do, one man bands must focus much of their attention on the technical execution crucial in newsgathering; operating microphones, cameras, and editing software.

Anecdotally, the number of one man band job postings included in online media job boards has increased dramatically over the past few years. However, the industry has experimented and struggled with the implementation of one man bands for much longer.

The results are clear; one man bands are generally not capable of producing the quality and quantity of work a two or three person team is.

Still, the financial benefits have not prevented television stations from trying to make one man bands work. Entire television newsrooms have been gutted and replaced solely with one man bands. Veteran reporters who have worked with a teammate for decades are being told they must learn to shoot and edit their own materials or be laid off. In some instances, the quality of work created by one man bands has been so poor the newsroom has opted to return to two person teams to gather news despite the increased costs. Those instances are rare though.

The trend is too enticing; a corporation can eliminate nearly half its staff and health care costs associated with those employees. However, it often also immensely reduces the journalistic quality of its product.

The newspaper industry is facing a similar shift as well.

Newspapers are increasingly focusing attention on their websites to compensate for plunging circulation statistics. Websites are flush with content that increasingly includes video, news feeds, and social media applications. It means print reporters are being forced to learn new technologies.

Much like television one man bands, print reporters are now often required to lug cameras to news scenes, shoot video, and upload it to their paper's website. The time dedicated to accomplishing those chores was time that used to be spent ferreting out the facts.

The march toward doing more with less has only been magnified by other cost cutting measures in which broadcast entities have engaged. Programming is expensive. Television stations spend hundreds of millions of dollars buying up the rights to air reruns of popular situation comedies, cartoons, and court-related programming. However, as industry margins compressed it did not take television station mangers long to realize they had a money saving solution right beneath their noses.

Instead of continuing to pay for expensive programming, television stations are increasingly opting to fill the time themselves. When contracts for high dollar programming expire, television stations are increasingly opting not to renew the contracts or purchase additional programming. Instead, stations are adding newscasts to replace programming.

Years ago, viewers generally had three evening options: catch the local news at 5, 6, or 11 P.M.. (Late news may air at 10 P.M. depending on your time zone). But today the options are much more numerous.

Television stations across the country are plugging the early afternoon gap in programming with 4:00 and 4:30 P.M. newscasts. Quite often a 6:30 P.M. newscast has been added as well. In some cases, newscasts are even being broadcast at 7 P.M. Later at night, stations have added newscasts to bookend their late news broadcasts.

It makes financial sense: reduce programming costs, use the staff you have remaining to fill the time programming once did, and create new revenue by selling commercials during all of the newscasts that have been created.

It also helps television stations mask massive ratings declines. Rather than having to answer tough questions from advertisers about ratings declines for individual newscasts, stations can total up their individual newscast audiences to create a composite number that's more attractive to an advertiser.

Sell the package. Not the individual show.

News outlets would like you to believe they have beefed up their commitment to news. With proper promotion, they believe viewers will see additional newscasts as a sign the station is willing to work longer and harder uncovering the truth in their communities.

In reality, it's a smokescreen.

The only winner in this scenario is the station's parent company. Television news is being broadcast by skeleton crews. Often, hours of weekend newscasts are produced by a small handful of people. Most local news stations are 5-day a week operations.

One day soon, a company's public relations staff may not even be dealing with a human being on the other end of a call from the media.

Narrative Sciences, a company in Chicago, has created a computer program that writes news stories. The company's website boasts its product, "...transforms data into high quality editorial content." The explanation continues, "Our technology application generates news stories, industry reports, headlines, and more- at scale and without human authoring and editing."

*The New York Times* reports the company has twenty customers and that the company's, "...technology would be primarily a low-cost tool for publications to expand and enrich coverage when editorial budgets are under pressure."

One of the company's founders has reportedly predicted that the computer program will win a Pulitzer Prize in journalism within five years.

The trend is clear. Staff is being cut and trained to do what a team once did. In adding newscasts, newsrooms now have fewer people to fill a much larger news hole. Computers are being programmed to write stories on topics humans once had to witness before writing about. At the same time television station promotions departments are telling the public the entity is still dedicated to real investigative journalism.

Nothing this weak can hurt you, right?

# Quick Hit Investigations

So how does an industry in fiscal and qualitative decline compensate?

Answer: Quick hit investigations.

That self-defining phrase is how a generation of reporters across the country is being trained to conduct journalistic investigations. It's also an economic reality forcing true investigative journalists to make difficult choices; reduce quality as a means to increase story quantity thereby ensuring continued employment, or find another line of work.

Either choice is a threat to corporations.

Quick hit investigations are defined as pieces that can be promoted as investigative but require a minimal amount of time or resources to complete.

Today's investigative reporter is being trained to complete investigatory projects with minimal research, often without inclusion of proper context, and often without the time needed to include perspectives from all relevant stakeholders.

Woodward and Bernstein need not apply.

The curriculum for the current crop of investigative reporters does not include cultivating "deep throat" sources, sifting through reams of data for context and perspective, or engaging in time-consuming surveillance work. While Computer Assisted Reporting (CAR) has allowed today's journalist to compile, sort, and compare data that would once have taken months to scour, the mass abandonment of the core principles and investments that provide a foundation for true investigative reporting overshadows the benefits technology provides. There simply isn't the time, money, or resources today allotted for the type of work no one but wrongdoers should fear.

Nationwide, investigative news units are being dismantled. Years ago, multi-person teams would spend months gathering

143

elements necessary for a single story. The cost of doing investigative journalism is great and requires substantial manpower and time. It's why many media outlets no longer have investigative units. Units have been whittled down to individual reporters who are often tasked with trying to complete an investigation along with their daily assignments.

Despite the tangible decline media outlets are obsessing like never before to seem as if they are engaged in investigative reporting.

The reason behind labeling something as "investigative" is grounded in logic and supported by research. True investigative reporting is often cited as the only type of work that can meaningfully and consistently boost television viewer ratings or newspaper circulation statistics. That allows media outlets to charge advertisers more money. Journalistic investigation is the only product that can truly distinguish a media outlet from its competition.

Today's quick hit investigations do little or none of that.

Editors choose investigative stories based on two metrics today: timing and teasability.

First, timing refers to the month of the year in which the quick hit investigation will be broadcast. "Sweeps" months are the four months each year when a television station's ratings historically count (February, May, July, November). During these months the ratings television stations garner determine the amount of money they can charge for commercials. A well-rated sweeps month can mean millions of additional dollars for a television station.

Second, teasability refers to how well the promotions department can tease viewers into watching a story. For instance, a content-rich investigation that is dry and boring but highly important to public health or safety may not be chosen simply because it is not easily teasable. Conversely, a story with little content or importance may be chosen for broadcast during a "sweeps" month simply because some aspect of the story is easily teasable and appeals to a mass audience.

You've seen them. The Hollywood-like promotional trailers that often attempt to scare you into watching the newscast. For instance, the item all of you have in your fridge that could make you sick, the toy in your child's room that could be deadly, or the disgusting fluids we found on your hotel bedspread tonight at ten!

A recent tease produced for *NBC Nightly News* reveals even the major television networks do not yet comprehend or refuse to acknowledge the changes that social media and the directional reversal of data dissemination have forced. In January of 2012, NBC began running a spot teasing a story about a medication millions take that could actually do more harm than good. The tease does not name the medication or the potential consequences of taking it. The tease ran all weekend and informed viewers they could tune in Monday night to learn whether they were in fact taking a medication that may be harming them.

If NBC was genuinely concerned about viewers' health why would it wait 48 hours to identify the medication in question? If NBC truly believed the medication could be harmful why wouldn't it broadcast the information immediately as a public service? And why did it believe in today's media landscape it could keep secret the identity of the medication?

The answer to all three questions is money.

NBC believed it could scare every person currently taking medication into watching its Monday night newscast. Despite plenty of evidence, this outdated mindset has not yet been replaced in the world of television news.

A quick Google search can immediately answer the questions most television news teases leave unanswered. For some reason, even network news producers fail to realize this and continue to operate as if it is 1980.

At a training conference for investigative journalists, one panelist was asked how she knows whether her pieces are accurate given she spends such little time on them.

The journalist replied, "We do worry we will miss something or make an error due to lack of time. I'm turning the story so quickly I don't have time to call everyone."

Didn't have time to call everyone!

It's understandable if your toes curled or a chill shot down your spine.

This panel explained to attendees it's no longer about the "big" investigation. "Big" meaning a work on which a reporter has spent substantial time. Presently, maintaining employment requires quick hit investigations one can turn quickly and often. Panelists then tell the room full of reporters these quick hits are easy to do, when you target corporations.

Targeting corporations is enticing because often governments or regulatory bodies have already done much of the work necessary for an effective story tease.

For instance, reporters are taught they can mine key documents for a steady stream of tips and stories on corporations in their hometowns. Inspection reports at state or county Health Departments are places reporters can find groceries, restaurants, hospitals, and nursing homes to target. Reporters are taught where they can quickly find warning letters, citations, fines, and punishments levied against corporations.

It is newsworthy when a company screws up and is fined or otherwise reprimanded by a regulatory body or governmental entity. It's newsworthy at the time the punishment is handed down. It's newsworthy and fair to bring up long after the punishment is meted out if it's relevant during a crisis situation (think BP's safety record during the 2010 Gulf of Mexico drilling rig fire and oil spill). But these reporters are being trained to fish.

Fishing was once something to be avoided. I was trained that before you cast a line you had to have a reason to get out your fishing pole. Are you fishing because you got a tip, document, or phone call urging you to look someplace specific? If not, your pole shouldn't even be brought to the pond.

However, today's reporters are training to be commercial fishermen; casting wide nets in the hope something good will be caught up when the net is pulled out of the water and onto the boat. For instance, reporters are being trained to fish via PACER, an acronym for the online federal court system. Reporters who have a moment of down time are taught they can just plug a hometown company's name into the search function of PACER and immediately find out who is suing the company. Doing so will provide reporters with an ample amount of lawyers and plaintiffs immediately willing to talk on the record about where the company has fallen short legally, ethically, or environmentally.

In terms of local television affiliates, there are generally only about five stations dedicated to quality investigative journalism. Hundreds of others are using these quick hit investigations to stem the financial bleeding. However, it's worth noting that Comcast, which bought a controlling stake in NBC recently, is making a commitment to investigative reporting at its local affiliates. Comcast recently announced it would hire approximately 135 employees to beef up the investigative units at the affiliates NBC owns and operates.

Whether Comcast is sincere in its desire to do real investigative journalism with integrity is not yet clear. Even if it is, some in the industry worry competitors unable or unwilling to match Comcast's financial investment will cut corners to keep up.

This means more quick hit investigations.

And more risk for corporations.

# Breeding Bulldogs

Despite the prospect of a low paying job in an industry decimated by cutbacks and digital competition, journalism schools are bursting at the seams. Record or near-record enrollment at many journalism schools has only increased the industry's supply-demand imbalance. Privately, j-school deans scratch their heads when asked why so many students are majoring in journalism.

Statistics included in the *Columbia Journalism Review* provide data to support the phenomenon; the *Review* reports 83,000 undergraduate students were enrolled in j-schools in 1985. The number balloons to 205,000 in 2009.

The possibility of a quick ascension to media superstardom has always attracted a number of students. In fact, many of the students at one well-known broadcast University enter the program believing that, upon graduation, they will immediately be hired to be the next six-figure anchor at ESPN or will be doing play-by-play for a professional sports franchise. The egos these teenage students enter school with are not always countered with the economic realities that now define the industry.

To be fair, there are journalism professors who were once working industry professionals who speak the truth to students. However, these students often have their minds made up in advance and are already arrogant enough to believe the low paying local news jobs that professors warn of are positions they will never be required to fill on their way to the top.

As is a criticism in other fields, University j-schools are teaching to the test. In other words, rather than equipping students with a thorough understanding of journalistic investigative fundamentals, schools are teaching students that which will most quickly help them become employed after graduation. Quite often teaching new technologies and methods of delivery trumps teaching content generation and the methods by which it is acquired.

Equipping graduating students with the skills in greatest demand by employers is why we send our children to college. But in the case of journalism there appears to be a disconnect between the skills that were once valued and characterized as the "fourth estate" and the skills most attractive to present-day employers.

Even greater in number than the students who choose journalism as a path to stardom are the students who choose the major by default; those who are not especially proficient in mathematics or other left-brained dominant challenges. It's one reason business executives and other left-brained dominant people often have such a hard time understanding journalists.

To compensate, Universities have created special schools to train journalists to execute quick hit investigations. They start at square one. *The Lumina Foundation for Education* sponsors on campus workshops in which marketing materials boast that j-school attendees will learn how to "read budget documents" and "use legal tools to pry open foundations". Additionally, *The National Center for Business Journalism* at Arizona State University offers scholarships and all-expenses-paid seminars entitled "Strictly Financials".

The goal, in essence, is to teach professional business journalists and journalism students the skills they'll need to read and understand a corporate balance sheet. The four day seminar advertises it will teach students the essentials needed to cover financial stories. This includes teaching students about stocks and bonds. The University says the seminar is a response to, "...requests from many participants in our one-day workshops who want to raise their sophistication level in all financial aspects of business coverage."

The *Investigative Reporters and Editors* organization is now offering "Watchdog Workshops" which are designed to bring "affordable training" to reporters across the country. The workshops suggest attendees will become better business and government watchdogs in a time when, "...governments are restricting the flow of information." In reality, corporate and government disclosure requirements have never been greater or easier to access.

Members have access to data illustrating how stories focused on executive compensation or executives using corporate jets to attend golf outings were executed. Members are also taught strategies to localize national crises. For instance, members are taught how to check to see if local credit unions made some of the same mistakes big banks and mortgage originators made, leading to the financial crisis of 2008.

Journalists who execute these strategies the best are rewarded financially.

Reporters who put their training to use and generate business stories are encouraged to enter the *"Bartlett & Steele Awards"* which honor that which is deemed to be the year's best in investigative business journalism. Besides the prestige of an award and being recognized in front of peers, investigative reporters earning a "gold award" are given $5,000. Second and third place honorees also finish in the money.

It can be even more lucrative.

*The Joan Shorenstein Center* on the press, politics, and public policy at Harvard's Kennedy School advertises a $25,000 prize for investigative reporting.

There is a bounty on your corporation's reputation.

*The National Center for Business Journalism* at Arizona State University boasts that since 2003, it has trained more than 10,000 journalists in these techniques.

Do you doubt there's one in your town?

# Crystal Balls

Imagine being able to see the next news story on your corporation before it's actually printed or broadcast.

It's possible.

Corporations do have the ability to know exactly what type of story an investigative reporter is looking to do, what information the reporter is seeking about a company, and even when a story about a corporation might be printed or broadcast.

Think of it as a crystal ball into a corporation's journalistic future.

Reporters use Open Records Requests and Freedom of Information Act (FOIA) requests to acquire public records related to matters such as a company's safety record, environmental history, and disciplinary measures taken against the company.

However, these tools are not just for reporters.

Understand that these records requests, once received by the public body they're meant for, become public records themselves.

Journalists do not have a monopoly in regard to sunshine laws that provide access to public records. Attorneys, businesses, and regular citizens are all able to use these laws as a means to obtain records classified as public.

Smart PR staffs should be using these laws as well.

In other words, corporations should FOIA the FOIA. Since a news outlet's records request is a public record, corporations have the same right to that record. There is nothing then to stop a corporation from filing its own public records request to obtain records requests submitted by news organizations.

News outlets have been doing it to one another for years.

For instance, San Antonio has been characterized by some as one of the more competitive television markets in the country. Detractors criticize the city's stations as being too focused on crime and gore. However, San Antonio has a tradition of producing some high quality investigatory pieces. And the competitive nature of the market is on full display as the city's television stations use the FOIA to, in essence, spy on one another's investigatory staffs.

KSAT, the ABC affiliate in San Antonio, is known to frequently FOIA its competitors' FOIAs. Doing so allows KSAT to know in advance the types of stories the other stations in San Antonio are working toward. This information is especially useful during the all-important sweeps months, where viewer ratings historically count and determine how much stations can charge advertisers for commercials.

Television stations have always wrestled with how far in advance of a story's date of broadcast to begin promoting or teasing a story. Promotional support of a story includes placing advertisements in newspapers, running advertisements on radio stations, or even teasing the story within the station's own newscasts.

However, competitors closely monitor a station's promotions and teases during sweeps months. If a station begins promoting an investigative story too far in advance, it gives a competitor time to quickly produce the story itself and then broadcast it before the station that originally did the story.

Doing this decimates the station that originally created the piece. News Directors have been known to kill the original story so it does not appear to viewers that it is his or her station copying the station that, in essence, actually stole the story. Being leapfrogged by a competitor during sweeps also renders the money spent gathering and promoting the story as wasted.

It's a tactic that has been around for some time. It is analogous to a baseball player intently observing the signs a third base coach flashes to batters, identifying what they mean, and using those signs to anticipate whether the batter is swinging away or bunting.

Stations that FOIA the FOIA are even more obtrusive. Requesting copies of a competitor's records requests is like sneaking into the baseball team's dugout, through the clubhouse, and into the manager's office where the signs are posted and explained on a chalk board.

KSAT's News Director, Jim Boyle, would not speak with me about how successful the practice has been or how the idea originated. But competitors in the market say KSAT began to FOIA the FOIAs several years ago after being beaten by competitors on some major stories.

One of KSAT's competitors says it is now policy at KSAT to FOIA the FOIAs of every news outlet in San Antonio. But this competitor says, "That's not how we play the game." This News Director goes on to say, "I personally don't think this is a good practice, while on one hand you are always on top of what your competition is doing, but on the other it sends the wrong message to your team. We should all be about the business of enterprising our own stories."

Another of KSAT's competing News Directors, who at one time offered me a position as an Investigative Reporter, suggested the tactic was underhanded. While interviewing for the position, the News Director asked how I planned to combat KSAT's aggressive pursuit of my future records requests.

I told him I'd "out-create" the competition.

When pressed for detail, I explained how I'd file hundreds of FOIAs I never actually intended to do anything with until KSAT went broke trying to do them all first!

Criticism of the FOIA the FOIA practice is not limited to Texas.

After using a similar practice in Florida in 1998, the *Tampa Tribune* responded to criticism with an article entitled, "Tampa Tribune Denies Spying on Competitors". Reports indicate the Tribune had requested the FOIA logs from the Governor's office. The request would reveal what type of information the Tribune's competitors had requested. However, the Governor's press secretary was reportedly uncomfortable with the request, citing a concern regarding the ethics of such a request.

The National Freedom of Information Coalition outlines on its website why FOIA logs are public and how best to go about requesting them. The Coalition also addresses the question of whether the tactic is ethical for journalists. A portion of the Coalition's argument is below:

> "And in case we didn't mention it, here is another good reason to FOIA the FOIAs: it is a good way of checking up on the competition, whatever your profession might be.
> From time to time, we hear complaints that obtaining FOIA logs violates some code of ethics. Journalists, in particular, tend to think that a record of

their FOIA request should be shielded from prying eyes, i.e. competing reporters working on the same story.

We, however, believe that an open record is an open record -- which is what a FOIA request becomes once it is filed."

The purpose of including the Coalition's response is not to begin a debate about the ethics behind the tactic. The purpose is to further illustrate how disruptive to a reporter or news outlet gathering this type of intelligence can be. It also provides insight into how reporters view themselves and the laws in place that help them do their jobs.

It is hypocritical for a reporter to be bothered by the same request he or she routinely uses to gather information. Reporters who are bothered by such behavior tell on themselves and indicate they believe they have a right to public records others should not.

If your corporation is not employing this tactic, it should begin doing so immediately.

A batter standing at home plate would be labeled a fool if he were to turn down an opportunity to secretly learn which pitch the pitcher was about to throw. A corporation that chooses not to seize this kind of freely available intelligence deserves a similar label.

Knowing what kind of story is in the works, the specific data a reporter is requesting, and when the reporter might come knocking on your corporation's door is invaluable. It provides a corporation with a warning it would otherwise not be afforded.

A corporation which actively retrieves these types of warnings buys itself time. While a reporter is waiting for his or her request to be filled, a corporation can thoroughly prepare a defense in relation to the reporter's request. It prevents the corporation from being caught off guard.

A smart PR staff might even "break" the news itself.

Employing this tactic allows a company's executives or spokespersons to be comfortable and confident when it is finally time to interview with the reporter. Why shouldn't the executive being interviewed be confident? He or she already knows the answers before the questions are even asked.

# Content Counters Content

Corporations can learn something from a bolt-action rifle. When the cable business news network CNBC embarked on its award winning documentary *"Remington Under Fire: A CNBC Investigation"*, Senior Correspondent Scott Cohn and Senior Producer Jeff Pohlman had no idea they too would become targets of an in depth investigation.

CNBC's piece, which was broadcast in 2010, targets gun manufacturer Remington Arms Company and the company's popular 700 series bolt-action rifle. The rifle, and its unique firing mechanism, was first introduced after World War II and quickly became popular among hunters, police, and the military which CNBC reports, "…prized its accuracy and smooth trigger pull."

However, CNBC's investigation uncovered a darker, even deadly side, of the Remington model 700 that the company allegedly tried to keep secret. CNBC's report suggests the model 700's trigger mechanism has a deadly design flaw that can lead to inadvertent discharges.

In other words, the gun can go off without the trigger being pulled.

CNBC's investigation found, "…at least two dozen deaths linked to inadvertent discharges of the rifles, more than 100 serious injuries, and more than 75 lawsuits- most of them quietly settled, the details hidden from the public by confidentiality agreements." CNBC interviewed people who attribute the deaths of loved ones to inadvertent discharges and cited internal company documents in which even the engineer who patented the unique trigger mechanism proposes a design change. Following the investigation, CNBC boasts a police department stopped using the rifles, the U.S. Border Patrol retrofitted its rifles, and hundreds of viewers wrote the network with similar allegations to those featured in the report.

For its part, Remington counters the accusations in the piece with a statement suggesting poor gun safety procedures and improper maintenance are to blame for accidental injury or death. The company also contends after extensive testing it was not able to duplicate claims of inadvertent discharge.

However, Remington did much more than just issue a statement.

In fact, Remington's tenacity and lengths to which it went to counter the CNBC documentary alarmed and disturbed the CNBC staff that produced the investigation. Unbeknownst to Correspondent Cohn and Producer Pohlman, Remington had been following them every step of the way during the documentary's gathering process.

At a training seminar for investigative reporters Cohn and Pohlman told the audience they were upfront with Remington about their intentions to create the documentary and had contacted the company immediately. CNBC says instead of sitting down for an interview Remington immediately hired two Public Relations firms. Cohn and Pullman told the seminar audience the PR agencies kept asking the network to meet for an "off the record" discussion.

CNBC said it refused each offer.

Then, two days before CNBC's documentary was scheduled to air, Cohn and Pohlman say the PR agencies asked one last time to meet privately and discuss the matter "off the record". This puzzled Cohn and Pullman. They did not immediately understand what Remington or its PR agencies were trying to accomplish.

It soon became apparent though.

Remington and its PR agencies were gathering information for their own documentary; a documentary that would counter, point-by-point, the claims made in CNBC's report which had not yet even been broadcast.

It became a war of dueling documentaries.

When Remington unveiled its www.remington700.tv website, Correspondent Cohn and Producer Pohlman finally realized why Remington had wanted to meet off the record. Remington had, in essence, been trailing Cohn and Pullman while the two compiled their story. Remington and its PR agencies re-interviewed the same people CNBC interviewed, poured over the same documents that CNBC had cited, and produced a refutation documentary that rivaled, if not bettered, CNBC's documentary in terms of production value.

In requesting an "off the record" meeting with CNBC, Remington was aiming for a "gold mine" for its own documentary: interviews with Cohn and Pohlman. Even without being able to pick the brains behind CNBC's documentary, Remington was able to produce a broadcast quality documentary along with an array of supplemental multimedia materials.

For instance, the Remington documentary starts with a "television anchor" telling viewers, "Reporting the news is a serious business, especially when it comes to allegations that can damage reputations...sometimes though reporters don't get the whole story...Remington Arms believes shooters should know the truth...and it's a story they won't see on cable t-v...".

Cohn was even criticized for having his finger on the gun's trigger during a stand up rather than positioning it alongside the gun's stock as he should have- a no no for gun enthusiasts. Would you trust a guy who doesn't even know how to hold a gun properly?

Remington's documentary features Marines who suggest the model 700 has saved lives during times of war, snipers who say the rifle is critical to their work, and a detailed review of CNBC's report that uncovers, "…numerous inaccuracies, misstatements, and mischaracterizations."

Remington uncovers information that calls into question the credibility of the "company insiders" featured in CNBC's report. Remington produces documentation suggesting statements these "insiders" made to CNBC are contradictory or inconsistent with statements they've made under oath in legal proceedings.

Remington is also critical of CNBC's ethical practices in regard to tracking down the elderly man who designed the trigger mechanism in question. Remington claims the man initially declined an on-camera interview with CNBC, but suggests CNBC showed up with its cameras at the man's retirement facility anyway and pressured the elderly man into speaking with it.

Remington's documentary is also critical regarding CNBC's use of a particular gunsmith in its report. Remington contends the gunsmith frequently testifies against gun manufacturers and is paid to do so by trial lawyers. Remington produces documentation indicating that, under oath, the gunsmith is not nearly as critical of the model-700's safety history as he is in CNBC's documentary.

In addition to Remington's refutation documentary, the company also provides a point-by-point written response to many of the allegations made in CNBC's documentary. The response accuses CNBC of being sensational, using documents out of context and smearing Remington's reputation. The response is in a two column document with CNBC's "allegation" on the left hand side and Remington's counter of "fact" on the right hand side.

When describing Remington's efforts to refute CNBC's allegations, Cohn and Pohlman appear to be shocked and even a bit offended. Both were flabbergasted and visibly uncomfortable with the idea that Remington would go to such a length to discredit CNBC's documentary. In fact, the pair describes an almost chilling scene as the folks at CNBC became aware of Remington's efforts to counter the news organization's work.

While the journalists at CNBC are constitutionally allowed to gather, produce, and broadcast work critical of Remington, the journalists seem to feel it was inappropriate for Remington to do the same.

Cohn and Pohlman had a sympathetic audience in the journalists who had gathered to listen to the tale at a recent investigative reporting training seminar. In fact, the general consensus of the group seemed to be that Remington must be guilty of everything CNBC had accused it of in the documentary. Otherwise, why would the company make the financial commitment it did to defend itself?

It never crossed the minds of most at the seminar that Remington likely did not see its actions as frivolous expenditures, but rather an investment in maintaining its reputational integrity when the company felt it wasn't getting a fair shake.

For their work on the Remington documentary, Cohn and Pohlman were awarded a prestigious *"Investigative Reporters & Editors"* award in June 2011. Those attending the awards ceremony marveled at the duo's work and the injustices it uncovered for the public.

However, Cohn and Pohlman failed to volunteer to the audience how they hatched the idea for the story. It's something viewers of CNBC's documentary were never told. And it's likely something not even Remington knew about.

Pohlman has roots in the West. Bozeman, Montana just happens to be where Richard Barber lives. Barber is prominently featured in CNBC's documentary. His nine-year-old son died in a hunting accident that involved a Remington 700 in 2000.

Turns out Pohlman and Barber go way back and have known each other for years. There's nothing inherently wrong with a journalist featuring the opinions of someone he or she might know. But when a journalist and a source are close personal friends, some would argue the journalist is ethically required to disclose that to the audience in a piece like the one here.

Finally, Cohn and Pohlman reveal to an audience of journalists at that training seminar how CNBC knows the documentary is a success; soon after the documentary aired, Remington's parent company withdrew its plans to file for an initial public stock offering.

# The Courage to Create

Remington pulled the trigger a bit late.

Remington's efforts are admirable. The company created valuable content. It presented it in a compelling way.

But it was late to the party.

It only created out of desperation.

And it paid big bucks to do it.

You can do it better.

And cheaper.

Remington provides us a window into what's possible. But it's a model with flaws. What the company did can and should be improved upon.

What if it were first?

What if the company had divorced its fear and become the first to create a documentary addressing the controversy surrounding its most popular gun? What if it had the courage to distribute the documentary for free?

Would CNBC have even done its own piece?

Would it even be news anymore?

Even if the answer to both questions is yes, Remington would have established itself as the primary narrator of the controversy. CNBC and anyone else who dared would simply be following. They'd be the party reacting. They'd be playing catch up. Remington would enjoy the first mover advantage.

We all have skeletons in the closet. We hide them there so no one sees them. So no one finds them. What if we dug out those skeletons? What if we stopped hiding them? What if we used those skeletons to create something beautiful? Something that made life better. Something that changed a life. Something we could be proud of.

Finding the courage to create is a choice.

We all possess it. But we lock it up inside. We hide it with the skeletons. After a while we forget it's there. We forget we have it. It fades. We don't need it as long as the skeletons stay in the closet.

But what happens when someone else yanks a skeleton from our closet?

What happens when the skeleton is visible to all?

We don't have our courage. It's still buried in the closet. Those who yank skeletons into public view certainly don't help us find our lost courage. In fact, they're banking that we won't be able to muster the courage to create. To rise to the occasion. To do good.

It's too late to begin searching for your courage after your skeleton is made public.

We must find our courage first.

Before we need it.

Rediscovering our courage provides us with freedom. Freedom not available to those who lack it. Those who've lost it.

Those with the courage to be the first to confront their skeletons rather than being forced to confront them by someone else wrest control of their fates. They control their destinies. They become the map makers. They create the rules others must play by. They create their own advantages.

The courage to confront and create frees you to focus on being better. On giving people something valuable. Something they can use. Something that'll better their lives. Something that makes a connection. Something that'll prompt them to come back to you.

Courageously creating will transform your organization. You'll no longer be a luxury. You'll become a necessity. Why would you choose to be optional? Why not choose to be necessary?

Let's pivot again.

Let's find out how to be sure what we create is exceptional.

# Pivot Point #3

On the way to unearthing the secrets to creating premier content it's useful to pivot here and address two uncomfortable topics: bias and subjective judgment.

How will we know whether our content is truly magnificent? How will we know when we have a winner? How will we know when we've created something truly innovative?

We'll have to measure.

Measuring our work can be scary. It illuminates failure. It highlights ineffectiveness. It shows how we are underperforming.

Isn't measurement great?!

This is why we divorce fear. It's why we embrace and learn from our bad ideas. It's why we've created a culture that pays homage to mistakes. Mistakes that ultimately lead to the creation of something special.

Pivot here.

Measure your way to success.

# Measure What You Make

*M*easurement is the ultimate truth teller.
Measuring the effectiveness of the content you create is the only way to guarantee a content creator is not lying to herself. Objectively measuring content forces the creator to be honest about the impact of his creation.

# Measurement

What does premier content look like? How will you know if it's special? If it's of high value?

Smart PR staffs dedicated to artfully creating something unique and valuable must prove what they've created is of high quality. However, the creators are not likely to be objective analysts. Impartiality is not a creator's strong suit. They're married to their creation. They should love it. They should treasure it.

Removing that bias is key.

The only way a smart PR staff can rid itself of subjective judgment and the biases inherent in creativity is to measure the content and its effect on others. Content must be measured from a variety of angles to ensure an accurate assessment.

Content creators and those who may use the content you create should be measured as well. Doing so will guide content distribution.

Measuring the effectiveness of the content you create is the only way to guarantee a content creator is not lying to herself. Objectively measuring content forces the creator to be honest about the impact of his creation.

Measurement is the ultimate truth teller.

It is often painful. Hurtful. And unkind.

But if done correctly and thoroughly it is always honest. That's why it's beautiful. That's why it demands your respect. Your admiration.

Those with the courage to measure will learn more about themselves and their environment than those who shy away from the fear. Those with the resiliency to look failure in the eye by checking to see how their creation stacks up will become tougher than those who cower. They'll be sure when their competitors are just hoping.

When measurement reveals a creation lacks necessary potency smart PR staffs will not deem their effort as failed. Instead, they'll be thankful measurement saved them the time and money they would've devoted to distribution.

While competitors without a measurement program are hoping what they've created is exceptional- you'll know for sure. If what you've created is not as effective as you had dreamed, you'll be onto the next project and one step closer to success while your competitors are still waiting and hoping.

Many corporations at this point understand Public Relations is measurable and devote at least a portion of their budgets to measuring their PR activities. However, debates continue to rage over what to measure, how to measure it, and whether the measurements are reliable.

A number of competing models or frameworks are available to corporations interested in measuring the effectiveness of public relations campaigns. However, there does not appear to be a consensus or generally agreed upon standard for a common measurement framework among PR practitioners as there is in other industries. For instance, consultants and academics are still debating whether measuring "outputs" or "outcomes" is proper. Others argue whether measuring cognitive outcomes should be bypassed in favor of solely measuring behaviors attributed to public relations activities.

I'm not convinced it is required or appropriate for the public relations industry to develop and agree upon a common measurement framework. I also happen to believe it is shortsighted and overly simplistic to believe the entire industry would benefit from adopting a standard set of metrics for each of a corporation's various publics.

One could argue there are generally agreed upon measurement frameworks for marketing professionals: think marketing mix models. Likewise, a generally agreed upon set of financial metrics exists; think Net Present Value (NPV), Return on Investment

(ROI), or Internal Rate of Return (IRR). Additionally, generally agreed upon metrics exist for specific industries as well; think same-store sales (Retail), Cost per Available Seat Mile (CASM-Airline), or Barrels of Energy Produced (Oil and Gas Industry).

So why should public relations be any different?

I would argue accurately measuring the successful engagement of various publics is actually more complex than simply totaling same-store sales, accounting for airline seat miles, or measuring the amount of oil pulled from the ground. However, the broader debate over what to measure, how to measure it, and whether a common measurement structure is viable is of little use to an organization aiming to make decisions based on data rather than gut instinct. If interested, you may acquaint yourself with the constructive verbal jousting taking place within the industry at the *Institute for Public Relations* website (instituteforpr.org).

What this book provides a smart PR staff is a set of tools designed to accurately measure messaging strategies from multiple angles. This book smartly equips corporations with the creative mindset necessary to develop or adapt their own set of situational or project-specific metrics. The advantage this book provides a public relations staff intent on transforming its perspective is a narrow focus not found in other works devoted to measurement. The book provides a framework for measuring relationships corporations have or do not have with their publics, their competitors, or their industries in general.

Begin thinking differently about measurement. The intent here is to question conventional metrics; those you may have used in the past or those your industry has deemed as standard. Industry standard metrics may be of great value. But periodically challenging existing assumptions and beliefs by adopting a different set of metrics that provide perspectives and angles not considered in the past will identify strategic strengths and weaknesses corporations may not even know they possess.

Spirit Airlines is a prime example of how profitable it can be to question how the sector to which you belong currently measures itself.

*Investor's Business Daily* interviewed Spirit's CEO Ben Baldanza in March 2012 in regard to what Spirit actually measures. In an effort to avoid availability bias, or measuring what's easily available, Baldanza told the newspaper he puts little credence in the industry standard metric passenger load factor. Passenger load factor is simply a calculation of the percentage of seats filled on a flight and is generally assumed to be an indicator of profitability.

However, *IBD* quotes Baldanza as challenging conventional thinking saying passenger load factor, "...historically has no correlation to profitability." Instead, Baldanza looks at profitability on a more granular level. Spirit, which charges ultra-low fares, prefers to measure the profitability of individual activities such as carry on luggage and drink and snack options. Additionally, Sprit selects and rejects distributors based on individual profitability.

Spirit's long-term profit growth is far superior to its competitors. The company's leaders attribute the success, in part, to its unconventional measurement strategy.

Some of the metrics in this section are familiar. Others have been adapted or modified from those used in the financial and marketing sectors. In both cases, metrics included here have been specifically tailored to help smart PR staffs measure the effectiveness of their work.

The purpose is to create in you the ability to measure intangibles like influence, relationships, and skepticism. Not only is it possible to measure the abstract, it is crucial for organizations dedicated to creating premier content. To being exceptional. To being the best.

Rather than outline a number of hypothetical scenarios and create meaningless charts and models to illustrate a given metric's usefulness, the intent here is to provide corporate PR staffs with the freedom and flexibility to choose appropriate situation-specific metrics.

Think of the array of metrics included on these pages as a metric buffet. Smart PR staffs can pick and choose which metrics to use and when. Clearly, some of the metrics developed here will measure similar phenomena. But an effective measurement program must employ multiple metrics to achieve a well-rounded view of whatever is being measured.

By no means are the metrics included here a comprehensive or complete list of the metrics available to measure relationships or other phenomena. The intent is to show corporate PR staffs how to creatively adapt metrics born in other fields and apply them to public relations. More specifically, the goal is to mentally force corporate public relations staffers to engineer measurement solutions themselves. If a tool does not currently exist to measure whatever it is a company wants to measure, invent and create the tool. If a tool exists but is rather costly and may only be used once, adapt or modify the tool to generate the data desired.

A robust measurement program keeps a smart PR team from lying to itself. Measurement ensures the content you create is actually premier. Is actually of high value. Measurement eliminates the subjectivity present among those who are creating content. It removes the bias.

Squeezing the content orange yields both juice and pulp.

Distinguishing between the two in real-time can be tough.

You can do it though.

You must.

The measurement tools and metrics are right here.

Help yourself.

# Software vs. Do-It-Yourself

A smart PR staff can utilize a number of measurement tools and strategies to collect and analyze key data sets that enable corporations to more efficiently allocate media investment dollars and better guide communications strategy. However, the decision on how to collect and measure will be largely based on how much money a corporation allocates for public relations measurement. This in turn will likely dictate the tools a PR team has at its disposal.

Public Relations staffs with large measurement budgets can afford some of the fancier tools and services available. For instance, *VOCUS* offers cloud-based public relations software that boasts of constantly monitoring 65,000 news sources, 20 million blogs, and the entire social web. The company claims its software measures company spokesperson mentions, message prominence, and can determine the tone of media coverage as it relates to your company. The yearly price tag for a software suite like this for one user is more than $20,000. That price can nearly double with qualitative measurement add-ons like social media sentiment, which are not always included in the original package.

Likewise, *Adobe Systems* has introduced its Adobe Social Analytics package for public relations and marketing professionals. Adobe advertises its tools allow PR practitioners to, "...track, measure, and optimize your social media efforts." The company claims its suite removes the guesswork from this type of analysis. It boasts its tools show corporations how marketing efforts impact profitability.

Additionally, *Dow Jones & Company* has developed its own set of tools dubbed Dow Jones Insight that the company says enables corporations to measure their, "...global media impact." The company says its tools provide, "...in-depth media analysis tools for global PR and media analysis teams." The service boasts of monitoring millions of sources and uses, "...consistent metrics that tell a single cohesive story."

Software suites like these often also include a variety of plug-and-play templates designed to quickly churn out custom reports complete with pie charts and bar graphs illustrating how a corporation measures up against its peers. Some also include journalist databases, the ability to categorize journalists by subject or prior coverage of the corporation, and the ability to quickly send news releases to a core group of selected journalists.

These tools have the potential to expedite and in some cases simplify the measurement process. They can also eliminate much of the heavy lifting or grunt work required of a thorough measurement campaign.

However, there is a downside.

Besides being expensive, measurement software tools are often not fully utilized by the companies purchasing them. While the software can often be customized for individual companies, PR and Marketing staff members do not always fully utilize the tools offered in these packages. While there are a variety of technological and institutional reasons for this lack of full adoption, what's clear is that some corporations are paying full price for a partially used service.

For well-funded public relations departments this full adoption shortfall may not have much of an impact on the corporation's overall measurement strategy or bottom line. But for smaller companies unable to pay for tools they may not fully utilize, the issue is paramount.

It's good to know measurement software suites are luxuries not necessities.

This is why the book and the metrics contained herein are laid out buffet style. A metric that might taste good or be useful to one corporation may not be needed or useful for another. That said, just because a corporation enjoys the luxury of having a measurement software suite at its disposal doesn't mean the metrics and strategies outlined here aren't applicable. On the contrary, it is important for corporate PR staffs to understand the measurement building blocks that comprise the backbone of these high-tech software suites.

Understanding the fundamentals of media measurement enables a corporation to customize and execute its own measurement campaign without expensive cloud-based software suites. Similarly, a deeper understanding of these measurement tools allows those with access to premier software suites to better interpret and analyze the data the suites provide.

Either way, a fundamental knowledge of media measurement tools and strategies will empower corporations to self-create customized solutions that provide a competitive advantage by comparing key data sets against the company's past and the company's competitors.

# Data Collection Tools

Corporations interested in measuring their public relations activities by hand will utilize a variety of data collection tools. Web Analytics programs provide corporations with data regarding web traffic, origination, and click-through behavior. Analytics can pinpoint the specific stages of a corporation's website experience in which visitor behavior is not consistent with company objectives. Attention may then be directed toward those specific stages to alter visitor behavior or clickstreams. However, even corporations that have extensive analytics programs or measurement software suites will benefit from familiarizing themselves with two dominant data collection tools: surveys and media content analyses.

# Surveys

We'll spend little space discussing survey construction and use since corporate PR departments are likely already using them to measure some aspect of their strategy.

However, surveys should be constructed around measurable company objectives and based upon what the corporation is measuring at the time. I often see survey questions with little relation to company objectives or current measurement goals. Efficient and cost-effective surveys are narrowly tailored to focus on a specific measurement goal. Survey data are transformed into metrics by numbering survey responses on a continuum. Often, numbered survey continuums are built around the agree/disagree, more/less likely, or extremely poor/extremely good lines of questioning.

Most often, surveys will reveal insight regarding a corporation's relational strength with stakeholders, perceptions stakeholders hold, or logical disconnects that may exist between perceptions and realities. Corporations may also survey stakeholders on brand awareness, top of mind, more or less likely to recommend corporation or its products etc.

Corporations that have built a large email database that might include customers or people visiting a website, blog, or corporate social media site are in a position to collect survey data relatively quickly. Those that lack such a database or do not require website visitors to register may still conduct online surveys quickly and cost-effectively by using online survey tools.

A free basic service plan offered by Zoomerang includes an unlimited number of surveys and real-time results, though survey questions and responses are limited. Always be certain the sample selected for survey is representative of the population a corporation wishes to survey. The company offers additional pay-for-service options, as do online polling concerns like PollDaddy and SurveyMonkey.

Mail and phone surveys may also be useful for corporations, especially keeping in mind the importance of surveying a representative sample. Additionally, in person surveys are often useful at trade shows or live events in which the corporation can directly interact with the public. However, to ensure the data generated via in person surveys is valid, post-event surveys should be conducted with the same participants.

*Note: An entire industry has sprouted around collecting opinion data from social media like Twitter and Facebook. The allure is great; people are providing their opinions free of charge. For instance, tweets are being quantified and translated into sentiment indexes. However, care must be taken when using an algorithm to quantify tweets and likes. Algorithms are often unable to accurately discern sentiment from jest. Additionally, if it is true that Twitter users skew younger, questions will arise as to whether you have a representative sample. Conversely, there is also research indicating that Twitter sentiment correlates accurately with traditional sentiment surveys. The point here is to remind corporations to vigilantly monitor the integrity of survey activities.*

# Survey Fatigue

Technology has made measurement easier and more affordable to accomplish. Corporations are measuring customer behavior, marketing efforts, financial results, and the degree of engagement they have with various publics. While basing decisions on data is allowing corporations to operate more efficiently there is a downside. Those being surveyed are growing tired of responding to surveys. Others are willfully avoiding them.

This trend is calling into question the accuracy of surveys.

Executing valid and reliable surveys is key for managerial decisions based on data. However, surveying samples representative of the population a corporation aims to gather data on has become more difficult due to survey fatigue. There are a number of reasons consumers have grown tired of taking part in surveys.

Consolidation in the airline industry is part of the problem. As airlines merge or acquire one another flyers are frequently asked to take short surveys following their flights. Most recently airlines appear to be focusing on customer satisfaction as it pertains to flight attendants. This data will be used to determine which flight attendants remain and which no longer have jobs with the merged entity.

Increased competition in the automotive industry is adding to survey fatigue as well. Following the recession, several auto makers reduced the number of models they offer, sold underperforming or luxury brands, and heavily weighed customer opinion prior to designing new vehicles. It's why you see vehicles with a dozen cup holders, muscle car throwbacks, and quad-cab pick-up trucks designed for family use instead of work.

Political surveys are another reason people are turned off by surveys. Politicians attempting to determine which primary states they should focus their time and money are constantly polling potential voters. News organizations are continuously attempting to gauge voter sentiment toward candidates. Independent pollsters are doing the same in hopes of being hired by a politician running for office.

Besides survey fatigue, bloggers, social media influencers, and consumers with independent streaks are at times quietly refusing to take part in surveys out of principle. Some people argue they are simply not interested in providing data to a corporation that is going to use that information to better market products or services in an effort to squeeze more money out of them.

The *Pew Research Center* says telephone survey response rates have been declining for the past decade. CNBC cites Pew's response rates as declining from 36% in 1997 to 11% in 2011. However, Pew concludes that despite falling response rates it is still possible to obtain representative samples.

One way Pew believes it can continue to obtain representative samples is by conducting cell phone surveys to compliment land-line surveys. However, this may not be cost effective for corporations attempting to measure their PR activities. As Pew points out, cell phone surveys take more time to conduct since Federal regulations require that cell phones be dialed by hand. Moreover, cell phone respondents are at times paid for their responses as compensation for costs incurred from cell service providers.

Corporations can often bypass these challenges by relying on media contact lists, customer email address lists, and shareholder registration lists when attempting to survey various publics. Additionally, surveys can often be completed online at no charge or cost-effectively using sites such as Survey Monkey.

The point is to be aware members of your various publics may be experiencing survey fatigue. With that in mind, corporations can keep a sharp eye on obtaining representative samples so the data on which they are basing decisions is valid and reliable.

# Media Content Analysis

Media Content Analyses are conducted by corporations interested in determining what is being said about them in various forums. Think of these as media cat scans. Analyses illuminate how a corporation's brand is being communicated on television, online, in print and elsewhere. They provide quantitative and qualitative data by which a corporation can measure itself against its past and its peers.

Corporations rely on continuous media content analyses to detect changes in journalistic sentiment, sentiment provided to media by key stakeholders, and consumer perceptions of an organization. When evaluating qualitative phenomena it is also important to note the context in which the corporation is mentioned. Is the corporation mentioned in an opinion piece? A television news report? By a blogger with little or no influence?

Corporations can also glean important data from media content analyses that identifies how prominently the corporation is mentioned. Is the corporation mentioned in a headline? The top 20% of a news piece? The bottom 80%? Examining media content also enables corporations to gauge the frequency with which key messages are being conveyed. When combined with data regarding sentiment and tone toward the company, media content analyses are quite revealing.

The key when conducting media content analyses is to first identify the media a corporation deems important to analyze and measure. It makes little sense and is practically impossible to collect measurement data from every source that opines on your corporation. Selecting which outlets to include in a content analysis should be based on the outlet's influence.

It's now possible to measure the influence a journalist possesses. Similar metrics may be created to identify which media outlets a corporation should include in content analyses. Corporations that base decisions on television ratings or newspaper circulation numbers are making big mistakes (Television stations and newspapers routinely manipulate audience ratings to preserve revenue generation).

Corporations engaged in content analysis must select which media to include only after they select specific measurable objectives. These objectives will relate back to specific stakeholders a company wishes to impact in some manner. Clearly, the media these stakeholders consume must be identified and included in content analyses. To create a data-driven strategic communications plan, a corporation must compare itself with its past and its peers in news pieces important to stakeholders. For instance, determining whether your corporation's key messages are being conveyed with a greater frequency than competitors in mediums relied on by stakeholders will dictate strategy going forward. Many of these key mediums will likely be intuitive. However, some will not. Later, I'll show you how a corporate PR staff can use the Origin of Awareness Metric (OOA) to identify where stakeholders are first exposed to news about the company and why it may or may not be in a corporation's best interest to alter.

Software is available to help corporations analyze media content. While automating the process may be helpful in certain situations, software does not always provide reliable information. For instance, a software program will likely not be able to discern proper sentiment in the following Facebook post; "Company XYZ is bad ass." Software may mistake "bad" as the sentiment present in this post. Similarly, software will also be less likely to accurately gauge sentiment in this tweet; "I just love Company XYZ's yogurt-j/k!" In this case the Twitter user is kidding and actually holds a sentiment completely opposite of the denotative meaning of the post. Accurately analyzing media content is often a tedious job humans must undertake.

# Valuing Public Relations

How valuable is a specific piece of PR?
The mere question can be blamed for sleepless nights and boosting the blood pressure of corporate PR executives worldwide.

It's understandable that executives would want to know exactly how much money a successfully executed piece of public relations is worth. If a company's product is prominently displayed on the front of the *The New York Times* is it worth the same amount of money it would take to purchase a similarly sized and placed advertisement in the Times? Is it worth more?

PR practitioners have been calculating PR value using Advertisement Value Equivalency (AVE) for years. For newspaper coverage, AVE is calculated by multiplying the column inches a piece of PR covers in a newspaper by the newspaper's advertising rate. For television, AVE is calculated by multiplying the length of time a PR piece is broadcast by the broadcaster's advertising rate.

In some cases, PR has been given a multiple of between three and six. In other words, pieces of PR have been valued between three and six times more than an equivalent advertisement. The rationale behind the multiple is that news items have more credibility than advertisements, therefore they are worth more than ads.

The problem: PR has likely been valued incorrectly all these years.

*The Wall Street Journal's* Carl Bialik wrote a piece in which he interviewed a publicist regarding a popular photograph of a Vancouver, B.C. couple kissing in the middle of a semi-riot. The article points out the publicist ordinarily values PR as five times more valuable than an advertisement. The publicist allegedly valued the kissing couple photograph at $10 million. However Bialik writes, "That, it turns out, wasn't based on his rule of five. Instead, the publicist says he, 'pulled the figure out of thin air'-because the reporter was on deadline."

Advertising Value Equivalency is based on an assumption *The Institute for Public Relations* argues is not supported by factual data. AVE assumes advertisements and news pieces are equally impactful. However, a paper written in 2003 by Bruce Jeffries-Fox, Mark Weiner, and Katie Paine for the *Institute* argues there is no research to confirm the veracity of this underlying assumption.

The Jeffries-Fox paper points out, "...there have been many studies in the field of journalism showing that over the past two decades the credibility of the news media has been declining...".

If you've read this far, you know I argue the credibility deficit journalists are facing is accelerating in the face of declining advertisement revenue and the birth of new influencers.

Furthermore, The Journal article sites a research project conducted by David Michaelson of David Michaelson & Co. in which news piece publicity was compared with traditional advertising. In the end, the study found that the article tested, "…was no more effective than the ad in building brand awareness."

At the least, there is clear evidence indicating that attaching a multiple to a piece of PR is a flawed way of calculating value.

Additionally, calculation becomes even hazier when one attempts to value public relations efforts designed to reduce media coverage. For instance, the goal during a crisis is to make media crisis coverage go away. How does one go about totaling the number of stories that could have been done? Even if one could, do you think the reporter who opted not to do a story is going to be able to tell you his or her decision was based on a specific public relations activity in which the company engaged?

I would argue corporate public relations departments are better serving their companies by measuring the effects of specific public relations efforts. For instance, when a corporation measures its Cost Per Message (CPM) across multiple contexts it can determine the return on investment for each and allocate future resources more cost-effectively. Likewise, a corporation that learns it shortened the duration of a crisis versus peers involved in similar crises can calculate the money it saved in legal fees for each day the PR staff shaved from the duration of the crisis.

Decision makers are better served by smart calculations like these than they are with fuzzy AVE figures that are often inflated beyond reason.

Nick Winkler

# Quantitative Metrics

Counting and measuring how a corporation compares with its past and its peers is the foundation on which a comprehensive public relations measurement program is built. Identifying how often your corporation is mentioned, where it is mentioned, and by whom it is being mentioned by are key sets of data that will dictate future measurement decisions and ultimately strategic communications strategy.

Identifying whether your corporation is top of mind, being mentioned more frequently than a competitor, or how often your spokesperson is relied upon as a thought leader are important pieces of data that enable a corporation to become more efficient and better allocate marketing budgets.

The metrics outlined in the rest of this section are structured in a manner designed for quick comprehension. Immediately following the introduction of each metric I'll highlight four points which are key in fully understanding the metric. Each is found in bold type and in parentheses. First, I'll define each of the metrics for you (**Define**). Then I'll show you how best to collect data to calculate the metric (**Collection method**). Afterward, I'll teach you how to calculate the data collected (**Calculation**). And finally, I'll show you how the metric may be used to analyze or interpret your organization's strategic communications strategy (**Insight achieved**).

**Media Market Share (MMS)- (Define)** Determining your corporation's "share of ink" versus its competitors is a routine measurement corporations often use to gauge the effectiveness of PR efforts. It quantitatively identifies a corporation's share of media coverage. (**Collection method**) Media Content Analysis (**Calculation**) A corporation selects the media outlets for which it wishes to measure, identifies a specific time frame over which to measure, identifies industry competitors it wishes to measure against, and collects the total number of instances in which the company is mentioned and divides that total by the total number of company and competitor mentions collected. (**Insight achieved**) The metric identifies where the corporation ranks versus its peers in terms of its share of media coverage. For corporations that believe "all press is good press" the metric is a useful gauge. However, the metric lacks qualitative data regarding the corporation's share of media coverage. In other words, an industry leading MMS may not be desirable if a large percentage of that share contains messages harmful to reputation and profitability. A minimal MMS may be more desirable for corporations in politically sensitive or controversial industries.

*Note: Quantitative metrics may be of little value in and of themselves to a smart PR staff. During the 2012 Republican Presidential nomination process a research company conducted its own MMS evaluation of the candidates. The firm calls itself an "innovative, online research tool". However, the data the company pitched to reporters was worthless in that it generated absolutely no coverage in at least one television market immersed in a caucus. The company's version of MMS lacked any sort of complimentary qualitative metric needed to produce a more balanced picture. For instance, what does it actually mean in the 2012 presidential primaries, that Rick Santorum got 29% of the media's attention leading up to the Minnesota caucuses? What if the majority of that 29% was actually negative in sentiment? Would that still make Santorum the "winner" in terms of media attention?*

**Awareness, Attitudes, & Usage Metrics (AAU)- (Define)** For our purpose, AAU metrics are useful in identifying what stage a media member or outlet is in regarding its knowledge, beliefs, or behavior toward the corporation. (**Collection method**) Survey and Media Content Analysis (**Calculation**)

> **Awareness-** calculate awareness for corporation and competitors to determine where corporation ranks.

Likewise, open-ended survey questions reveal and allow for an industry ranking of specific companies that are top of mind or industry thought leaders.

**Attitudes**- survey allows corporation to identify the beliefs or intentions select media have toward the corporation, where a corporation is perceived as strong or weak, and how a specific media attitude compares with attitudes toward competitors.

**Usage**- media content analyses will help a corporation identify data such as the frequency with which select media are including key messages in coverage.

(**Insight achieved**) Identifying logical inconsistencies among phenomena such as media awareness and usage or awareness and attitudes highlights specific areas of a strategic communications strategy that may need attention or altering. Categorizing journalists and media outlets by their AAU stage provides corporations the data needed to appropriately tailor and prioritize communications strategy.

**Pitch Redemption Rate (PRR)- (Define)** Measures the frequency with which corporate PR staff media pitches ultimately become news pieces. This metric will assess the effectiveness of a corporation's pitching strategy. (**Collection method**) Survey and Media Content Analysis (**Calculation**) Divide number of media pitches that become news stories by the total number of pitches made to select media over a defined period of time or the total number of stories done on the corporation for that time period. (**Insight achieved**) Corporate PR staffs lacking strong media relationships invariably have lower PRRs than PR staffs that have nurtured relationships with journalists. The PRR will clearly indicate cold call or mass email dump pitches are ineffective and costly. A dismal PRR indicates a corporation has been negligent in building relationships that can protect and enhance its reputation. A mistake corporations often make when hiring outside PR firms is assuming those firms are better pitchers than people the corporation has on staff. Before hiring an outside firm, ask what its PRR is. You're not likely to be impressed.

**Source Dependency Index (SDI)- (Define)** Journalists often rely on a small number of sources in regard to story generation. Identifying those sources journalists most often depend on for story ideas is useful in narrowing public relations strategy. **(Collection method)** Survey and Media Content Analysis **(Calculation)** Divide the number of stories originating from a single source by the total number of stories the journalist has created over a defined period of time. **(Insight achieved)** This metric is valuable for companies attempting to mitigate risk posed by problem journalists. Identifying who those journalists rely on enables a corporation to focus on weakening that specific source of information flow or influence. Dependency will ebb and flow over time and circumstance. Monitoring dependency over time reveals newly acquired sources a corporation may deem important to influence. Corporations may calculate SDI for a number of journalists and learn multiple journalists are overly dependent on only a handful of sources.

*Note: Collecting data for this metric will likely prove difficult, especially when it comes to investigative reporters relying on anonymous sources. Often, corporations will be able to determine a story source by simply examining a journalist's work. In instances in which identifying a story source is a bit murkier, corporations will need to utilize resources outside their public relations department. Some entities have been known to quietly hire private investigators to identify story sources. Before doing so, keep in mind it is much more cost-effective to tap company lobbyists, elected officials, outside attorneys and other stakeholders who will likely be able to help determine a story source.*

# Placement War

Behavioral research suggests even avid news connoisseurs often read no more than a fifth of any given print news piece. Combine this notion with a generation centered on a maximum 140 characters per message and corporations may be dealing with audiences with the attention spans of gnats.

Hence the importance of winning the placement war.

Corporations that find themselves mentioned in news headlines, at the tops of television broadcasts, or "above the fold" in newspapers versus their peers may carve out a competitive advantage in the marketplace for themselves. But being featured more prominently than competitors may not always be beneficial given the situational context or corporate objectives. However, if a corporation desires to win the placement war, it must first identify where it ranks compared to its peers. Here is how:

**Premium Mention Ratio (PMR)-(Define)** Refers to the location in which the corporation's name, quote, or picture is placed in a news item or conversation. PR practitioners often use the term prominence to gauge placement. For instance, is the corporation mentioned in the headline, top 20% of the news item or conversation, or bottom 80%? Metric may be used to measure placement superiority in print, online, broadcast, or social mediums. **(Collection method)** Media Content Analysis **(Calculation)** Divide the number of headline or lead mentions by the total number of news items or conversations during a defined time period. Repeat for statistics related to top 20%/bottom 80%. May calculate for a specific media outlet, for only those outlets the company has identified as crucial, or all outlets that follow company. **(Insight achieved)** Compare with the company's PMR from a prior comparable time period or compare with competitors' placement to identify media perceptions and relationship to reality. Metric may also be used to quickly gauge coverage or conversations surrounding special events.

**Headline Inclusion Metric-** Smart PR staffs understand the importance of winning the headline battle. Headlines are increasing in number as television stations and newspapers routinely post content online. In the past a newspaper would simply print a single headline for a single story. Now papers are posting those stories online which can create an additional headline. Additionally, headlines have the potential to change as online content is updated to reflect changes or the latest information. Likewise, traditional headlines did not exist in regard to television stations prior to the web. Headline creation has been amplified as television stations are now tasked with writing headlines for television content posted online. Since many of these headlines will be the first thing readers see when searching online for a corporation, winning the headline battle is key. But first, a corporation must know whether it's winning the battle. The Headline Inclusion Metric (HIM) enables corporations to gauge headline success or failure versus prior time periods and versus their competitors. (**Define**) Identifies the frequency with which a corporation, its products, services, or key messages are included in the headline of a news item. (**Collection method**) Media Content Analysis (**Calculation**) Gather all pertinent industry headlines over a given time period from select mediums that are of interest to corporation. Divide the number of headlines mentioning corporation, its products, services, or key message inclusions by total number of headlines included in the data set. (**Insight achieved**) Ratio may be compared to prior comparable time periods to gauge headline inclusion progress or lack thereof. Ratio may also be compared to competitors for insight into where corporation ranks in the industry in regard to headline inclusion. Metric may also be adapted for real-time use at live or special events to gauge social headline dominance versus competitors.

*Note: The HIM provides corporations with only quantitative data for analysis. Assuming that your corporation is winning the headline war simply because your corporation's HIM is greater than those of your competitors may not be accurate. The messages headlines convey must also be measured for a well-rounded perspective on headlines. A richer understanding of the headlines in which a corporation is included may be gained by additional measurement. Combining other metrics, for instance Key Message Conveyance, with the HIM will provide a corporation with qualitative data that can then be weighed against the HIM. For example, a corporation with an industry leading 34% HIM may, upon further qualitative measurement, learn that 18% of headline inclusions are inaccurate or negative. Realizing that just 16% of headline inclusions are actually beneficial to the company reveals the corporation may not qualitatively be an industry leader in terms of headline inclusion. Companies collecting this type of data gain a competitive advantage by quickly being able to strategically target the unflattering 18% for change.*

# Qualitative Metrics

As important as it is to measure where a corporation is mentioned in a conversation or news piece or how often a corporation is mentioned versus its peers, quantitative analysis alone is not enough. In addition to quantitative data, corporations must also seek out qualitative data for a more complete measurement picture. Corporations that employ qualitative metrics to compliment their quantitative data gain better visibility into how their corporation compares with its past and its peers.

**Negative Sentiment Ratio-(Define)** Measures the negativity associated with a corporation's mentions in news items or conversations. Care should be taken to specifically define what qualifies a mention or conversation as negative. The metric is defined as containing two levels: 1) Unintentional Negativity 2) Intentional Negativity. Unintentional Negativity may include apathetic indicators such as: not aware, not top of mind, not a preference, would not recommend. Intentional Negativity may include maliciousness such as: recommends product or service of competitor, prefers competitor's product or service, or identifies weakness or deficiencies in corporation's product. Mentions and conversations may be further segmented by degree or type of negativity. (**Collection method**) Media Content Analysis (**Calculation**) Collect the number of Intentional and Unintentional negative mentions or conversations and divide them by the total number of mentions over a defined period of time, among a specific set of media outlets or conversation hosts. (**Insight achieved**) Data may be compared with a prior comparable time period to determine sentiment or conviction direction. Data may also be compared with comparable data from competitors to determine overall market satisfaction. Analyzing differences between Intentional and Unintentional ratios may indicate how a corporation allocates strategic communications investments.

*Note: It's not clear why some corporations might measure only for volume or media market share. If you are of the mind that "all press is good press" then collecting only quantitative data would give you what you need. However, corporations concerned about their reputations will find measuring for sentiment is the only way a corporation can derive qualitative detail to compliment volume or share data. In fact, sentiment determines how tens of millions of dollars are invested on Wall Street. Institutional investors are using social media sentiment to supplement stock trading strategies. Johan Bollen at the University of Indiana-Bloomington conducted research and published a paper in December 2011 that concluded the mood on Twitter can accurately predict moves in the stock market. Bollen also contends that Twitter sentiment and Google search queries are leading indicators and are, "...statistically significant predictors of daily market log return." Additionally, The Wall*

*Street Journal reported in February 2012 that, "More than a dozen hedge funds and high frequency traders now make trades guided, in part, by data from social media sources such as Facebook, YouTube, and Twitter...". A cottage industry has developed around analyzing social media sentiment and selling the data to traders. If traders use sentiment data to make million-dollar investment decisions, PR staffs are obliged to at least consider sentiment when determining how best to allocate strategic communications investments.*

# Key Message Repetition

Corporations invest heavily in creating memorable content aimed at achieving a specific objective. But how often do corporations measure to see whether the time and money invested in these communications is being accurately conveyed by third parties? I recently asked a corporate PR staffer how often the company's key messages were being accurately conveyed. Her response, "Well, the newspaper did a decent job the other day of summing up our position."

If that's good enough for you- please stop reading.

But if you want more...

If you want an edge in an ultra-competitive business environment- stay with me.

Identifying whether a corporation's key messages are being accurately communicated affords the corporation insight as to whether any adjustments to strategy are in order. Measuring whether key messages are being accurately articulated in media accounts allows a corporation to determine if something is wrong with the message, dissemination channel or method, or the influencer or medium involved.

**Key Message Conveyance Ratio (KMC)- (Define)** Identifies the frequency, if at all, a corporation's key messages are included or conveyed in news mentions or conversations. The metric is defined as containing three levels; 1) Completely 2)Partially 3)Incompletely **(Collection method)** Media Content Analysis **(Calculation)** Gather the number of mentions in news items or conversations over a defined time period, divide the number of Complete/Partial/Incomplete Message Conveyances by total number of mentions to determine percentages for all three. **(Insight achieved)** Ratio may indicate how well corporation is communicating with influencers. It may also identify the portion of a message that may need special attention or altering. It may also identify a specific influencer who, for some reason, is not conveying a key message. Data may be compared with that from a prior comparable time period or compared with competitors' Key Message Conveyance Ratios. Metric may also be used to quickly gauge coverage or conversations surrounding special events.

**Inaccurate Message Conveyance- (Define)** Identifies the frequency, if at all, a corporation's key messages are inaccurately included or conveyed in news mentions or conversations. **(Collection method)** Media Content Analysis **(Calculation)** Gather the number of inaccurate message inclusions in news items or conversations over a defined time period, divide the number of inaccurate inclusions by the total number of mentions to indicate deficiencies in strategic communications strategy. **(Insight achieved)** Data may identify specific reporter who, for some reason, is not accurately conveying corporation's message. Data may be compared with that from a prior comparable time period or compared with competitors' Inaccurate Message Conveyance Ratios. Metric may also be used to quickly gauge accuracy during special events.

**Message Differentiation Index (MDI)- (Define)** Critics argue the term "product differentiation" is practically useless due to the difficulties associated with attempting to measure or analyze the concept. However, corporations engaged in commodity industries can creatively quantify key messages to identify message differentiation, or lack thereof. (**Collection method**) Media Content Analysis (**Calculation**) Corporations engaged in commodity businesses must first identify the most common key messages associated with a given industry or for a specific commodity. Afterward, corporations must construct a scale on which key messages may be plotted numerically. These scales will differ by commodity and industry. For our purpose, assume a metals miner constructs the 5-point scale below:

| 1 | 2 | 3 | 4 | 5 |
|---|---|---|---|---|
| Finding Cost Leader | Largest Producer | Highest Margin Producer | Least Leveraged Producer | Least Susceptible to Price Volatility |

Next, the corporation must plot on the scale the position for which its key message falls. Key messages for each of the four competitors are plotted similarly. This allows for each key message to be assigned a number. Below is an example of a key message plot:

Metals Miner = 1.5
Competitor 1 = 3.2
Competitor 2 = 1.7
Competitor 3 = 5
Competitor 4 = 2.5

A corporation may analyze this data two ways depending on its objectives. First, if the corporation is concerned with just one competitor, it is now able to quantify differentiation in key messages and can adjust strategy accordingly. For instance, assume our metals miner is only concerned with Competitor 4. The metals miner can see its key message differs from Competitor 4 by 1 point, or 20%. Comparatively, our metals miner can see its key message differs from Competitor 3 by 3.5 points, or 70%. Likewise, the message differentiation between our metals miner and Competitor 2 is 4% and with Competitor 1 is 34%.

Alternatively, scores on the message plot may be averaged which provides the corporation with a different perspective in terms of differentiation. In the above example, the differentiation mean is 2.78. For our metals miner, this means its key message differs from its competitors by a score of 1.28 or 46%. The corporation can compare that with competitors to illustrate the average difference. For instance, Competitor 3 differs from the average by a score of 79%.

(**Insight achieved**) Constructing and analyzing an MDI to decipher message differentiation allows a corporation engaged in a commodity business to quantify that difference. An industry group closely clustered around a differentiation mean will likely have a greater potential to differentiate its message. Conversely, an industry group more evenly distributed away from the differentiation mean will likely find it more difficult to create space or uniqueness in terms of key messages. A company's communications strategy will obviously be limited by acknowledged industry facts such as "finding cost leader" or "largest producer". However, corporations that deem message differentiation beneficial to the bottom line should not be constrained by existing key messages identified within the industry. The MDI affords a corporation the ability to see how closely clustered industry messages are. After that it must tap its creative energy to break free of the index's confines.

**Media Penetration Share (MPS)- (Define)** Penetration refers to how popular a corporation's key messages are among influencers. This metric is not a simple calculation of key message volume or conveyance. It weighs popularity against that of the total key message marketplace and alongside that of competitors.

(**Collection method**) Media Content Analysis (**Calculation**) First, a corporation must figure for Industry Key Message Penetration and Corporation Key Message Penetration:

a)    Industry Key Message Penetration =
      Mediums Including Industry's Key Messages
      Total Number of Messages Communicated

b)    Corporation's Key Message Penetration =
      Mediums Including Corporation's Key Messages
      Total Number of Messages Communicated

c)    Penetration Share=
      Corporation's Key Message Penetration
      Industry Key Message Penetration

Or, shown an alternative way:

d)    Penetration Share =
      Mediums Including Corporation's Key Messages
      Mediums Including Industry's Key Messages

(**Insight achieved**) Calculating a corporation's MPS within its industry allows a corporation to rank itself among its competitors in terms of media or influencer popularity. It identifies industry thought leaders and thought laggards. Once a corporation identifies where it falls on the continuum it may then determine why it holds that position. Analyzing these insights may then dictate strategy going forward.

**Key Message Recency Metric (KMR)- (Define)** Measures the length of time since select media have conveyed a corporation's key messages. (**Collection method**) Media Content Analysis (**Calculation**) Collect key messages conveyed by date from select media over a defined period of time. Data may be expressed in days, weeks, or months. Data may then be compared to historical recency averages for perspective. (**Insight achieved**) Comparing recency with competitors may indicate a change in media sentiment or a corporation's position as an industry or thought leader. KMR is a useful metric in tracking media behavior. If KMR suddenly increases as a competitor's KMR decreases, it is useful for the corporation to diagnose why. It is important to keep in mind variables like crises or other disruptive events may temporarily skew this metric. However, continuously monitoring for recency may alert a corporation a specific relationship is in need of attention.

**Quote Accuracy Tracker- (Define)** Identifies how frequently a quote attributed to a company spokesperson or executive is conveyed accurately. (**Collection method**) Media Content Analysis (**Calculation**) Gather the number of accurate quotes attributed to company executives and divide by total number of quotes gathered from selected mediums over a specific period of time. Metric may be adapted to measure partially accurate, incomplete, or accurate but out of context quotes attributed to corporate employees. (**Insight achieved**) Data identifies the frequency with which a corporate representative is quoted accurately. Data may reveal message conveyance issues related to the spokesperson or executive being quoted or could identify a problem journalist unable, for some reason, to accurately convey the attributed quote. Metric may also be adapted to include secondhand quotes, or those that appear in news pieces not directly receiving the quote. News outlets often use quotes in their work that first appeared in a news piece featured by a competing news outlet. *Note: This is becoming more common and increases the risk that an inaccurate quote will be repeated and may deserve separate measurement.*

**News Consumer Tracker-(Define)** People consuming content online are invited to and often leave comments or sentiment indicators regarding the news item they have just consumed. These comments may be used to quickly gauge the perception consumers have of a corporation based on the manner in which the corporation was included in the news piece. (**Collection method**) Media Content Analysis (**Calculation**) Corporations may adapt metric to best meet situational-specific needs but will likely benefit from categorizing comments in the following manner:

1) Company Defender
2) Company Antagonist
3) Likely to seek out additional information about the product/company
4) Likely to recommend product/company
5) Believes company was portrayed accurately
6) Believes company was not portrayed accurately
7) Would not likely recommend product/company
8) Comment is based on rumor or falsity
9) Comment is neutral in sentiment
10) Not pertinent, nonsense, humorous

(**Insight achieved**) These categories are meant to be starting points for organizations intent on tracking consumer perceptions. The list is not exhaustive, but rather a means by which a smart PR staff may begin to craft a categorization strategy that best meets its individual needs.

**Rumor & Speculation Metric-** (**Define**) Corporations often set internal goals to be included on lists identifying the company as one of the best places to work within a given industry. Being included on such a list shapes perceptions about the company. It also helps the company attract top talent for open positions. If inclusion on theses lists generates enough interest from job seekers, a company may also be in a position to reduce wages for certain positions due to increase in job demand. However, companies constantly rumored about or speculated upon may become less desirable for job seekers and current employees. Rumors of job cuts, mergers or acquisitions, or managerial change may not only be distracting to current employees, but may also deter job seekers and cause them to become interested in a competitor. Identifying the frequency with which your corporation is rumored or speculated about is a basis for creating a work environment attractive to current and prospective employees. (**Collection method**) Media Content Analysis (**Calculation**) A simplistic version of this metric simply divides the number of rumors or speculative news items involving the company by the total number of rumor or speculative pieces in a given industry, for select content producers, and over a defined time period. However, truly calculating rumor and speculation may be much more complex. A corporation must take into account intentional "leaks" aimed at generating a predetermined outcome beneficial to the company. These intentional leaks initially may not be flattering but should be taken into account when collecting and measuring. Further complicating the calculation is the merit of the rumor or speculation. If the rumor or speculative portion of a news piece is ultimately true, a corporation must determine whether to include this during the collection process. At its core though, this metric assumes rumor and speculation are not conducive to an attractive working environment and simply provides a means by which a corporation can quantify the phenomena. (**Insight achieved**) A corporation must compare its Rumor and Speculation ratio with its past and its peers. This allows a corporation to identify whether rumor and speculation have increased versus the last time it measured and also allows the corporation to identify how it compares with its competitors in regard to rumor and speculation.

**Content Contradiction Metric-** (**Define**) Corporations may discern much when they measure the frequency with which content includes contradictory information or a counterpoint immediately following the corporation's key message. A number of variables must be considered when using this metric such as the amount of experience a content producer has, biases a journalist might possess, or a more effective strategic communications plan offered by a competitor. That said, identifying how often your company's key messages are conveyed unopposed is key when determining when, how, and to whom to deliver key messages. (**Collection method**) Media Content Analysis (**Calculation**) Number of countered key messages collected from select mediums over a defined time period divided by the number of the total key messages conveyed. (**Insight achieved**) This metric may provide insight in regard to the strength of an organization's key messages versus its past and its peers. It may also illuminate which journalists or mediums are more apt to allow a corporation to convey a key message without countering the message with a critical counterpoint. The metric is particularly useful when determining which media outlets are chosen for live interviews with company executives. An entity less likely to counterpunch may be deemed a more efficient message delivery channel than an entity more likely to confront the executive with unflattering counterpoints.

**Social Loyalty Score (SLS)- (Define**) Metric aims to discern the strength of an organization's relationships with new influencers. The metric may also yield intelligence regarding how engaged an organization is socially. SLS measures the degree to which key social influencers are willing to recommend a corporation, its products, services, or other efforts. (**Collection method**) Survey (**Calculation**) Percentage of those surveyed willing to recommend to others minus the percentage unwilling to recommend (**Insight achieved**) A dramatic drop in SLS warns a corporation it must immediately identify the cause of the SLS decline and take steps to mend and strengthen the relationships SLS measures.

# Measure Frequently

Routinely deploying metrics like these is vital for corporations interested in measuring the strength or weakness of their reputations and relationships in real-time. Perceptions can change with headlines and corporations relying on outdated data will undoubtedly make less than optimal decisions. Routine measurement will also position a corporation to avoid mistakes.

For instance, the housing slump that started prior to the financial crisis in 2008 was actually much worse than many thought. As 2011 came to a close The National Association of Realtors announced an embarrassing mistake. It had drastically overestimated the number of homes sold during the crisis. The NAR overestimated home sales by 14.3%, or 2.9 million homes between 2007-10. The group blamed the error on its failure to realize fundamental changes in the industry such as fewer "for sale by owner" sales, expanded regional listing services, and other factors.

The NAR example supports the notion organizations should measure often and with multiple metrics as a way to ensure the data on which they are basing decisions is accurate.

It is imperative that corporations dedicated to measurement continually measure relationships to obtain accurate data. This can be done by arbitrarily scheduling data collection and measurement or immediately after a corporation senses a possible change in sentiment among its publics after a headline-grabbing event.

For instance, Canadian oil & gas company EnCana Corporation generated unenviable media coverage in December 2011 when the Environmental Protection Agency announced that chemicals found in a Wyoming town's drinking water were likely the result of the company's use of hydraulic fracturing (a technique in which water, sand, and chemicals are shot down a well to fracture hard shale rock containing oil and gas).

Hydraulic fracturing has come under attack recently and has been blamed for everything from drinking water contamination to increased seismic activity (the oil and gas industry argues there has never been a documented case of aquifer contamination). The companies engaged in fracking are routinely affected by negative media attention focused on the method. For example, the day the Wyoming news broke, shares of EnCana fell six percent.

Corporate PR staffs at these companies are forced to make a decision; proactively address the fracking issue to protect the company's reputation and commitment to the environment or take a more passive role and react only when forced to. Which is the right strategy? It likely depends on how a given corporation stacks up against its peers. Rather than relying on instinct or gut feeling, an optimized smart PR staff will rely on data.

For instance, a media content analysis focused on identifying Negative Sentiment Ratios of several independent oil and gas companies engaged in or affiliated with fracking prior to the Wyoming incident revealed the following:

- Halliburton -26%
- Cabot Oil & Gas -24%
- Concho Resources- 22%
- Chesapeake Energy -21%
- Anadarko Petroleum -18%
- Devon Energy- 16%
- EnCana- 13%
- EOG Resources -11%
- Continental Resources -9%
- Pioneer Natural Resources -8%
- Carbo Ceramics- 5%

The Negative Sentiment Ratios above do not differentiate between intentional and unintentional. Vastly different results may be derived from your own content analysis based on differing parameters such as how negativity is defined, media outlets included in analysis, and time period covered by analysis. The point is to establish a baseline by which change can be measured over time or incident.

Performing another media content analysis immediately following the EnCana news in Wyoming reveals the following changes in Negative Sentiment Ratios:

- EnCana- 39%
- Chesapeake Energy -37%
- Halliburton -32%
- Anadarko Petroleum- 29%
- Concho Resources- 29%
- Cabot Oil & Gas -27%
- Devon Energy- 19%
- EOG Resources -16%
- Continental Resources- 14%
- Pioneer Natural Resources- 12%
- Carbo Ceramics- 9%

EnCana's Negative Sentiment Ratio increased 200% after the media began reporting on the EPA's announcement. Not surprisingly, EnCana aggressively attacked the EPA's announcement and argued the agency failed to take into account naturally occurring chemicals in the deep wells drilled.

However, Chesapeake's Negative Sentiment Ratio increased 76% from its baseline- substantially more than some of its peers. This may be explained by Chesapeake's aggressive efforts to dispute the Wyoming news and defend the practice. The company argued the hydrocarbons the EPA found in its test wells were naturally occurring, not the result of fracking.

Political considerations will obviously be taken into account when developing strategic communications plans for sensitive issues like fracking. However, data sets like those above provide corporations key insight when determining how aggressive a company should be in its response or if it should respond at all. While the companies at the top of the Negative Sentiment list may feel obligated to defend the practice, those at the bottom may feel differently after observing only minor increases in negative sentiment.

Acquiring data sets like these also offers the companies involved opportunities to measure the effectiveness of their communications strategies. For instance, EnCana may benefit from measuring its Negative Sentiment Ratio in the days following its aggressive rebuttal of the EPA's findings. A dramatic decrease in negative sentiment following the rebuttal campaign may indicate how successful EnCana's strategy has been. If negative sentiment increases further, the company can adjust its strategy accordingly. For instance, follow-up measurement may identify specific channels or content producers that may benefit from more or less attention. Likewise, a company at the bottom of the negative sentiment list that collects an updated data set will know whether it would be beneficial to adjust its hands-off approach. No matter where a company ranks on a list like this, continually measuring sentiment equips the company with data needed to dictate strategy.

# Establish Benchmarks

Establishing benchmarks for your corporation and its competitors and continuously measuring against those benchmarks must also be complimented with event driven measurement. Relationships and perceptions are likely to change during and after instances such as a company sponsored event, an executive speaking at a conference, or when a company is featured by high profile business media outlets.

# Break Out of PR Prison

Television programs like Jim Cramer's *Mad Money*, which airs on CNBC, is one of those programs. Cramer is a former hedge fund manager who routinely interviews Chief Executives as part of his show. I single out the widely followed Cramer in regard to event driven measurement because so many websites attempt to artificially boost traffic by linking to or including his opinions and analysis. Many websites appear to have built a portion, if not all of their business model, around drawing Jim Cramer traffic. While not fair at times to Cramer, there is a certain logic to the strategy.

Cramer has a half million followers on Twitter. He founded *TheStreet.com* where he provides insight. And his *Mad Money* program is one of the most popular on CNBC. He is highly influential and has an extremely loyal following of viewers who rely on him for company specific information and analysis. Reputable media outlets like *Investor's Business Daily* even note when Cramer mentions a company on his program when attempting to explain to readers why a particular stock may have moved dramatically the day before.

Besides moving a company's stock, a mention by Cramer can spark vast online conversations about a company, its products, or reputation. It is important to monitor and measure these conversations. A PR staff not scheduled to measure Origin of Awareness, Sentiment, or Key Message Conveyance for another several months will not be in possession of accurate data sets if it ignores events such as a Jim Cramer mention. Cramer passes judgment on a variety of publicly traded companies each weeknight. Measuring change immediately following such an event arms smart PR staffs with current data that will better guide strategy going forward.

However, the only way an organization can accurately gauge the impact of an event is to have established a baseline against which it can measure. Without a benchmark an organization will have nothing to which it may compare event measurement data.

The lesson here is to measure even when you think you don't need to measure. Benchmarking exercises may be tedious but they will certainly reveal their value as they'll allow organizations to identify change following an event.

Put another way; you won't know where you're going unless you measure where you've been.

**Executive Narcissism Metric- (Define)** Identifies the degree of narcissism present in a corporation's Chief Executive. (**Collection method**) Media Content Analysis (**Calculation**) Gather the number of instances on conference calls or media interviews in which CEO uses first person singular pronouns such as "I, me, and my" or refers to self in first person and divide total by the frequency with which other first person pronouns such as "we" and "our" are used. (A similar calculation can be done by creating a temporal ratio in which the amount of time a CEO spends talking on a conference call, versus other company executives and competitors, is expressed as a ratio). (**Insight achieved**) The data collected with this metric may be compared to that of former company CEOs, compared to prior comparable time periods for the current CEO, or against CEOs at competing companies. A Chief Executive interested in possibly altering or adopting a communication style most conducive to a specific goal such as merger & acquisition activity may also find this metric useful.

This metric has been adapted from research conducted by a group of French and U.S. economists in December 2011. Nihat Atkas, Eric Bodt, Helen Bollaert, and Richard Roll created a way to measure CEO narcissism and its impact on the merger and acquisition potential of the companies the executives head. The research was based on conference calls and media interviews with Chief Executives at the helm during 146 M&A attempts between 2002-2006.

In its paper, *CEO Narcissism and the Takeover Process: From Private Initiation to Deal Completion*, the group determined the following:

"CEO narcissism affects the M&A process. More narcissistic target CEOs obtain higher bid premiums. Acquirer shareholders react less favorably to a takeover announcement when the target CEO is more narcissistic. Among acquiring CEOs, narcissism is associated with initiating deals and negotiating faster. Higher narcissism in both target and acquirer CEOs is associated with a lower probability of deal completion. Interactions between acquirer and target CEO narcissism play a significant role."

The utility of a metric like this may be debated. It is likely to be obvious whether the Chief Executive at your company is a narcissist. It is just as likely that no one in the public relations or marketing departments will be eager to point this out to him or her. However, measuring executive narcissism and being aware that research of this nature could be used by investors looking for an edge in the midst of M&A rumors may prove beneficial to a corporation's relationships with its various publics.

A PR or IR department should be mindful of this research when scripting remarks to potential media questions or answers to analyst inquiries in advance of conference calls. Especially during periods in which the company is rumored to be involved in M&A activity. Realizing various publics may be measuring not only an executive's words, but even his or her pronouns, is useful when selecting which words are to be used when addressing M&A speculation.

**Origin of Awareness Metric- (Define)** Identifies how members of various publics became aware of your company, its products, services, or community-related endeavors. **(Collection method)** Surveys and Web Analytics **(Calculation)** Depending on which public a corporation is interested in learning about, a corporation simply divides the origin of awareness for a specific public by the total number of origin of awareness instances counted. The metric can be creatively used to identify the most common origins of awareness for various publics including customers, reporters, elected officials etc.

**(Insight Achieved)** Identifying where your publics first become aware of your company and its offerings is vital when developing a strategic communications plan. First impressions are crucial and understanding where those first impressions are occurring enables corporations to allocate resources to ensure those first impressions are prompting key publics to further engage with the corporation.

**Content Origination Metric- (Define)** New influencers and journalists are often most influenced by the first and last people with whom they speak about a topic. In many cases a corporation will find it beneficial to speak with a content producer just prior to a story being posted, printed, or broadcast. However, it's not always in the corporation's interest to be the first to talk with a content producer unless the producer is first talking with a critic, competitor, or entity that does not have the corporation's best interest in mind. While a corporation will often benefit immensely when a third party advocate initiates a discussion with a journalist regarding the corporation, third parties unfriendly to the corporation can be equally destructive. Therefore, it is paramount corporations identify the origin of stories in which they are mentioned. **(Collection method)** This metric may be the most difficult to collect data for. Origination will not always be clear within a news story and surveying journalists is not likely to yield much success and could even damage relationships. Corporations will likely have to become creative when investigating exactly where a story originated. However, a corporation will likely be required to use resources it is not accustomed to using for these purposes; think lobbyists, public affairs staff, and employees with social media connections to reporters. **(Calculation)** Corporations will likely be interested in categorizing the most common story origins when calculating the metric. The origination categories below may be tallied and divided by the total number of news pieces collected:

1) Company originated (this category may be broken down into subcategories based upon intentional origination and unintentional origination)
2) Customer originated
3) Company liaison originated
4) Elected official originated
5) Ex-customer originated
6) Competitor originated
7) Critic originated
8) Crisis originated
9) Regulatory requirement originated
10) Vendor originated
11) Supplier originated

(**Insight achieved**) A corporation that identifies where news items originate gains the ability to narrowly focus its strategic communications strategy. Doing so enables a smart PR staff to better steer origination.

# Event Measurement

To further narrow the focus of a smart PR staff and more efficiently allocate PR dollars and resources corporations must understand how, if at all, corporate tangibility (B to C or B to B) impacts sales. More specifically, corporations that identify marketing methods or sales techniques that result in greater capital returns are better positioned to most effectively allocate PR resources.

The practice aims to identify whether a corporation should invest resources into live events or business-to-person sales tactics. If a corporation determines sales increase dramatically during or shortly after a live event in which customers have direct contact with the corporation, PR resource allocation may be shifted away from lower returning investment efforts.

For instance, an independent book publishing company measured the impact of live events on sales during and after events allowing the public to interact with authors of the book. While live author "meet and greets" did not immediately dramatically increase sales at the live events, these events foreshadowed and were a prerequisite for increased book sales following the live events. Identifying this phenomenon allowed the authors to more efficiently and effectively allocate PR and marketing resources.

The book authors collected data prior to live events, during live events, and in the weeks following those events. They complimented the data sets with an email survey targeting people who had purchased the book. Data derived from the measurement process then guided future marketing and PR strategy.

To begin, web analytics tools provided the authors with weekly book website visitations and compared the data against online book sale totals. More specifically, the authors were able to divide the number of online sales by the number of people visiting their book marketing site. The data was collected in the weeks leading up to a live event. This ratio established a benchmark to which future measurement would be compared.

At live "meet and greet" events visitors to the authors' booths were asked to provide email addresses for future contact. The number of live event book sales was then divided by the total number of booth visitors to compile a live event book sales ratio.

The authors' weekly online book sales ratio revealed 26% of website visitors purchased a copy of the book during their visit. This compared with just 13% of total live event booth visitors purchasing the book at live events. The data struck the authors as counterintuitive since both were aware of research suggesting that face-to-face or live event marketing is one of the more effective ways to impact consumers.

However, because the authors employed a continuous measurement strategy they noticed that online book sales spiked following live events despite little or no increased website traffic. The numbers looked like this:

- Pre-event online sales / website visits = 26%

- Live event sales / booth visits=13%

- Post-live event sales/ website visits= 39%

In the week following a live event the authors determined online sales increased 50% versus the online sales benchmark. While pleased with the data, the authors were puzzled as to what could be causing the phenomena. A qualitative measurement was needed to determine why this was happening.

The authors conducted an email survey with each person who had volunteered their email address while visiting meet and greet booths. The survey revealed the following in regard to booth visitors:

- 23% did not recall visiting the authors

- 3% intended to purchase the book prior to visiting the booth but waited to do so to meet the authors

- 41% had no intention to purchase the book prior to or after visiting the booth

- 21% intended to purchase the book after but not before visiting with the authors at the booth

*Note: The remaining 12% of responses were not relevant or easily categorized.*

A second email survey of the 21% who delayed their purchase decision until the week following the live event revealed a myriad of economic, personal, and technological reasons for the purchase delay. The results reveal the importance of measuring relationships from different points of origin. Had the authors simply stopped measuring after quantitative data showed live meet and greets were not cost-effective versus other sales channels, future live events may have been cancelled in favor of more efficient marketing and public relations efforts.

However, qualitative data revealed live events were much more cost-effective versus other marketing and public relations activities such as television, radio, and newspaper advertising. Without qualitative measurement the authors might have attributed the pickup in online book sales following a live event to something other than the live event. Not only did qualitative measurement identify a lag between the live event and actual purchase, it guided marketing and PR strategies going forward. More specifically, qualitative data allowed the authors to implement a more customer-friendly payment acceptance system at live events which converted a greater percentage of booth visitors with intent to purchase into actual purchasers.

*Note: The authors are now tracking live event sentiment in real-time by using a Twitter hashtag. Booth visitors are advised to use the hashtag to discuss the book when tweeting about the event. By creating a hashtag for a specific event the authors are able to search Twitter for comments about the live event currently taking place. This allows them to adapt or modify their sales and PR strategies in real-time to enhance book sales.*

# Measuring & Weighing Buzz

Not all buzz is equal.
And parsing the wheat from the chaff becomes more difficult as buzz increases about a product, service, or live event.

Collecting data from web analytics software, hashtag social media searches, media content analyses, and Google Alerts among others, provides a PR staff with the data necessary to use any number of the metrics described thus far. However, simply measuring for Negative Sentiment, Key Message Conveyance, or Inaccurate Message Conveyance may not provide a corporation with enough color. Additional granularity can be gained by weighing the buzz a corporation generates against competing buzz. More specifically, simultaneously measuring what is being said and by whom will provide details pertinent in shaping strategy.

But first, more must be known about those engaged in the conversation.

Influence Indicator ratios may be calculated to determine the most influential journalists, bloggers, or social media kingpins. Pertinent data points in regard to influence measurement include but are not limited to: how frequently content producer breaks news, the degree to which it manifests itself across other platforms, and audience reach. Identifying the degree of influence belonging to those engaged in conversations about your organization provides needed context to the buzz being generated and will be used to calculate the Buzz Influence Index.

Nick Winkler

# Buzz Influence Index

This index weighs the buzz being generated about a company based on the importance of the buzz. Weighting the buzz generated based on the influence one has enables an organization to prioritize its response efforts and guides future strategic initiatives with those at the top of the index.

After defining a specific time period over which to measure a corporation must then identify the metrics it wants to weigh and compare. For instance, the Buzz Influence Index may be comprised of "Key Message Conveyance" and weighted by a reporter's "Influence Indicator". In another context, it may be more useful to measure buzz influence using "Inaccurate Message Conveyance" and weighted by a key new influencer's "Social Influence Ratio".

For example, one corporation may have a top 20% "Premium Mention Ratio" of 18%. After comparing this ratio against a comparable time period or against a competitor's ratio, a corporation might determine its PMR is relatively low. While this provides a certain level of insight, it does not provide qualitative intelligence a corporation might find valuable. A corporation interested in a more complete measurement picture must also assess the influence of the medium or reporters responsible for the PMR. Doing so provides an additional layer of context for corporations interested in this type of detail.

For instance, the corporation with an 18% PMR might determine the "Influence Indicator" associated with the medium or reporter responsible for the PMR is 7.3 on a ten-point scale. Further investigation might reveal that while a competitor's PMR is 26% over a defined time period, the "Influence Indicator" associated with the medium or reporter responsible for the PMR is just 3.6 on a ten-point scale.

To determine placement quality weighted by influence the Buzz Influence Index (BII) is calculated by dividing the reporter or medium's Influence Indicator (II) by the PMR and multiplying by 100. In the example above the calculation would look like this:

**Corporation 1**) .073/.18 = .405 * 100 = 40.5 on the BII

**Corporation 2**) .036/.26 = .138 * 100 = 13.8 on the BII

The BII reveals Corporation 1's premium mention status is of a higher quality or more influential than Corporation 2. While Corporation 2 may be winning the premium mention race in terms of frequency, it is not outpacing Corporation 1 in terms of placement quality or influence. In other words, quotes from or mentions of Corporation 1 are being placed in the top 20% of news items created by the more influential reporters at more than double the frequency of Corporation 2.

Had Corporation 1 stopped measuring after initially identifying a seemingly disappointing PMR as compared with its competitor, the company might have been persuaded to invest or refocus its strategy on boosting its PMR. However, since a more thorough investigation reveals Corporation 1 is actually better off than its competitor in terms of placement quality and influence, the company might determine its investment dollars and strategic attention may produce a better return when focused elsewhere. (**Note**: *placement on the BII indicating higher placement quality or influence versus competitors with a larger PMR may indicate a need to reasses which reporters, new influencers, or media outlets a PR staff is including in its PMR calculation*).

Nick Winkler

# Measuring Key Relationships

Much of the book thus far has focused on how a corporation can measure content producers, their influence, and the relationships the corporation has or does not have with producers who follow the corporation. However, some would argue it is just as important to measure relationships a corporation has with those who influence the media. In other words, how the third party experts often called upon to add context or perspective to a news piece think and feel about the corporation is just as important, if not more, than the relationship the corporation has with a journalist or new influencer.

Determining how you are perceived in the marketplace among your various publics: elected officials, media, university professors etc. versus your competitors can help dictate investment and strategic decision making. You may actually learn much more by understanding the relationships competitors have with various publics. Understanding competitor-stakeholder relationships allows a company to identify weak relationships a corporation can then exploit and ultimately gain market share, decrease churn, increase brand loyalty or achieve some other measurable objective.

While implementing a relationship measurement strategy may be new for some corporations, the concept is nothing new in academia. For decades, scholars have studied, researched, and published works about the virtues and ambiguous shortcomings of measuring relationships with various publics. Scholars like Dr. Linda Childers Hon and Dr. James E. Grunig offer three "guidebooks" that lay out strategies and tools corporations can use to measure relationships with their publics. Those materials may be found on the *Institute for Public Relations* website (instituteforpr.org). In fact, Katie Delahaye Paine, who develops measurement systems for corporations, devotes much of her latest book, *Measure What Matters*, to the benefits of measuring relationships with a popular survey developed by Dr. James E. Grunig at The University of Maryland.

However, relationship measurement critics argue the complexity and fluidity of most relationships calls into question the validity of such measurements. Joy Chia, of the University of South Australia, writes, "...relational characteristics such as commitment, trust and satisfaction are so subjective that attempts to measure them have been extremely difficult as they change with each situation, with different clients and organizations and with varied perceptions and interpretations of those in a relationship."

While critics question the validity of measuring relationships characterized by continuous perceptional change, supporters like Paine counter with the notion that critiques like these bolster the idea that companies must continually measure for change in relationships. The corporations with the freshest data and analysis gain a competitive advantage versus those lacking data.

It is outside the scope of this book to settle the dispute. The dispute is simply highlighted here so corporate PR staffs can decide for themselves what they deem to be worthy of measurement. However, few would likely dispute that the ability to measure, analyze, and compare that which is intangible affords corporations a competitive advantage versus their peers (so long as the data is accurate). Again, the strategies and tools offered here are not likely to benefit every corporation conducting business in every sector. The tools are simply being offered here in the event a corporation might find some value in using them.

As outlined in other sections, identifying publics that influence reporters and new influencers is key in developing a proactive strategic communications strategy. Often, a PR staff may first want to measure its relationships with these publics (financial analysts, elected officials, University professors etc.) prior to measuring or attempting to strengthen relationships with reporters. The key here is to understand how the relationship your corporation has with these key publics compares with the relationships your competitors have with these key publics.

In general, measuring relationships can be accomplished in five steps:

1. Create measurable objectives
2. Identify which relationships you wish to measure
3. Choose the metrics or measurement tools best suited for execution
4. Remeasure for comparison purposes
5. Analyze data to guide strategy

Measuring a corporation's relationships with thought leaders, key influencers, and media savvy academics may alert a corporation to subtle relational changes that can be stemmed or leveraged to the company's benefit prior to such changes becoming evident to others.

# Identifying Logical Disconnects

A logical disconnect exists when a gap is present between a public's perceptions and situational realities. Additionally, these gaps may also exist between situational realities and a company's key messages. Understanding how those key messages are affecting a public's perceptions better allows a company to strategically bridge any gaps that are present when need be.

It may be easier to conceptualize the relationships graphically:

**Identifying Logical Disconnects**

Perception → Reality
Reality → Key Message
Key Message → Perception

A gap between any two of these subjects means there is a credibility deficit, that if determined to be negative, must be bridged.

Identifying a logical disconnect between any two of these subjects indicates the corporation's credibility is not optimal within a given public. In other words, a gap means a credibility deficit is present and must be addressed if the corporation determines the gap is negative.

*Note: not all gaps must be bridged.*

For instance, if a corporation identifies a gap between a situational reality and the perceptions held by journalists is positive, it may be in the company's best interest to continue to allow the gap to exist. For instance if journalists perceive a corporation is much more dedicated to employee safety than it actually is, there is no incentive to bridge the gap.

Qualitatively analyzing gaps will determine whether a gap is positive or negative.

The focus here is on identifying and fixing negative logical disconnects. For instance, if journalists perceive a company to be environmentally insensitive or reckless despite a reality indicating the company is actually an industry leader in terms of environmental responsibility, a negative logical disconnect exists. In this case, identifying the existence of a gap is the first step in understanding how the gap was created and why it persists.

Identifying gaps between perceptions and realities requires surveys, media content analyses, and honest self-evaluation. Surveying various publics provides a corporation with data regarding perceptions. So too can examining media content including comments offered online and socially. These perceptions may be coded according to the specific context from which they were gathered.

For instance, if a corporation is interested in perceptions held by a key public pertaining to the company's environmental responsibility, it can survey the public in a manner that allows the company to code responses.

A survey example is below:

1) Strongly agree company is environmentally responsible
2) Agree company is environmentally responsible
3) Don't know whether company is environmentally responsible
4) Neutral on whether company is environmentally responsible
5) Disagree company is environmentally responsible
6) Strongly disagree company is environmentally responsible

Assigning each response a number (1-6) allows a corporation to average the responses and quantify the overall average perception the key public has regarding the corporation's environmental responsibility. For our purpose, let's assume the average is calculated at 4.8.

Afterward, a corporation must develop a measurement strategy that allows it to quantify its environmental safety record versus its past or its peers. Here's where honest self-evaluation must be present. Data collected will obviously be industry-specific and may include: environmental quality violations, environmental-related fines or penalties assessed, emissions quality or quantity etc. These data sets may be weighted if appropriate and then coded so an environmental responsibility score may be assigned. For our purpose, let's assume a company chooses to measure its environmental record versus that of its competitors.

For example, let's also assume that of the six companies for which environmental responsibility scores were calculated your corporation ranked second best, or 2nd out of 6.

Perceptions and realities may then be assigned an axis and expressed graphically to identify the existence of logical disconnects:

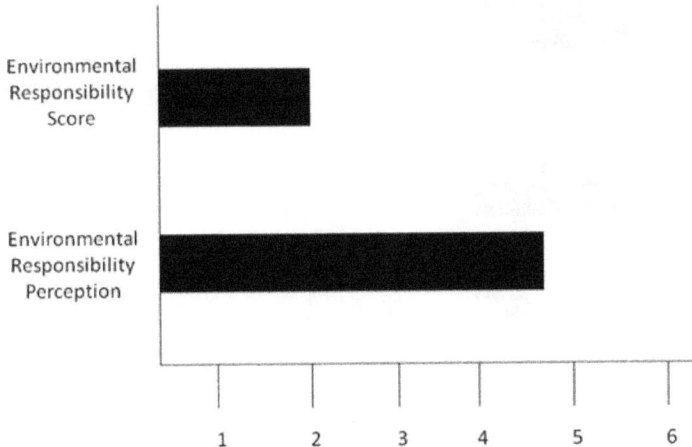

Notice the gap between reality and perception. The graph illustrates the logical disconnect present. Although the corporation ranks in the top third of its industry in terms of its environmental responsibility score, it ranks toward the bottom in terms of average perception associated with the company's environmental responsibility.

If perceptions were consistent with the reality of the company's environmental responsibility score, the graph would look like this:

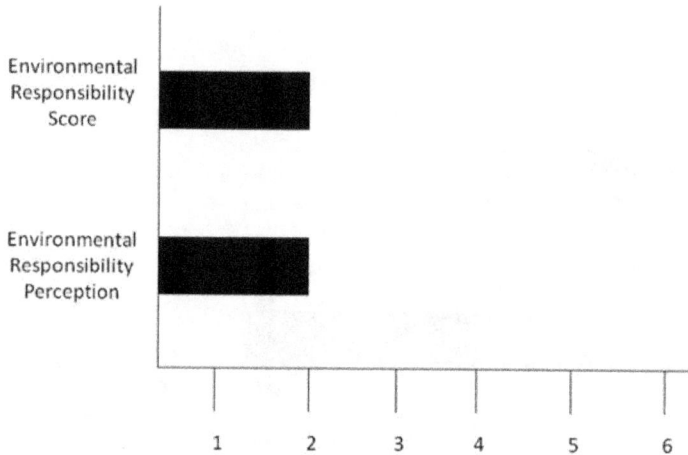

Identifying logical disconnects and why they might exist requires a three-dimensional measurement approach. Once a gap between a public's perception and a company's reality is identified, a corporation must determine what role, if any, its strategic communications are playing. Put another way, is there a logical disconnect between a reality and a key message the corporation is attempting to communicate?

The reality has already been measured and established; the corporation is in the top third of its industry in terms of its environmental responsibility score. A corporation must now determine whether a logical disconnect exists between the reality and the key messages it is communicating. In other words, if the corporation's reality is contradictory to its strategic communications it must determine why.

Corporations may utilize previously discussed metrics such as Key Message Conveyance (KMC) or Inaccurate Message

Conveyance (IMC) to accomplish this. If environmental responsibility is not a key message the corporation is attempting to communicate, the disconnect between perception and reality may guide your strategic communications strategy. Strategy may be adjusted if the corporation sees value in bridging the gap.

However, if environmental responsibility is a key message the corporation has been attempting to convey, it is useful to chart the reality discovered earlier alongside the KMC ratio. For our purpose, let's assume the corporation's KMC ratio is 72%. Let's also assume that prior to embarking on a measurement strategy designed to identify potential logical disconnects, the corporation was content with a 72% KMC that ranked among the top 15% when compared against its peers.

As illustrated below, the corporation's top 33% environmental responsibility score (reality) appears alongside its top 15% KMC ratio:

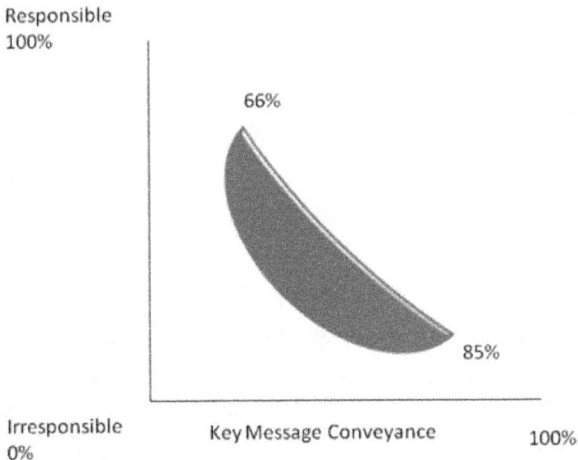

219

The gap between the KMC ratio and the company's reality is evident. Were the two subjects at equilibrium, the graph would look like the one below:

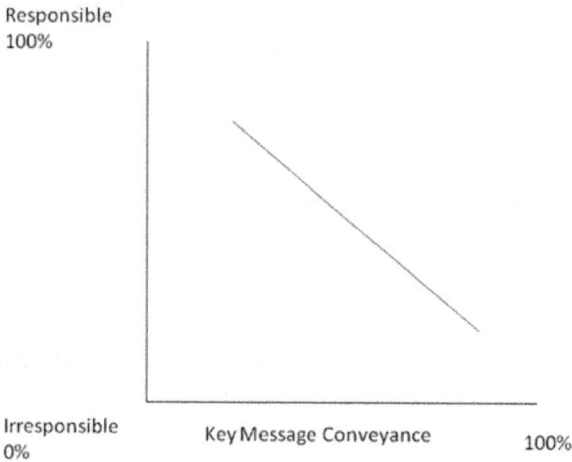

Responsible
100%

Irresponsible
0%                Key Message Conveyance            100%

Achieving equilibrium between a corporation's reality and its KMC ratio is a lofty goal and likely not continuously achievable for some. A more realistic framework would include minimizing gaps between reality and KMC. However, the point here is to identify the existence of gaps. If gaps are identified, corporations are then in a position to better understand why the gaps exist. For instance, if KMC severely lags reality, a company might focus on increasing KMC for the reality it wishes a public to perceive.

Conversely, if KMC is far outpacing the reality a corporation wishes a public to perceive, a corporation must determine whether its communications strategy is responsible for the logical disconnect. If not, variables outside the corporation itself may be responsible for the gap. For instance, identifying whether a competitor's strategic communications plan is responsible for a logical disconnect is key in determining how a corporation should go about bridging the gap.

Once a corporation understands where logical disconnects exist and why, it can begin attempting to convey key messages to change perceptions held by key publics. However, this assumes it is in the corporation's financial interest to align perceptions and realities. As long as it is, using data to drive your communications strategy removes the guesswork often involved in determining how to communicate key messages.

Credibility deficits destroy value and can reduce a corporation's profitability. When logical disconnects exist between perceptions, realities, and key messages, a corporation begins each endeavor with a handicap it is not likely to overcome. Bridging or reducing these gaps is one of the most important activities in which a smart PR staff may engage. However, only after a corporation identifies logical disconnects can it begin the sometimes tedious process of minimizing the gaps and reducing credibility deficits.

# Internal Communications Measurement

Corporations have spent inordinate sums of money communicating internally. Many of these internal communications not only fail to yield a return on investment, but actually increase risk to the company's reputation. Whenever something is published and disseminated, a corporation assumes the risk it might fall into hands wishing to do it harm. I'm not advocating corporations stop communicating internally. I'm arguing corporations can better protect themselves and become leaner by communicating smarter.

Measuring the effectiveness of a corporation's internal communications is not something some companies have even considered. Internal communications is often viewed as a necessary evil more aligned with Human Resources than with the public relations staff. Internal communications is often viewed as an activity that will never yield a return.

Nothing could be further from the truth.

Using some of the metrics set forth thus far to measure the effectiveness of internal communications can not only increase employee productivity, it also has the potential to reduce costs associated with employee turnover. Wall Street titans, like *Goldman Sachs,* fire 5% of their least productive staffers each year. Constantly measuring productivity removes much of the subjectivity involved with employee reviews and evaluations. Why corporations outside the financial industry choose not to adopt an approach based upon measurement and analysis makes little sense.

Can your employees recite the company's objectives? Can your mid-level managers? While specific employees may only be relied upon for specific tasks that seem far removed from the corporation's overall strategic objectives, shouldn't internal communications efforts have the goal of informing and uniting employees regardless of pay grade or status within the company?

When companies realize it is financially beneficial to measure intangibles like morale, they begin the process of becoming more efficient by weeding out dead or nonproductive weight. Do not mistake this argument as supporting a goal of attempting to ensure employees are happy. Theoretically, employee happiness should not be a consideration since it does not directly or empirically relate to profitability. However, the reality is employee sentiment plays a significant role in terms of employee efficiency and employee churn rates.

Reducing turnover has the potential to save employers a significant amount of money that can be reallocated and used to increase investment returns elsewhere. Paying departing employees accrued vacation is only one aspect of the expense. Expenses associated with listing an open position combined with the costs of interviewing candidates along with moving expenses often afforded important new employees are all investments that are often not recouped when employee turnover is high, due in part, to poor internal communications.

You may think gossip rags are reserved specifically for grocery checkout lines. However, it may be in a corporation's best interest to actually host a gossip rag or online venue in which employees in a specific industry can go to vent and gossip. Whether a corporation deems it valuable to host a site like this itself, it should be clear there is a competitive advantage apparent in at least monitoring the conversations employees are having even if those conversations are not flattering to the company.

Aside from measuring for internal key message conveyance, negative sentiment, and logical disconnects between employee perceptions and realities, corporations may find it useful to measure the relationships they have with employees. More specifically, organizations may find value in routinely measuring employee morale.

**Employee Morale Metric- (Define)** Metric quantifies employee morale and the relationship employees perceive they have with company. **(Collection method)** Employee survey *Note: an accurate assessment of morale requires that employees not be concerned they will be identified via their work computer or in some other fashion. Precautions must be taken to ensure employees truly believe their survey answers are given anonymously.* **(Calculation)** Survey will be constructed in accordance with company's specific objectives. Survey will likely include Agree/Disagree types of questions regarding how employees feel they are treated, how they feel toward the company, its different divisions, its executives etc. Questions may be tailored to ascertain specific morale issues. Survey answers may then be plotted across a continuum or illustrated graphically. **(Insight achieved)** Corporation may compare data to past morale surveys. It will not likely be able to compare data with its peers since such data will not be easily obtained. However, corporations are able to gauge how

223

employees feel competitors treat employees versus how they are treated by your corporation. If a "grass is greener" sentiment is found to exist among employees, internal communications strategies may be tailored with the goal of diminishing the sentiment.

**Employee Stress Indicator- (Define)** Quantifies employee stress by measuring whether employees are more or less likely than they were to listen to a job offer from a competitor, percentage of time spent discussing crisis consequences, etc. **(Collection method)** Survey **(Calculation)** After a benchmark study, a corporation mathematically evaluates the change in the number of employees willing to listen to a competitor's job offer or percentage of time discussing crisis consequences. **(Insight achieved)** In any form this metric can measure the impact a crisis has had internally. It may also be used to ascertain the degree of risk as it relates to employee poaching. This metric, or some variation, is especially useful for corporations with technical or specialty workforces that are generally more difficult to replace.

# Crisis Measurement

When a major crisis hits, the last thing a corporation is likely concerned about is collecting measurement data to graphically represent the mess it is in and the challenges it faces. It's why this book takes a different approach to crisis measurement. The key to making data-driven decisions during crises is having immediate, or real-time data, whenever possible.

Much of the research or case studies a corporation might find on crisis measurement deals with coverage volume. Measuring the volume of media coverage, and charting its decline as a crisis begins to subside may appear useful on the surface. But I would argue it's rather meaningless and fails to provide executives any data they don't already know intuitively. A corporation is the first to know when it has a media bull's eye on its back. Those that deem it valuable to quantify the onslaught are free to do so.

However, doing so is often a waste of time, money, and resources.

Successful crisis mitigation hinges, in part, upon creating a dashboard of key metrics a corporation can monitor in as close to real-time as technologically possible. The concept is analogous to the dashboard inside a vehicle; a driver has immediate access to a plethora of real-time data that immediately dictates how a driver ought to behave. Ignore the vehicle's temperature gauge and the engine may seize up and compound the crisis. Conversely, a driver closely monitoring a vehicle's gauges gains the visibility needed to make quick decisions that mitigate crises.

While it's vitally important to keep an eye on the road ahead, it's equally important to accurately gauge how a corporation is performing on multiple levels during a crisis.

# Crisis Dashboard

Choosing what to measure during a crisis will depend on the crisis at hand. Metrics important to a corporation during one crisis may not be as strategically helpful in the midst of dissimilar crises. Additionally, the metrics most useful initially may not be as crucial to monitor toward the end. What is important to keep in mind though is that navigating a crisis will become much clearer to decision makers when key metrics are continuously monitored. When a corporation allows data to determine where and how to allocate resources the crisis window shrinks dramatically.

Corporations that implement a continuous measurement program will have a head start during times of crisis as they'll already enjoy benchmarks to measure against. This is key when decision makers glance for the first time at their Crisis Dashboard. Immediately being able to compare initial crisis data against a benchmark is crucial in measuring for change. Without the benchmark a corporation will lack actionable data until it measures a second time.

Besides the nature of the crisis, choosing metrics to include on your Crisis Dashboard will likely be dictated by the goals you set at the outset of the crisis. Knowing ahead of time what successfully navigating a crisis looks like allows a corporation to choose the correct measurement tools. Key metrics a corporation may want to include on its Crisis Dashboard are included below:

1. **Key Message Cannibalization Rate (KMCR)**- When news of a CEO's extramarital affair or a takeover rumor makes headlines rather than a corporation's key message, key message cannibalization is occurring. (**Define**) Normally, cannibalization refers to the introduction of a new product that decreases sales of another product within a company. For instance, analysts anticipated iPod sales would be cannibalized after Apple Inc. introduced the iPhone which had the same music playing capabilities as an iPod. For our purpose, cannibalization refers to the introduction of non-key or unflattering messages that take the place of a corporation's key messages. This metric is particularly helpful during times of crisis or when rumor and speculation are included in news items. (**Collection method**) Media Content Analysis (**Calculation**) First, calculate the decline in Key Message Conveyance versus a benchmark. Afterward, total all or specified non-key messages found in select media over a like period of time. Dividing the two looks like this: Cannibalization Rate= Key Message Conveyance Lost / Non-Key Message Inclusion rate. (**Insight achieved**) The KMCR can have a dramatic

impact on a corporation's bottom line. It underscores how important it is for corporations to invest heavily in crisis mitigation. Below is an example:

If a corporation's KMC Lost is 70% and its Non-Key Message Inclusion rate is 25%, then the corporation's KMCR is 280%. Therefore, if a corporation has a CPM (cost per message) basis of thirty-cents, its new CPM, when KMCR is accounted for, is $0.84

2. **Media Abandonment Rate (MAR)- (Define)** This metric measures the progress a corporation is or is not making in terms of shortening the duration of a crisis. This metric relies, in part, on the Premium Mention Ratio (PMR). A corporation that finds itself included in media headlines and the top 20% of news items less often signals the corporation is being abandoned in regard to premium mentions- which is exactly what a company desires in a crisis situation. **(Collection method)** Media Content Analysis **(Calculation)**

Media Abandonment Rate = $\dfrac{\text{Premium Mention Ratio}}{\text{Total Corporation Mentions}}$

**(Insight achieved)** The MAR serves as an early indicator a crisis is beginning to lose its ferocity. When a corporation sees MAR increase it means the media is no longer prominently positioning the corporation in its product. Determining why MAR begins to increase is much more difficult but also important. If a corporation can determine what specifically is responsible for a spike in the MAR, it can then amplify those activities to continue boosting MAR and ultimately shrink the duration of the crisis.

3. **Intra-Media Sentiment Metrics**- Much of the advice public relations firms or measurement practitioners offer corporations during crises regarding sentiment is too broad. The strategy offered here is much more narrow and provides corporations with a degree of granularity not found elsewhere. In the midst of a crisis, utilizing Sentiment Metrics to measure the overall tone of media coverage lacks the specificity corporations must have to develop effective mitigation strategies. A one-size-fits-all crisis mitigation plan fails to acknowledge the complexities and tonal individualism present among various corporate stakeholders included in media reports. However, Intra-Media Sentiment Metrics slice media coverage into subcategories and measure the sentiment present for each. Subcategories are simply the stakeholders included within news items related to the crisis. Intra-Media subcategories may include:

   a. Journalists or new influencers creating the news items
   b. Antagonists or special interest groups
   c. Industry regulators
   d. Government officials
   e. Elected officials
   f. Defenders of the Company
   g. University professors or academics
   h. Financial or industry analysts

   Identifying the tone or sentiment held by stakeholders included in daily crisis media coverage enables corporations to more efficiently allocate resources.

For instance, Intra-Media sentiment for a hypothetical crisis may be graphically represented below:

Negative
Sentiment

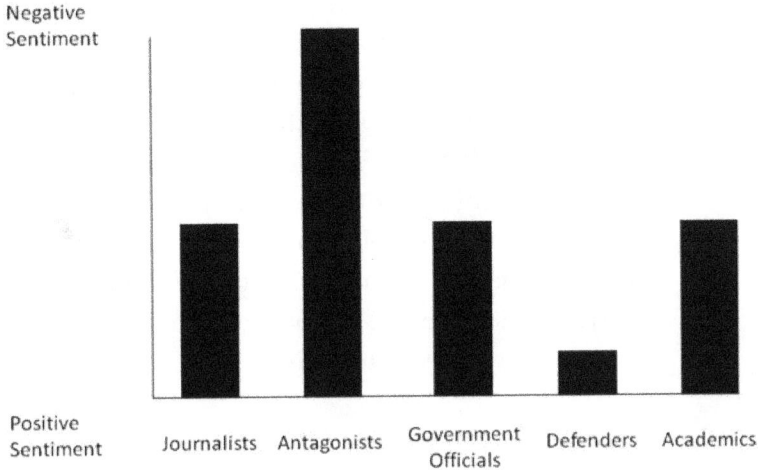

Positive
Sentiment

Journalists　Antagonists　Government Officials　Defenders　Academics

Illustrating sentiment enables a corporation to focus its mitigation efforts on those most responsible for lengthening the duration of crises. While measuring for coverage volume or overall sentiment provides corporations with a macro-crisis view, that view is relatively useless in developing mitigation strategies. Conversely, measuring Intra-Media sentiment provides corporations with a micro-crisis view that allows them to customize specific strategic communications directed at the most problematic individual stakeholders. Reducing negative sentiment in these stakeholders dramatically reduces the length of crisis media coverage.

Nick Winkler

The importance of identifying Intra-Media
Sentiment is illustrated in the recent debacle
involving the Susan G. Komen Race for the Cure
charity. The breast cancer charity did an about-face
after it announced plans it would ultimately cut
funding it provided to Planned Parenthood
affiliates. After the announcement, abortion rights
activists protested the planned cuts on social media
sites and rallied around the mantra of "shame on
Komen". NetBase Solutions Inc., a social media
measurement outfit, provided *The Wall Street
Journal* with the following measurement data; 1)
online chatter regarding Komen increased 80%
during the debacle 2) 66% of the conversations
about Komen were negative.

I would argue that data is strategically and
functionally useless.

If Komen's decision to reverse course was based
only on volume and overall sentiment metrics,
maybe it deserves the crisis it found itself in. What
Komen should have based its decision on, at least
in part, are Intra-Media Sentiment Metrics.
Identifying the sentiment held by other key
stakeholders besides a loud and organized abortion
rights lobby may have altered the company's
strategy. While volume counts, qualitative analysis
would seem more important to a charity that
depends on the generosity of donors, not those that
rely on the charity for funding. Extending Intra-
Media Sentiment Metrics to stakeholders beyond
those included in media coverage would also have
helped Komen form a strategy based on data rather
social media heat. For instance, had Komen

checked the sentiment pulse of its top 10 donors, or its top 50 "Race For The Cure" organizers, it may have found that its donor base is standing loyal and firm despite the backlash from abortion rights activists. Allowing abortion politics to dictate strategy rather than Intra-Media Sentiment Metrics appears to have cost Komen some face. The hundreds of thousands of dollars at stake may be spent any way the charity wishes. However, remembering that charitable donors have the same freedom should be just as important to Komen.

*Note: Intra-Media Sentiment Metrics may also be indexed for greater clarity. More specifically, subcategorized stakeholders are not created equally. Since each possess a varying degree of influence, a more complex measurement tool can further narrow strategy. Weighing sentiment based on subcategory influence gives corporations the ability to identify subcategories that may need to be eliminated or included in a mitigation strategy that Intra-Media Sentiment metrics alone failed to identify. For instance, a relatively high negative sentiment ratio for a subcategory holding only minor influence may not need the attention a corporation initially thought after measuring for sentiment. Conversely, a subcategory with a rather modest negative sentiment ratio but holding a relatively high influence indicator may need more attention than a corporation first thought after measuring only for sentiment. Refer to the Buzz Influence Index (BII) for calculation method.*

4. **Crisis Perception Metrics-** Assumptions are certainly dangerous foundations on which to base decision making during crises. So don't. What may appear to be a crisis internally may actually be far less of a crisis in the eyes of lenders, customers, suppliers or other stakeholders. Before a detailed crisis response can be formulated, smart corporations first identify whether logical disconnects exist between realities and perceptions. Most importantly, corporations deluged by crisis media coverage must identify the perceptions held by key stakeholders. Do customers believe what is being reported by the media? For instance, a growing number of news consumers distrust certain mainstream mediums or generally only seek out news from mediums that reinforce existing beliefs. A corporation does itself no good attempting to correct or mitigate unflattering media coverage if the medium is not perceived as credible or relied upon by key stakeholders. Obtaining qualitative data from stakeholders that have a direct impact on the company's bottom line will dictate the strategic communications strategy aimed at entities with an indirect impact on the company's profitability. Corporations faced with a crisis often immediately throw the kitchen sink at the crisis. While it is crucial to respond immediately and aggressively, especially when public safety is an issue, simultaneously measuring for perception positions a corporation to model not only an effective response plan but also one that is efficient and less detrimental to profitability.

5. **Stakeholder Trust Gauge-** Constantly monitoring the trust various stakeholders have in the company during a crisis is also key in dictating response strategy. Trust refers to the enduring confidence stakeholders have

that the corporation may be relied upon to execute its obligations as it has in the past. Measuring for trust is crucial in identifying strong trust relationships that may need additional care to maintain. Gauging trust may also identify relationships strong enough to withstand a period of time in which the corporation's efforts are focused elsewhere during a crisis. Corporations must not forget crises are matters of degree. For instance, the Costa Concordia cruise ship that wrecked off the coast of Italy in January 2012 created an obvious and costly crisis for parent company Carnival Cruise Lines. Victims were offered compensation, the company was likely required to pay millions of dollars in insurance deductibles, and refunds had to be offered to customers who had booked future trips on the ship. The news media speculated this would hurt the industry overall and produced news items anticipating fear-related cancellations. However, newsroom insiders, as hard as they tried, could not identify mass numbers of people canceling their cruise plans out of fear their ship might crash. Measuring for trust affords a corporation in crisis data that can prevent costly and unneeded response efforts. It will also identify loyal customers who are still looking forward to their trips who may then be offered up to the media to counter speculation regarding industry fallout. Measuring trust is accomplished by surveying stakeholders with a series of Agree/Disagree questions and comparing the data to a company's past or its peers.

6. **Loyalty Erosion Indicator**- Loyalty is different from trust in that it refers more specifically to the faithfulness or devotion stakeholders have to a

company. While a specific stakeholder might maintain his or her trust that a corporation will fulfill its obligations during a crisis, the stakeholder may simultaneously be less devoted or faithful to the corporation. Clearly, the difference between trust and loyalty is greater than the connotative meanings might suggest. Having a pre-crisis loyalty benchmark is crucial for corporations interested in measuring for erosion. While measuring for loyalty will vary by industry and product, a tailored relationship survey that includes a series of Agree/Disagree and Likely/Not Likely questions will identify whether loyalty is eroding during a crisis. If measurement reveals even a hint of erosion, retention efforts may be started immediately.

7. **Key Message Metrics**- Corporations must constantly measure for Key Message Conveyance (KMC) and Inaccurate Message Conveyance (IMC) in traditional and social media. The frequency with which a corporation's key messages are conveyed accurately must continually increase if it is to minimize the duration of the crisis. Immediately recognizing when KMC is decreasing and IMC begins to increase prepares corporations in crisis for a potential shift in strategy. This is similar to what fast food restaurant chain Taco Bell did in 2011. A lawsuit filed against Taco Bell alleged the restaurant must stop labeling the meat it serves as "beef". The suit suggested the concoction was comprised of "extenders" and "binders" and did not meet the federal requirements to be labeled as "beef". The news prompted unflattering headlines around the globe. The restaurant immediately addressed the issue in the media but complimented the response with a much more direct

and aggressive set of tactics. To combat the firestorm, Taco Bell's parent company Yum Brands Inc. spent roughly $4 million dollars attacking the allegation with full page newspaper advertisements. It followed up with television ads and a YouTube campaign defending its meat as "88% beef". The direct approach proved effective. The lawsuit was withdrawn four months after it was filed.

*Note: Increased KMC ratios in sidebar and bounce pieces are early indicators a corporation's mitigation plan is working effectively. Sidebar and bounce pieces are often smaller news pieces, more narrowly focused, and are included to compliment a headline news piece. Often these pieces provide a corporation an opportunity to convey key messages unopposed by counterpoints or contradictory information. These pieces offer corporations opportunities to humanize their companies. The corporation that wins the sidebar war often shortens the crisis duration and begins changing negative sentiment more quickly. Often the sentiment and tone contained in these bounce pieces have the potential to bleed into headline coverage. When bounce piece KMC begins to increase a corporation is seeing light at the end of the crisis tunnel.*

8.  **Sales Metrics-** Real-time sales data are crucial to monitor during a crisis but a number of corporations become so wrapped up in the crisis they fail to actively monitor them. Sales are one of the most tangible indicators of public sentiment during times of crisis. Less than dramatic sales declines during times of crisis may indicate the corporation's crisis response plan is working well or may indicate a company is investing too heavily in its response. Tracking sales also affords a

corporation an opportunity to survey the customers buying the product or service. Insight into customer values, attitudes, and beliefs will aid corporations measuring for trust or willingness to recommend or purchase again.

# Identifying Emerging Threats

Now that the capability to broadcast exists for the masses not just the mass media, it should be clear that corporations, at least to some degree, are in a constant state of crisis. Whether the crisis stems from unhappy customers, disgruntled employees, obstructionist regulators, or politically motivated elected officials, corporations that choose to ignore even the most minor of sparks may quickly find themselves engulfed in flames.

Vigilantly identifying, measuring, and mitigating emerging threats that have the capability of growing into full-fledged crises may be the single most important activity in which a corporate PR staff is involved. Preventing threats from morphing into crises requires intensity, aggressiveness, and foresight. More specifically, it requires that a corporation customize its own Emerging Threat Detector.

# Emerging Threat Detector

An Emerging Threat Detector (ETD) identifies potential threats to a corporation's reputation and profitability. Think of it just like a radar screen a meteorologist might use to identify and track changes in weather conditions and patterns. Without radar, a forecaster is less likely to accurately predict whether a batch of flurries has the potential to turn into a crippling blizzard. Similarly, without an Emerging Threat

Detector corporations are more likely to find themselves flat-footed or caught off-guard by a crisis that could have easily been identified and handled in its infancy.

Customizing your corporation's Emerging Threat Detector will depend on a myriad of variables: industry, company goals, private or public, etc. However, the components and strategy behind building a customized Emerging Threat Detector are similar. The process is outlined below:

1) **Identify Measurable Objectives-** Does the corporation wish to reduce negative customer feedback, criticism from the political establishment, negative sentiment in local media coverage, negative social media volume? Objectives must be quantifiable and time frame specific.

2) **Identify Publics to be Monitored-** In this context, a corporation must identify company antagonists, critics, competitors, labor unions, special interest groups or others who may wish to do it harm.

3) **Identify Appropriate Metrics-** The objectives and publics selected for monitoring will dictate what the corporation measures.

4) **Measure Continuously-** Collecting data will only be valuable when a corporation has something with which to compare it. Creating a threat radar requires continual benchmarking.

5) **Analyze Threat Degree-** Continuously tracking threats in accordance with quantifiable and time-specific objectives will dictate if or when a company responds to an emerging threat. For instance, if the objective is to reduce negative social media volume by 15% in the next 90 days and the company's ETD shows negative volume is flat at the 60-day mark, a corporation might choose to become more strategically aggressive during the last one-third of the defined time period.

# Components to Monitor

O nce a company has identified which publics it wishes to monitor for emerging threats it must then identify the communications preferences unique to each of the publics selected. Once a corporation determines how and to whom the public communicates it can begin monitoring those communications. This may prove more difficult than it appears on its face. For instance, special interest groups often communicate internally to shield planning efforts from the public or those that might inhibit those plans. To monitor such a group it may be necessary for a member of the corporation or a company liaison to pay or donate money to become a group member to gain access to these communications.

Corporations wishing to monitor public communications for emerging threats can do so in a number of ways. Several strategies are listed below:

1) **Hashtag Threats-** Corporations must identify unflattering or potentially threatening Twitter hashtags related to the company. A threatening hashtag that is promoted powerfully can attract additional users to the discussion and become viral. On Twitter this phenomenon is called "trending". Twitter users have employed hashtags to organize mass protests like those seen during the Arab Spring, Occupy Wall Street, and to create flash mobs. Corporations must track the frequency with which an unflattering hashtag is used to gauge the momentum a potential threat possesses.

2) **"Likes" Threats-** When an influential Facebook user posts a disparaging comment about a corporation it is crucial to monitor the number of "likes" the comment receives. While "friending" antagonists and others a corporation

wishes to monitor is an ideal way to eavesdrop on potentially threatening "likes", databases and search engines are being created to make the job a bit easier. The startup *Likester* provides a service in which one can search more than a half-billion Facebook "likes". Noticing a dramatic increase in the number of unflattering "likes" alerts a company to a problem that is much easier to fix now versus later.

*Note: While functionally useless in a variety of other contexts, measuring for unflattering hashtag and "like" volumes can be illuminating, especially in the case of "likes" where little or no additional content exists. However, basing a response solely on hashtag threat volume is dangerous without first qualitatively analyzing twitter content since company proponents may also be using a disparaging hashtag to defend the company.*

3) **Competitor Threats-** Corporations interested in monitoring emerging threats must also subscribe to RSS feeds related to competitor blogs and websites. Doing so will save time for the corporation as it will not have to manually visit each of these blogs or websites for information. Additionally, subscribing to competitor RSS feeds may also alert a corporation to potential threats emerging internally. Internal threats may become apparent when a corporation subscribes to a competitor's employment RSS feed. A particular job opening may alert a corporation to a poaching threat. Also, using Google Alerts is another efficient manner of immediately learning what competitors are up to.

4) **News Consumer Threat-** When traditional media post content online, opportunities often exist for consumers to post comments regarding the content. Many of these

comments may contain little or no substance or even be meant as humorous. However, this is also a forum in which antagonists feel their voices may be heard. That's a big reason traditional media offer the opportunity. Particularly poignant comments are often used as starting points for follow-up stories. While smart corporations will be sure to weigh the poster's influence, they must also understand that traditional media are monitoring these comments to find follow-up stories and people who are dissatisfied with a company for some reason.

Once a corporation selects a component for monitoring it must then decide what it wants to measure for in each component. Metrics often associated with identifying an emerging threat include: Inaccurate Message Conveyance, Negative Sentiment Ratio, Quote Accuracy Tracker, News Consumer Tracker, Origin of Awareness Metric, and Influence.

# The Fear Index

Identifying slight changes in terms of sentiment, message conveyance, message cannibalization, and other metrics, in regard to topics, issues, or matters potentially harmful to the corporation's reputation is vital. Corporations that deem it valuable to proactively mitigate threats before they become disasters can only do so by having access to pertinent data. Quantifying fear is one method on which a corporation can rely for such data.

Years ago, the financial industry began measuring and profiting from fear. The Chicago Board Options Exchange created a Market Volatility Index, otherwise known to equity and options traders as the VIX. The VIX measures the implied volatility of S&P 500 index options and affords investors a measure of the market's perceived volatility over the next 30 days. Without going into greater detail, the VIX measures the degree of fear traders possess in regard to the market decreasing in value. For instance, the investment tool that tracks the VIX rose to an all-time intraday high of $81.65 on October 27, 2008- the height of the stock market plunge during the financial crisis.

Adapting the VIX to measure volatility or fear as it relates to public relations may be accomplished similarly. A corporation's specific objectives will determine which metrics it uses to measure fear. Situational specifics will also be taken into account. However, I suggest combining metrics such as Key Message Cannibalization Rate, Media Abandonment Rate, and Key Message Metrics with web analytics tools to accurately measure fear.

For example, let's assume a key regulatory vote affecting a corporation is scheduled to take place in the next 30 days. A corporation may choose to use Key Message Cannibalization Rate (KMCR) to gauge the fear that exists in terms of the potential for media coverage to negatively influence the individuals set to vote. KMCR is combined with analytics measuring coverage volume for key media websites. *Note: Circulation data and Nielsen television ratings may also be included though keep in mind they are often manipulated.*

The Fear Index identifies changes in KMCR over time while simultaneously tracking coverage volume which will often increase similarly to KMCR during extreme periods of key message volatility.

An illustration of the example is below:

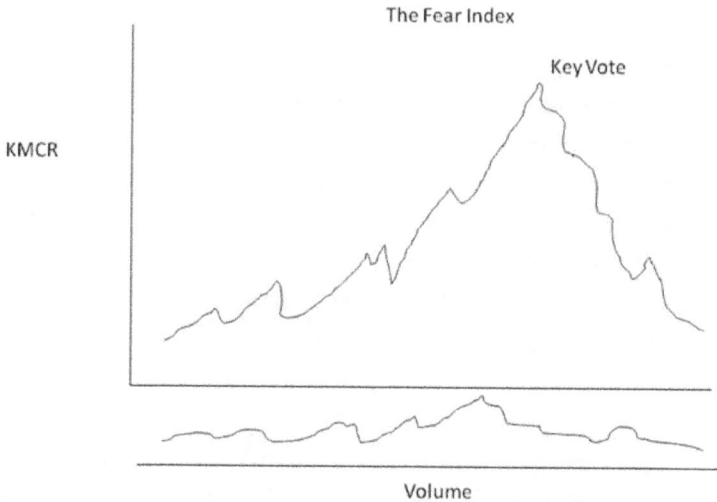

The Fear Index

Key Vote

KMCR

Volume

Notice the volume that tracks the fear. Monitoring coverage volume is crucial in creating a reliable fear index. Volume can act as a lie detector for a company attempting to quantify fear. For instance, increased fear on low coverage volume may not require a company to act. In fact, acting may draw more attention to a negative change in sentiment and increase coverage volume. Financial traders rely on volume to determine whether a stock is being purchased or sold with conviction. If a stock runs up on relatively light volume, traders generally assume big money institutional investors are not responsible for the surge which often indicates the stock will quickly give back recent gains. Conversely, a trader is more likely to believe in the authenticity of a big price swing if it occurs in lockstep with increased volume. The same principle is applicable when attempting to identify emerging threats or gather data during a crisis. Dramatic changes in sentiment are less likely to occur without increased coverage volume. However, a negative change in sentiment on low volume should not be ignored if it has the potential to impact reputation.

# Post-Crisis Measurement

Executives and public relations staffers who endure sleepless nights and increased stress levels during a crisis are likely the last people in a corporation interested in post-crisis measurement. The attitude may be, "The crisis is over, let's refocus and get back to the day-to-day management of the core business." The problem with this type of thinking is that while the crisis may be over for the corporation, post-crisis perceptions held by various stakeholders may be different than they were pre-crisis. Think of it like this, a surgery patient doesn't just get up off the operating table and walk out of the hospital never to see the doctor again. In fact, the contrary is true. The patient returns afterward for check-ups, follow-up care, and possibly even rehabilitation therapy. The lesson here is after a crisis, corporations must do check-ups on their relationships to determine whether therapy is required.

The good news with regard to post-crisis measurement is that benchmarks exist for quick and easy comparisons. Relationships with employees, the media, vendors, suppliers, customers, or other key stakeholders are to be measured to determine what impact, if any, the crisis had on those stakeholders. Some of the same metrics on a corporation's Crisis Dashboard may be used; the Stakeholder Trust Gauge and the Loyalty Erosion Indicator are both useful tools in determining relational strength following a crisis.

Post-crisis measurement is also a time in which corporations may identify the existence of logical disconnects. These gaps between a public's perceptions, situational realities, and a corporation's key messages were discussed in greater detail earlier. Why measure post-crisis for these gaps? After a crisis, gaps may exist where there were none prior to the crisis. Additionally, identifying whether a pre-crisis gap has grown wider is useful when allocating public relations resources. Measuring for logical disconnects three, six, and nine months after a crisis concludes will tell a corporation whether time is healing crisis-caused wounds or whether the corporation must be more aggressive in rehabilitating those wounds.

# Measuring Crisis Mitigation Success

Corporations that identify specific objectives at the outset know instantly whether their crisis response activities are successful. Defining success beforehand clearly identifies the path a corporation must take to end a crisis quickly, minimize damage to its reputation, and do so in the most cost-effective manner possible. While these three broad-based goals are admirable, we know they are not specific enough to be counted as appropriate crisis objectives. The post-crisis measurement tools included below will be helpful when the time comes to create specific measurable crisis objectives for your company:

1) **Crisis Duration**- Crisis duration may be compared to a corporation's past or its peers. Post-crisis measurement plans must be sure to compare like crises in terms of casualties, economic damage, environmental damage etc. Doing so allows for a valid duration benchmark against which a corporation can measure. Crisis duration may be a metric by which a corporation judges its public relations efforts and guides future crisis mitigation strategy. Corporations must be sure to clearly define what the end of a crisis looks like to calculate duration. Corporations that shorten the duration of crises may then calculate the cost savings associated with ending a crisis sooner than it did in the past or versus its peers.

2) **Crisis Cost-** Costs that might be included in calculating this metric include environmental clean up costs, costs associated with company assets damaged or destroyed, fines or financial penalties levied, the hiring of outside legal counsel, outside PR firm costs, legal settlements, governmental lobbying costs, etc. Comparing crisis costs with a company's past or its peers provides the company with insight into the effectiveness of its mitigation plan, provided like crises are compared. If a corporation determines its crisis costs were dramatically less than those of its past or peers, find out why. Reducing crisis costs often directly correlates with a company's public relations efforts.

3) **Customer Churn-** Identifying whether your corporation loses fewer customers versus its past or peers as a result of a crisis is important when conducting post-crisis analysis. More important though is why. Why did your corporation lose fewer or more customers? Was it due to crisis duration? Key Message Conveyance? Loyalty erosion? Surveying lost customers, after determining the crisis caused customer churn, is important in refining future crisis mitigation efforts. For instance, is a 3% customer churn during a two month crisis that costs the corporation $2 million acceptable? Is this an acceptable objective for future like crises?

4) **Share Price Volatility-** Crisis mitigation success may also be measured by comparing the share price of a publicly traded company with its past or its peers. While macro-economic conditions must also be taken into account when comparing the impact of crises on share price, identifying whether shortened crisis duration, lower crisis-associated

costs, or reduced customer churn may be responsible for putting a floor beneath a company's share price is crucial in prioritizing post-crisis metrics.

# Quantifying Character

At least one media conglomerate in the Midwest requires reporter candidates to open up their financial closets and bare it all. Like many employers, the company wants to check a candidate's credit history prior to making a hiring decision. Identifying any skeletons in a reporter's financial closet is important to the employer for a variety of reasons. A strong credit score may indicate the reporter is trustworthy and accountable. A poor credit score may indicate the reporter is less trustworthy and less inclined to fulfill his or her obligations.

These are deemed by many as extremely important insights into a reporter's character.

Identifying whether a reporter feels a moral obligation to pay his or her bills on time is seen by some employers as a measure of character. Understanding how a reporter handles his or her finances may indicate whether the reporter will be reckless in regard to the truth. A reporter living a life he or she cannot afford suggests the reporter may not be concerned with the consequences of his or her behavior.

Quantifying a reporter's character is useful to smart PR staffs as well.

Full disclosure; research regarding employer use of credit scores is contradictory. The Society for Human Resource Management says 60% of employers conduct credit checks as part of the employee screening process. A *Wall Street Journal* article from January 2012 cites an academic study that found, "Nearly one-third of employees with self-reported credit problems engaged in counterproductive work behavior such as theft or accepting bribes compared to about 18% of employees without financial problems."

Conversely, psychologists at Eastern Kentucky University found that credit scores are not valid predictors of employee job performance. Despite initially believing credit scores may in fact predict such phenomena, researchers concluded employees with lower credit ratings were not more likely to have poor performance reviews or leave the company in greater numbers than those with higher quality credit scores. In fact, researchers found employees with a higher number of late payments received higher job performance ratings.

Quantifying character in this manner is also under attack from privacy advocates and state legislatures. Privacy advocates say the foreclosure crisis damaged the credit scores of valuable employees nationwide. Likewise, credit scores often contain errors or are in dispute.

These concerns are also causing state lawmakers to crack down. Several states have banned employers from conducting credit checks on some employees. At least a dozen other states are considering measures limiting employee credit checks. The Society for Human Resource Management says federal legislation is also being considered, "...that would amend the Fair Credit Reporting Act to limit employer use of consumer credit reports."

It should also be noted that while writing this portion of the book the nation's three major credit bureaus are facing potential scrutiny from a newly created federal consumer watchdog. The Consumer Financial Protection Bureau (CFPB), brought to life by the Dodd-Frank financial regulatory law to prevent financial abuses evident in the 2008 crisis, has proposed a rule that would allow it to scrutinize credit bureau activities. The Federal Trade Commission oversees the ratings agencies but the CFPB wants the authority to examine and review the ratings agencies' books and records. The proposal is likely in response to increasing complaints from consumers alleging it's too hard to correct mistakes on credit reports that could cause them to be overlooked for a job or a loan.

Still, many employers argue credit scores reveal valuable character insights ordinary employment interviews do not.

Additionally, identifying the websites a journalist visits can compliment credit score data in terms of quantifying character. In February 2012 Congress began considering whether to require an online privacy bill of rights. This includes a "do not track" button that web browsers can click on. Why would this be needed? After Google was caught circumventing the privacy settings inherent in Apple's web browsing software, it should have become clear to all that tracking online behavior could be used on a much broader scale.

Besides customizing advertisements, individual online footprints are valuable to a number of industries. Tracking a person's behavior online is lucrative and can help companies determine who to hire, who to trust, and who might be a liability if acquired as an employee or customer. While web browsing giants have agreed not to use tracking data, "...for employment, credit, health-care or insurance purposes...", *The Wall Street Journal* makes clear there is plenty of wiggle room. The paper reveals companies will still be able to use tracking data for "market research" and "product development".

We're not advocating every corporation begin investigating the credit histories or online footprints of the journalists who follow them. What we are illustrating though is that this type of data, along with other personal information, are being used more frequently to predict future personal behavior. And predicting how a journalist or new influencer may behave is undoubtedly valuable to a corporation attempting to bolster or salvage its reputation.

For instance, the health care industry has at its disposal a behavioral prediction tool that may help it cut costs and improve medical outcomes. Fair Isaac Co., the same outfit that created the FICO credit score, has now developed a measurement tool it calls The Medication Adherence Score. The score assembles and weighs different metrics that when combined correctly aim to predict the likelihood that a person will actually take his or her prescription medications.

Fair Isaac Co. claims The Medication Adherence Score can identify the people at highest risk of not routinely taking prescribed medication. The score allegedly enables health care providers to target those people with email reminders or other direct marketing strategies. The company says using The Medication Adherence Score can dramatically reduce marketing expenses while simultaneously increasing the effectiveness of a company's public relations efforts. For instance, a pharmaceutical company might use the score to remind a forgetful prescription drug user it's time to do so, which can maximize profit per patient. Likewise, a pharmaceutical company with data showing a particular patient needs no reminder can avoid marketing spend altogether in that instance.

Credit reporting agency Experian PLC is now offering a product which aims to identify a person's income. The company says its Income Insight Score can quantify an individual's total income including wages, rent, alimony, and investments. Experian claims using the score can help corporations make profitable decisions based on an individual's ability to pay. Competitor Equifax has designed similar tools for credit card issuers such as the Ability to Pay Index (ATP) and the Discretionary Spending Index (DSI).

What's clear is that a variety of industries are combining data sets to predict personal behavior in an effort to mitigate risk and increase profitability. Information corporations were once only able to glean interpersonally and with a relatively large time investment is now being quantified in just moments using some of, but not limited to, the data below:

- Credit Score
- Foreclosure
- Bankruptcy
- Alimony

- Child Support
- Marital Status
- Duration of Marriage
- Home Ownership
- Duration in Residence
- Employment
- Duration in Job
- Automobile Ownership
- Outstanding Debt
- Debt 30 Days Past Due
- Discretionary Spending
- Gender
- Age

While it's important to be mindful of privacy concerns and the debate over the accuracy of these scores when attempting to predict future behavior, it's even more important for a corporation to conceptualize how data mining will shape the future along with your company's reputation.

A much talked about concept has led many to this prediction; one day a generally agreed upon Reputation Score will be created and used to rank people, places, and companies. A reputation score will be relied on much like a credit score; it will aid in determining whether you are approved for a loan, hired to complete a task, or chosen as a reliable business partner. However, a reputation score would be much more complicated to manage than a credit score.

While identity theft and certain uncontrollable financial hardships have blemished even the most sterling credit scores through little or no fault of the individual, for the most part an individual is the sole determinant of his or her credit score. The same cannot be said for reputation. Consultants and the like define reputation in a variety of ways. Pick whichever fits your company. But be mindful that a component of almost any of these definitions will include what others are saying about you.

Influencing what these people say and how they behave toward your corporation will likely be a top objective for every corporate PR staff interested in boosting or salvaging its reputation score. A reputation score will influence purchasing decisions which will ultimately determine a corporation's fate. In fact, variations of a reputation score are already being used.

Twitter has been scoring reputations for some time. Reputation scores determine who Twitter features in its "Who to Follow" section. Be assured the micro-messaging service is not selecting users for inclusion here randomly or by chance. The method or manner by which Twitter calculates its reputation scores is a secret. Though many tech bloggers speculate it's only a matter of time before Twitter makes public or attempts to monetize its reputation scores.

That's because others are already doing so.

Have you checked to see what your corporation's Klout score is? Klout.com boasts of being "The Standard for Influence". The 2008 startup attempts to quantify reputation or social influence by monitoring a number of online behaviors. For instance, it tallies your posts, comments, and likes on social networks like Twitter, Facebook, LinkedIn, and Google+. After calculating your social activities Klout assigns users a score between 1 and 100. The closer your score is to 100 the more social influence you possess. The company, which is backed by venture capitalists, says it has scored more than 100 million users.

Review websites like Yelp, which went public in March 2012, assign reputation scores based on a 5-star system. Google is constantly tweaking its search algorithms to outsmart search engine optimization (SEO) efforts that influence how high a particular website ranks in its search results. And your behavior on Facebook dictates, in part, how frequently your content shows up in news feeds.

An entire industry has bloomed around these phenomena. The reputation management industry makes its money attempting to influence your corporation's influence scores. These outfits attempt to remove or bury unflattering search results while boosting results that are complimentary. Several have taken some heat lately from customers who rediscover unflattering content they paid to have removed. In reality, understand that naked picture of your CFO will forever be enshrined on some Ukranian or Bangladeshi server and retrievable for those with a connection and some know-how.

The point here is not to scare corporations into investing heavily in boosting their reputation scores on Twitter or Klout. Do not allow the phenomena to distract you from your core mission. If you're a gold miner, worry about finding the metal and controlling extraction costs. The point here is to be aware and understand what is happening in the world of big data.

The quantification of intangible or previously unmeasured concepts or soft assets is underway. Analytics and data mining technologies will continue to evolve and reinvent the manner in which a corporation interacts with its publics. Privacy concerns will mingle with questions regarding validity and reliability, but these controversies will not stop big data from calculating reputation scores and the like.

There's too much money at stake to stop.

Trademarking or patenting the first universal, or at least widely agreed upon, method of scoring reputation will be lucrative. So too will be the cottage industries that spring up around what I call the age of Soft Quantification. For a fee, these companies will promise to improve your *Reputation Score,* your *Trustworthiness Rating,* or your *Willingness to be Forgiven for a Mistake* score. They'll attempt to convince you they are experts and that you'll be lost without their help.

The message here is consistent with advice found throughout the book; you can do most of this yourself. Save your capital. Determine which metrics appropriately measure progress toward the corporation's specific objectives and use them. If they do not exist, invent them. That's exactly what the big credit ratings

252

agencies have done. That's exactly what's being done online in terms of reputation. And that's exactly what a smart PR staff is capable of doing as well.

If a contentious situation arises that could pose a threat to the corporation's reputation and a PR staff is unsure of which reporter or new influencer it should engage, consider Soft Quantification. It may require some creativity to garner permission, but checking a journalist's credit score might be telling. Quantifying phenomena characteristic of a journalist's personal life can at times identify the safest and surest path out of a potentially damaging situation.

# Cost Per Message (CPM) Comparison

We know the U.S. Postal Service measures at least one thing: its financial losses.

The U.S. Postal Service estimates it'll lose more than $14 billion in fiscal year 2012. To stop the financial bleeding, the Post Office is considering boosting the price of stamps to 50-cents and halting Saturday mail delivery.

These results contrast sharply with Stamps.com, a startup company that sells stamps through its software products. The company allows clients to ship items without having to leave the office and visit a post office. The company's revenue increased 18% in 2011 compared with 2010. So how can Stamps.com enjoy accelerating revenue while the U.S. Postal Service is hemorrhaging cash?

One word: measurement.

When *Investor's Business Daily* featured the company recently, the newspaper attributed much of the company's success to its reliance on metrics. The article reads, "Stamps.com measures the return on investment of all of its marketing strategies to see how much revenue it generates and then makes adjustments." The article goes on to say, "When Stamps circulates direct mail to generate new customers, it analyzes the ROI to determine its cost per acquisition. Then it tweaks the mailer to get better results."

It's a strategy that can boost returns and messaging efficiency for smart PR departments as well.

Not all messages are communicated equally. Which channels provide the best return on investment as it relates to Key Message Conveyance (KMC)? When is the last time your PR staff checked? How often is your corporation comparing interdepartmental KMC costs? Corporations without financial data for KMC may be wasting a vast portion of their PR budgets. So why not take a small piece of that and measure KMC cost to identify where you get the biggest bang for your buck?

Cost per Message (CPM) calculations will quickly identify ways a corporation can cut costs. Identifying messaging costs across an array of channels inevitably causes corporations to become leaner and more strategically successful. Calculating CPM for live events, advertising, marketing, direct mail, news conferences, media tours, and other channels used to communicate will identify from where a company is extracting the most value.

For instance, I recently calculated CPM for a multimedia startup selling a nonfiction book without the marketing support from a large publishing house. I compared Key Message Conveyance (KMC) from the company's initial "Book Signing" event with the "Media Tour" it held several weeks later. The results proved counterintuitive.

The initial "Book Signing" event cost the company approximately $6,000. This included advertising and event space rental fees along with marketing, promotional, and event display materials. Invitations were sent to potential customers, members of the media, people mentioned in the book, and legislators among others. The "Book Signing" was widely promoted and covered by the media, however KMC was an unimpressive 29%.

The "Media Tour" the company hosted was held one evening at a restaurant and yielded far better results. The company was skeptical about inviting a few dozen journalists to an after work gathering on a weeknight. The "Media Tour" cost approximately $1,700 and included hors d'oeuvres, drinks, and some promotional materials. About 65% of the journalists invited attended. The book and its authors were featured by a multitude of media outlets and generated an astounding KMC of 86%.

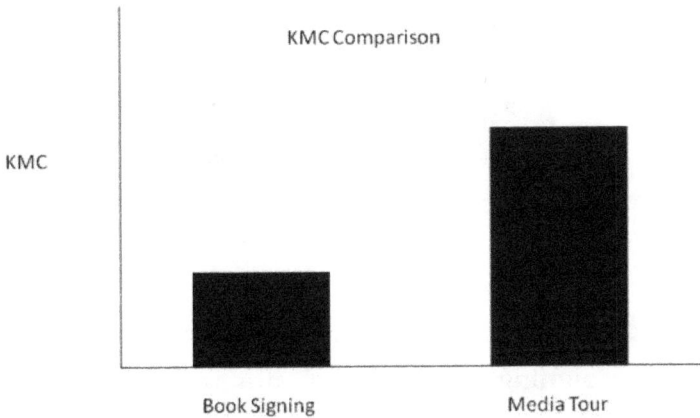

KMC Comparison

KMC

Book Signing          Media Tour

After calculating CPM for both events and then comparing CPM with KMC, one thing was clear; the event that cost the company the least, the "Media Tour", generated a far greater return on investment than the more expensive initial "Book Signing". More specifically, each key message conveyed in the media following the initial "Book Signing" cost the company $3.22.

That compared with a CPM of $0.62 for the "Media Tour. See illustration below:

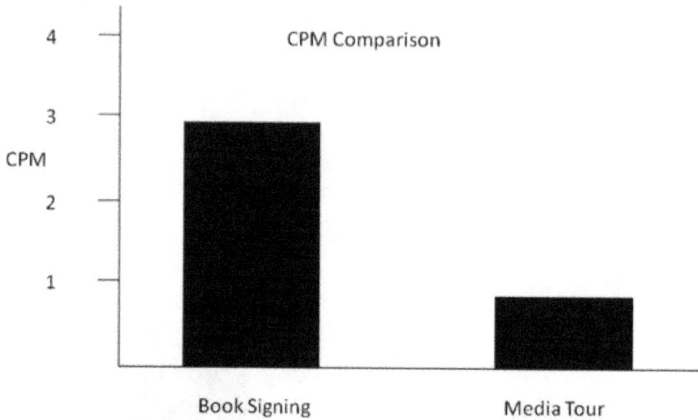

Clearly, the "Media Tour" provided a much larger ROI than the initial "Book Signing". This data dramatically altered the company's strategy going forward. Initially, the authors envisioned a series of book signings spread across different cities to maximize KMC. The authors thought the comingling of potential customers in love with the book with journalists covering the event would create third party credibility and lead to increased KMC ratios and better media coverage overall. However, after examining the data above the authors changed course quickly and held a series of media tours instead. Doing so saved the corporation thousands of dollars it was then able to redirect toward other more profitable means of communicating.

Corporate PR staffs can replicate CPM calculations to compare a variety of messaging events. The example of the authors should make clear the importance of routinely measuring message associated costs. A corporation that chooses not to identify the most cost-effective channels by which to convey key messages will ultimately be far less efficient than corporations that do. Tapping these channels for future strategic communications distribution trickles down to the bottom line.

# Pivot Point #4

We pivot here for the last time.
You've taken the long road thus far. One that has meandered through crisis, the rise of new influencers at the expense of traditional media, and the raw and sometimes painful honesty thorough measurement provides.

If you're still along for the ride at this point you know continuing to operate as you have will simply prolong a slow death. That mediocrity will slowly whither to failure and obsolescence. Deep down you know traditional PR assumptions, clichés, and tactics are no longer keys to effective messaging.

You're willing to strip it all away.

You're naked.

What now? This is where we are most vulnerable. Least able to protect ourselves. Most prone to failure.

Unbrainwashing yourself leaves you with a blank slate. It means you're free to make new rules. Create new things. Explore. Trailblaze.

You're already equipped with everything you need to begin creating premier content.

Pivot here one last time.

Creating exceptional content begins with a remade you.

# The
# 10 Content
# Commandments

*Whispering in a crowd of screamers forces listeners to draw closer. Telling on yourself exposes you for what you are: a courageous truth-teller worthy of loyalty and business. Worthy of another chance.*

# Pregnant With Ideas

Y ou are pregnant with ideas.

But giving birth to those ideas in the form of premier content is extremely difficult.

If it was easy, television news stations wouldn't be hemorrhaging viewers. Newspaper circulation rates wouldn't be cratering. Consumers of media content would be less likely to stray. Transforming yourself into a smart PR staff requires help.

It requires an idea midwife.

Smart PR is contingent upon creative ideas and giving birth to them in the form of premier content. Any old idea won't do though. You'll need unconventional ideas. Original ideas. Ideas that either haven't been executed before or haven't been widely distributed. These kinds of ideas are hard to come by. If it was easy everyone would be coming up with them.

Smart ideas contain two components: valuable content and compelling presentation. To stand out, both components must be present. Plenty of terrific ideas reside in newsrooms and reporters across the country. Without a compelling presentation though, valuable content languishes.

Value first.

Compelling presentation second.

# Elements of Value

L ike beauty, value lies in the eye of the beholder.

Real value varies among audiences.

However, creating value that reaches across cultural divides, financial interests, and arbitrary boundaries is achievable.

Al Tompkins of *The Poynter Institute*, a school that trains journalists, is an award winning reporter, news manager, and author of the book, *Aim for the Heart: A Guide for TV Producers and*

*Reporters.* Tompkins repeatedly trains television journalists to understand, "People remember how they feel longer than what they know." Tompkins' book details how successful stories are those told through memorable characters and with emotion.

Tompkins acknowledges it is often hard to get people interested in complex stories. The key, Tompkins argues, is identifying something most people hold dear, or motivators, and connecting the story with one of those motivators.

Tompkins lists the five items below as universal motivators:

1) Money
2) Family
3) Health
4) Safety
5) Community

Tompkins lists two additional motivators that relate specifically to investigative reporting:

1) Innate Curiosity
2) Public Outrage

Corporations that attach company products, services, or activities to these motivators dramatically increase the likelihood of creating premier content. Finding a way to wrap corporate accomplishments into one of these motivators and using compelling characters to deliver the narrative is a recipe for storytelling success.

Nick Winkler

# Compelling Presentation Elements

What if you fetched the paper for Fido?

What if you wore a hoodie rather than a business suit during an IPO road show?

What if you were to give everyone else presents on your birthday?

Behaviors like these grab people by the collars of their shirts and force them to pay attention. Such behavior demands notice. It makes you memorable. It demonstrates, without words, that you are unique. That you are courageous enough to see things differently. That you're not confined by learned ritual. By illogical constraint. Behaving like this prompts people to listen to you.

Presenting valuable content unconventionally is a requirement today.

Unfortunately, terrific content can be buried in this era of big data. Great stories can be lost in the chaos and confusion of technology. Informational diamonds may be passed over simply because they shine a touch less than another.

Valuable content that lacks a compelling presentation is likely doomed. Without a compelling presentation the time, effort, and money spent creating the content will be wasted.

Still, traditional PR continues to rely on conventional presentation methods: news releases, mass email blasts, impersonal pitches. Admittedly, traditional distribution methods are effective when strong relationships exist between a PR staff and a new influencer or reporter. But relationship-building is often absent from a large organization's basket of objectives.

Traditional PR tools lack surprise. They don't provoke curiosity. They don't demand an audience pay attention.

Routinely using traditional presentation tools gives audiences permission to look away. Continuing to use only these tools communicates you do not value the audience enough to create something new. An ordinary presentation tells people the message must be ordinary as well.

What if you violated the constraints of these tools?

What if you broke the rules?

What if you made your own?

Smart PR not only requires valuable content but also delivering it in a compelling manner. A compelling presentation may at times require more effort than the creation of valuable content.

Doing so disrupts the storytelling process.

Valuable content presented in a compelling manner will be adopted by others. It'll be passed among audiences. It'll be retold by the media. It'll be copied by competitors. By that time though, you'll already be creating high value content in new ways.

Violate norms.

When a written news release is expected create a video for distribution.

That's what kitchen products maker Blendtec does.

Blendtec manufactures commercial and home blenders. To distinguish its blenders from those of its competitors, Blendtec zigs when others zag. Instead of focusing on the subtle feature and benefit differences of a commoditized product, Blendtec uses its products to create premier content.

Blendtec created a website and YouTube channel entitled "Will It Blend?" A man in a lab coat and goggles appears at the beginning of these humorous videos and asks, "Will it blend, that is the question?" He then inserts items like cell phones, football tees, and video game systems into the company's blenders and documents the damage that ensues.

The videos have gone viral.

As I write this a video of an Apple iPad being dumped into a Blendtec blender has gotten nearly 13-million views.

Hundreds of these videos exist.

The return on investment is massive.

The videos can be produced cheaply. They increase brand awareness dramatically while boosting sales. The videos themselves can even turn into revenue generators. For instance, a video showing how a crowbar might blend has gotten more than 6-million views. Google, which owns YouTube, will pay video producers that generate this amount of web traffic a portion of the advertisements sold alongside the videos and web searches for the videos.

In case you're wondering, yes, the iPad blended!

# Broadcast Like Al Qaeda

I hate Al Qaeda.
I hate the terror organization's objectives, the tactics it executes to create authority, and the pain it has caused so many families.

However, the success Al Qaeda has enjoyed in terms of global reach and recruitment is, in part, attributable to the content it self-produces. Lessons may be learned from the proactive approach Al Qaeda employs in terms of its media strategy. In fact, Al Qaeda has been so successful in generating its own news, the Central Intelligence Agency has both studied and attempted to combat the terror organization's media prowess.

Al Qaeda could care less what a network nightly news anchor in New York City has to say about the group. Al Qaeda has single-handedly discredited and made Western media irrelevant to legions of people across the globe. Granted, these people often lack the interest or capacity to discern truth from fiction. However, no other organization in the world has used video to capture an audience as large or as effectively as Al Qaeda.

Critics might argue this characterization is an oversimplification. I would agree Al Qaeda's media making prowess takes a backseat to its anti-Western ideology that draws a global audience. A bias also exists in that the group's only product, terror, produces independent media coverage in and of itself. In light of all that, I still believe there is something to learn from Al Qaeda in terms of how it often generates its own headlines even without blowing up something.

For instance, Al Qaeda broke a huge merger and acquisition story in February 2012.

When Al Qaeda announced the African-based terror organization Al Shabaab was joining it to form a mega-terror group, it did so without the help of third party media. Al Qaeda produced a video explaining to the world how the acquisition was extending its global reach (in reality it was an admission of Al Shabaab's weakness). The video had major television networks and newspapers scrambling to catch up and disseminate news of this "match made in hell".

The lesson to be learned here is that Al Qaeda understands how aggressively using technology enables an organization to bypass traditional media gatekeepers. Long ago, these gatekeepers (editors) had the authority to anoint something as news or conversely keep something from becoming news. Al Qaeda realizes it can communicate directly to its target audiences. The terror group's message is then amplified when rebroadcast and printed by third party media outlets.

Examine this list of facts for a moment:

1. Al Shabaab confirmed the merger news via an audio recording disseminated on the group's website.
2. Al Qaeda leader Ayman al-Zawahiri is equipped with the video production tools and talent to create a 15 minute announcement and post it online.

Unfortunately, I've visited with corporate PR departments incapable or unwilling of independently accomplishing what these terror groups have.

Al Qaeda has accumulated its own video production gear out of necessity as there are likely few production houses headquartered in the caves of Tora Bora. And granted, sympathizers are likely providing the technological know-how regarding online video posting. The point here is that Al Qaeda and Al Shabaab are manufacturing original news items from remote locales plagued by war, genocide, and famine.

Why isn't every corporate PR staff able to do the same?

The cost of acquiring video production capabilities has plunged. Video editing, web design, and the know-how to marry the two have all been transformed from specialized skill sets to commodities. I've consistently argued doing much of this work on your own is not only possible but cost-effective as well. If you disagree or estimate doing it yourself is not practical for your budget, at least consider adopting Al Qaeda's penchant for establishing specific objectives regarding strategic communications.

# Bad Ideas Are Cannibals

Bad ideas eat good ones.

They are cannibals that erode value and cause audiences to disregard you. They prompt audiences to look elsewhere for premier content.

Be aware ideas are also cumulative.

Distributing a bunch of bad ideas, those that lack one of the key components, will weigh upon your good ideas. Bad ideas drag down good ideas. One good one will struggle to overcome many bad ones. Television news has largely made itself irrelevant by broadcasting bad ideas. Stale ideas. Common sense ideas. Worn out ideas. The bad ideas accumulate. Finally, when a television station comes up with a gem no one is watching. Viewers have already turned the channel. Too many bad ideas caused the good one to go unconsumed.

It's tragic.

Good ideas are murdered by gangs of bad ideas.

Don't murder your good ideas. Don't allow bad ideas to accumulate. Don't make yourself irrelevant.

# Good Ideas Are Promiscuous

Good ideas are attracted to one another.
They are drawn together magnetically.
In seas of technology and chaos they somehow manage to find one another.

Good ideas join together to create even better ideas. They create value neither would possess on their own. Merging good ideas increases their individual potential exponentially.

So where do good ideas hide? Where can you find them? How can you create them? First, stop looking outward for good ideas. Instead, look inside. Good ideas, or the tools to create them, are inside us all. We have to look hard. Think hard. Probe deeply. Challenge ourselves. Set aside pride. Set aside fear. The fear of being wrong. Be wrong. Be wrong some more. Throw away the bad. Keep searching for the good.

We have to birth great ideas.

We're pregnant with great ideas. We must nourish them. Take care of them. Give birth to them. And raise them well. Giving birth to greatness is a challenge. It may be one of the hardest things we ever do. It can be painful. It can seemingly take forever. It can also happen instantaneously, though it's rare.

**The 10 Content Commandments** are outlined in the following pages. Think of them as midwives you can rely on to help birth your ideas. Follow these commandments and you'll create something special. You'll create value. You'll give birth to greatness. Each of the Commandments is defined. And beneath each Commandment is a series of bullet points. These bullet points are not ideas specific to your organization. These bullet points are thoughts, metaphors, or directives aimed at making you think differently. They're designed to arouse your creativity. To inspire innovation. Use these bullet points to begin the search. Funnel your organization through these stimuli. Interrogate yourself. How does the metaphor apply to your organization? How could you use a directive to create something special within your company? How can your employees personalize one of the thoughts? How can you use the bullet points to create something tangible? Something unique. Something brilliant.

# The 10 Content Commandments

### I. Get Naked

It causes nightmares. It jolts people awake at night. It prompts feelings of terror. It's the rawest of insecurities. But ripping off your clothes and getting naked is key in creating smart PR. Fear will flee once an organization realizes the benefits of being naked. Premier content hides in plain sight. It's in the form of human capital. Why save it all? Why not spend some of it? Spending human capital is an investment. It will create a return. Show people who you are. Show them the smart people you have on board. Show how they are making a difference. Out yourself. Expose the ideas your people have, the things they create, and the good they do. Stop covering up. Stop hiding. Stop being bashful. Become an open book. Exude transparency. Initially, getting naked will shock people. They'll stare. Overcome the discomfort associated with the stares. You want them to stare. Now you have their attention. Expose them to who you are. What you want to be. And how you plan to get there. Engage those who stare. Show them why you are naked and how they can benefit. Reveal processes, strategies, and operational achievements. Get naked like this:

- Show how mundane products and processes make life better
- Show people the employee responsible for it
- Identify him or her publicly as an MVP
- Offer your MVP employees as experts and sources

- Show how lobbyists are trying to save money for customers
- Catch employees involved in acts of kindness
- Highlight customer, vendor, supplier achievements
- Show differences being made
- Show courage
- Show greatness

## II.  Have Funerals for Mistakes

The trust deficit is at an all-time high. People do not trust governments, corporations, or each other. This trust deficit impacts reputations and profits. It gives people a reason to try a competitor. It gives the media reason to be skeptical. Trust deficits are the kindling by which infernos are born. Filling these trust gaps is crucial. Filling trust gaps removes impersonal corporate facades. It engages. It creates loyalty. It brings a company closer to its customers. Smart PR fills trust gaps by having funerals for mistakes. Organizations mess up. They make mistakes. Burying those mistakes publicly fills trust gaps. People feel compelled to comfort those suffering loss at funerals. Allow them to comfort you. Let them in on something unpleasant. They want to help you heal. Eulogize and memorialize mistakes for what they are— stepping stones to success. The high price paid to become exceptional. Smart PR invites stakeholders to funerals like these:

- Hold a funeral when times are good
- Show how good times spring from mistakes
- Keep your bad ideas
- Bury them in the mistake graveyard
- Show people what you learned from them
- Show people why they were important in the process
- Mistakes are the early inputs of success
- Show people how resilient your people were following mistakes

- How they overcame setbacks to create something valuable
- Be an example
- Show how others can bounce back as well
- Say something nice about your mistakes
- Honor them
- Bury them for all to see

### III.  Kick a Pit bull

You're a leader. Others look up to you. They copy you. They use your successes as models. As the role model of your industry your standards are higher. Your responsibilities are greater. You have obligations your competitors do not. When you see something that's not right you have to say something. You have to call it out. You must show the world why it's wrong. You have to kick a pit bull. Kicking a pit bull has consequences. Those who kick pit bulls know they'll be bitten. They know they'll be attacked. But they also know it's their duty. When a leader identifies something that is inefficient, illegal, or impractical in their industry or sector they must call it out publicly. They must explain why it is in the world's best interest to fix the problem. They are fighting up. They are starting a war with something greater than themselves. They know they are outgunned. They know the consequences. But they continue because it's the right thing to do. They do it because it sets them apart. It is courageous. We all want to be brave. And we all want to do business with companies that are brave. Companies that have our backs. Companies that kick pit bulls like this:

- Pick a fight on behalf of the underdog
- Rescue a process or principle
- Restore manners
- Strip apathy
- Sink a ship promoting selfish peace
- Fix a leaky ship waging a selfless war

- Urge behavioral suicide for wrongdoers
- Talk the beloved but confused off the ledge

## IV. Tell on Yourself

Legal counsel, insurers, and government relations specialists will all try to convince you not to do it. Telling on yourself exposes an organization to liability, litigation, and regulatory scrutiny. It could harm profits and reputations. It could do irreversible damage. It could cause pain, embarrassment, and financial duress. It could also save your company and its reputation. Telling on yourself before someone else does affords an organization an opportunity to steer the narrative even in the stormiest of times. Telling on yourself makes a statement to the world. It says what words cannot. It communicates your organization's priorities. It tells the world it is more important than the blemish on the company's cheek. It communicates honesty and transparency. It begins the healing process immediately following the creation of a wound. It puts the world on notice that you are trustworthy. That you value people, the environment, and property. Telling on yourself exposes you for what you are: a courageous truth-teller worthy of loyalty and business. Worthy of another chance. It's the ultimate indicator of confidence. Being self-critical prevents organizations from being self-defensive. Telling on yourself forges bonds between your organization and those to whom you are confessing. Doing so will prompt customers to seek out your company despite inconveniences and in spite of less transparent competitors. Telling on yourself creates new markets. Markets that do not exist for competitors that hide their mistakes. Tell on yourself like this:

- Break your own heart
- Tell people the bad news
- Announce disappointments
- Embrace error

- Tell the world when you are mistaken
- Tell people when you are wrong
- Tell them why
- Show them how you've already fixed what was broken
- Show them how to avoid breaking their own hearts

## V. Whisper

Everyone is screaming today. They scream traditionally. They scream socially. They scream publicly. And they scream constantly. Individual screams are nearly impossible to decipher. They become faceless. They lose their individuality. They are forced into a kingdom of screams where none stick out. Where none excel. Where none hit their target. Screaming louder is futile. It's a waste of time. It's a waste of money. It's ineffective. Instead of screaming—whisper. Whispering is a smart PR technique that calls attention to your message. It violates boundaries rather than observing them. Whispering in a crowd of screamers forces listeners to draw closer. It creates mystery. It communicates importance. It sets you apart from the masses. It forces listeners to remember you. It creates loyalty. It communicates to listeners they are important. Important enough to break from the screaming pack and invest in something different. It tells listeners they are special. It respects audiences. It does not treat them as others do. Whispering singles out audiences as special. It communicates message importance. It trusts that audiences value quality content. Whispering prompts people to lean in closer. They'll work harder to receive quality. It respects a listener's time and well being. Whispering is rewarded when done like this:

- Whisper when you are right
- Scream when you are wrong
- Be modestly soft
- Be not arrogantly loud

- Run over budget for good reason
- Remain under budget during times of excess
- Tell everyone why
- Show customers what you learned from them
- Tell them what you did with those lessons
- Forgive them for straying
- Invite them back
- Learn the names of their children
- Ask for help
- Write a letter
- Run when you can walk
- Walk when others are running
- Slow down when everything speeds up
- Speed when others slow

## VI.  Reveal a Secret

A distance exists between large organizations and their stakeholders. Customers suspect the curtain is in place to keep them from seeing something. Something ugly. Something menacing. Something that may cause them to choose differently. The façade is built of self-interest. It is fortified by protectionism. It is maintained with secrecy. The barrier assumes people cannot or will not understand. It assumes people will make snap judgments. It assumes they will not forgive. Rather than add to the barrier, surprise people. Tell them a secret. Secrets are treasures. They are valuable. Those who receive them feel trusted. They feel special. They feel chosen. They guard the secret with all they have. They feel closer to the secret giver. The act of revealing a secret positions the secret giver as vulnerable. The secret giver trusts the secret receiver with this vulnerability. It is a big responsibility. One that comes with risk. The secret receiver feels obligated to protect the secret giver. Why? We are all vulnerable. We want others to be gentle with our vulnerability. So we are gentle with theirs. Revealing a secret spurs reciprocity.

Organizations that reveal secrets are in turn trusted with commitment and business. Reveal secrets like this:

- Rescue a competitor
- Help an industry avoid a mistake you've made
- Teach a reporter where to look
- Don't tell someone when they're lost
- Give directions to those who aren't
- Explain why you don't have to
- Tell them why you must
- Make time when you have none
- Don't waste it when you do
- Expect more
- Prepare for less
- Call even when you need nothing
- Answer the phone when you do

## VII. Blindfold a Clock

Clocks can't see but we see them. That's the problem. No matter what we do we have either too much or too little time. It's a universal problem. It both hinders and helps people across cultures, regions, and ethnicities. The same fighter saved by the bell in one instance will find himself needing additional time to make a comeback in the next. Vacations don't last long enough. Runs on the treadmill last too long. Time flies. Time stands still. Counting time is a distraction. It causes angst and worry. It does not allow us to be our best. Instead of counting time, smart PR requires us to ignore it. Blindfold the clock in front of you. Cover the treadmill clock with a towel. Stop looking at your watch on vacation wishing it weren't already the end. Blindfolding clocks removes distractions. It allows people to focus on a task not a time. Blindfolding clocks allows organizations to set healthy deadlines. Deadlines often push quality forward. People under deadline pressure often invest less upfront. They're in a hurry to get to the end. To meet the goal. So they are less focused on the task in the beginning. Later, as the deadline approaches and the person knows the goal is attainable, they are able to better focus on the task. Quality increases on the back end. They are not preoccupied with time. They are task-focused rather than time- focused. Being task-focused evenly distributes quality. It avoids mistakes and oversights associated with being hurried. Deadlines are important. They exist for sound reasons. They must be met. But work expands to fill the time allotted. It's inefficient. Quality is inconsistent. Organizations can remedy both by blindfolding clocks like this:

- Befriend uncertainty
- Invite belatedness
- Praise unexpected earliness
- Announce earnings misses early
- Announce earnings beats late
- Update regional sales midway through a quarter
- Don't update them at all the next
- Eat breakfast food for dinner
- Eat it again at breakfast
- Eat nothing the next day
- Offer a little now
- Work on the rest for later
- It's new again when it's complete

## VIII.  Hire Hookers & Steal from Kids

Expectations, like rules, are made to be broken. They are fluid and reset often. Managing expectations is one of the tallest orders a business faces. Set expectations too high or too low and you disappoint. Disappoint regularly and risk losing face, trust, and customers. Instead of trying to game the expectation game, smart PR requires you perform in a manner that violates expectations.

Routinely violating expectations erodes the power inherent in expectations. It hits the reset button. It forces people to pay closer attention to what you have to say. It forces people to measure you differently. It forces them to use the yardstick you provide. It affords you a greater degree of control over narratives, deadlines, and markets. Changing how you are measured externally allows you to reset the rules and manage expectations on your own terms. Fundamentally changing how expectations are set gains you a competitive advantage. Instead of narrowing the expectation range, broaden it. Give yourself room. Create your own measuring tape. Give it away. Prompt them to measure what you want them to measure. Exceed expectations. Miss them. Succeed in doing both. Create a state of mind. Shock them when they expect to be underwhelmed. Underwhelm when they expect you to shock.

Do it like this:

- Pay hookers to talk
- Swear in front of a pastor
- Be on your best verbal behavior around sailors
- Steal from a child
- Give away good ideas
- Keep the bad
- Don't give to a charity
- Explain why
- Donate to the rich
- They'll give to the poor
- Fight up
- Be kind down
- Work on vacation
- Vacation while you work
- Cry when you are happy
- Smile when you are sad

- Listen to the ignorant
- Ignore the know-it-all

## IX. Dump Your Fiancé

You're not right for everyone. You're not right for most people. You're only right for a select few. It's that select few who deserve your undivided focus. Organizations should not try to be all things to everyone. Those that do will be nothing to anyone. So stop being selfish. Smart PR requires that you dump your fiancé'. Be honest. Probe deeply. Look hard. If your fiancé' is not the one—cut her loose. Things may seem good. The two of you may get along just fine. You might even like your fiancé'. But once you determine your fiancé' is not the one—you must break it off. Your fiancé will not understand. In fact she doesn't even know there's a problem. That's the beauty. You are solving a problem someone else does not know exists. You are affording your fiancé' time to find a true match she otherwise would have wasted had you not dumped her. You are breaking a heart. You are the bad guy. You are giving a gift. You are being kind. You are setting yourself apart from the pack. You're not like the other guys. Initially there'll be anger. Your fiancé will not understand. She'll yell at you. She'll cry. She will no longer speak to you. Eventually though, she'll thank you. She'll thank you for the time you gave her. For the sacrifice you made. For your honesty. For your integrity. For making a difficult decision. For solving a problem she did not know existed. Seek out problems. Look hard for them. Look for them in unexpected places. Look for them in obvious places. Solve them like this:

- Alert competitors to danger
- Keep secrets from your friends
- Show people why they don't need your product
- Introduce them to a competing product they do need
- Minimize solutions

- Elevate distractions

## X. Listen to your Dad

It never goes away. It's always there. It's the little voice in your head telling you- you can't. Telling you, you're due to fail. Convincing you, you are not good enough. Ignoring the voice doesn't work. It laughs if you ask it to stop. The voice is blind. It doesn't see your successes. It doesn't see your wins. At least it doesn't let on that it does. It berates you regardless. As a child, my father routinely told me I could do anything I put my mind to. He was right. Corporations should listen to their dads. Believe. You already have the tools. Discover them. Get them out. Learn to use them. Screw up. Learn. Do it again. Make something. Demolish it. Start over. You can do it. You've done it. You can do it again. Your way. On your time. On your terms. That voice will not go away. It will always try to convince you, you'll fail. No matter the amount of success you'll always have a fight on your hands. But it's a fight you can teach yourself to win. Create your own voice to counter the negative voice. Nourish the created voice. Teach it to be strong. Teach it to win. Convince yourself the negative voice is wrong. That you are right. Make the rules. Change them. Win. You can do it. Listen to your dad:

- Predict the future
- Misremember the past
- Get help lifting something light
- Lift heavy weights yourself
- Befriend the lonely
- Leave the popular alone
- Celebrate loss
- Mourn victory

Congratulations!

If you've read this far you're part of the team. A team itching to break out. Loners who are scattered across geographies and industries. People whose voices have been drowned out by the institutional acceptance of mediocrity. You're looking to rid yourselves of the mental and physical PR constructs the world has been tricked into accepting as best practices.

**The 10 Content Commandments** are a guide by which you can live your new PR life. One that's free from the shackles of traditional messaging and distribution. **The 10 Content Commandments** are permanent-crafted to withstand changes in technology and time.

They are yours.

Allow them to guide you.

However, there are two strings attached.

The content these commandments inspire must be given away-available to thieves and those with the potential to harm you. When executed properly, content emanating from these commandments will be infrequent and scarce.

Both topics are addressed briefly in the final two sections of the book.

Thanks for coming this far- for taking this trip.

For breaking out.

# Scarcity Value

The era of big data is only getting bigger.

User-generated content is growing at unprecedented rates. Google's Eric Schmidt argues the amount of this information doubles every two years.

Very little of this data is actually new though.

Much of the user-generated data is simply a compilation of data already in existence that has been reconfigured or topped off with an opinion. Existing data is simply broken down, rearranged, and personalized for publishing.

Quantity is not to be confused with quality. Even the well-intentioned produce data junk. Failure and folly are produced. Conversations once had verbally are now translated via technology designed to create more data.

Increasing amounts of data junk make it harder to stand out. The more junk standing between your message and its intended target, the harder it is to make a connection. When connections are made they can quickly be disrupted. Big data can distract. Big data can interrupt. Big data can break connections prematurely.

The traditional reaction would be to create more content. Meet volume with volume. Scream louder. Scream more frequently. The more you produce the better your chance of hitting your target audience. The one that produces the most will be easiest to find, right?

By now you know it's more complicated.

Voluminously producing content in the form of a cheap commodity lessens the potential impact of the content. If people can get something similar, why consume yours? If there is a race to the bottom, why would they pay more for yours? That's the sad life of a commodity. If the content you produce is commoditized, this is what you can expect. This is your future. It's not much of a future. It's bleak and boring.

Instead, smart PR has scarcity value.

Not that it has much of a choice.

High value content is in short supply in a world filled with data junk. Creating premier content requires a large investment. Financial capital, human capital, and temporal capital are necessities. Fortunately for you, most organizations are unwilling or incapable of making these investments.

It means truly premier content is rare.

The value of authentic premier content will not be derived from the cost to produce it. Instead, its value will hinge upon its quality and rarity.

*"Saying too much of something is the same thing as saying nothing."*

*- Johnny Cash*

Your words, ideas, and content should be produced selectively. In a world of data junk, your choice of standards will either separate you from the pack or afford you a place within it. Those with the highest standards will stand out. They'll lead. They'll control their fate. And their narrative. It is extremely difficult and time consuming to produce content of such quality.

That's why it is in such short supply.

That's why there is such a demand for it.

It's similar to the power an elder holds over a particular group. The elder doesn't speak often. The elder rarely increases the supply of his words. However, when the elder does speak everyone listens. His words are in such short supply there is great demand for them. The elder's words contain insight. They are respected. They are trusted. They are special.

Be the content elder of your industry.

Speak infrequently.

But speak with importance when you do.

# The Thief Model of Distribution

Successful people who enjoy good fortune in love, money, and finance are just lucky, right?

Everything falls their way. They get breaks the rest of society doesn't. Their success is written in the stars and was predetermined by forces that simply don't smile down upon the rest of the world as kindly, right?

Professor Richard Wiseman disagrees.

Wiseman, an experimental psychologist at Britain's University of Hertfordshire, spent ten years studying luck, conducting experiments between the self-proclaimed "lucky" and "unlucky", and compiled his findings in a book entitled *The Luck Factor: The Scientific Study of the Lucky Mind.*

Wiseman concludes, "People are not born lucky. Instead, lucky people are, without realizing it, using four basic principles to create good fortune in their lives." In essence, Wiseman scientifically concludes that people make their own luck.

If we can create something as fascinating and intangible as our own luck, we can also create our own premier content.

After we do so, we must do something that at first blush may strike us as insane.

We must give it away.

It must be free.

I call this the thief distribution model but in reality it is charity. Media consumers will steal the content and re-disseminate it on their terms. In reality though, content that is given away cannot be stolen. It's a charitable donation to those craving content. To those who did not know intrinsically they needed our content. The benefit of a charitable donation is generally realized at tax time. But in this context the benefit to an organization is much greater than a single tax break.

The benefits of giving away the content accumulate.

Distributing content for free is counterintuitive to corporations that are often forced to legally protect their intellectual property; create something of value, then give it away or let others steal it and profit from it emotionally or financially. But the theft of your company's creation by a new influencer with sticky fingers is how an agile, smart PR department must function.

Theft is pervasive.

Corporations spend fortunes protecting intellectual property and preventing theft.

They are right to do so.

However, premier content is different.

That's not to say it's worth any less. It simply means optimum distribution depends on it. And why would you want to withhold or hide magnificent content?

An entire generation expects content to be free. Members of this generation grew up in a world of free or stolen content. This is the Napster generation. They've been empowered by technology. They feel they deserve it at no cost. The mindset has been reinforced by the newspaper industry which decided to give away its only product online.

Thankfully, your business model does not rely on the free distribution of content for its only source of revenue.

Content theft is a crime toward which many turn a blind eye. Rarely is anyone ever prosecuted for content theft in the court of public opinion. Why? Because a juror one day will be a thief the next.

Once again, smart PR staffs must transform their mindsets.

They must not view this distribution model as theft. Smart PR staffs will come to embrace the model as an investment. Distributing premier content is the fruit of a creator's labor. Seeing it elsewhere, in its original form, invigorates content creators. It's a sign of success when someone swipes it.

Sell your watchdog. Send back your surveillance cameras. And remove the lock from your content gate.

The news you produce is available to thieves without consequence.

You are an aggressive giver.

You are a creator.

Embrace it.

Enjoy it.

Break out!

# About the Author

## Nick Winkler

**N**ick started *The Winkler Group*, a strategic communications firm that helps entrepreneurs, risk takers, and small businesses create and steer narratives that add value. His book, *Break Out of PR Prison: Make & Measure Your Own News in an Era of Crisis*, shows readers how to disrupt the storytelling process, vaccinate their reputations against crises, and measurably reduce their cost per message.

It saves organizations money.

The book identifies the assumptions inherent in traditional messaging, replaces the status quo with counterintuitive messaging strategies, and helps organizations become less dependent on outside messaging firms.

The book has been a complete flop with outside firms.

Nick has been fortunate enough to create communications handbooks, messaging guides, and crisis communications manuals for a number of industries and professions. A few have actually used them! His professional development workshops are often packed with doers, fixers, and starters who simply haven't recognized themselves as such.

As an entrepreneur he's started several companies. Most of them have failed. He worships the lessons each has taught.

Nick is a farm kid. He grew up raising cattle, hay, and hell. When something on the farm would break, he had little choice but to engineer a country solution without help from a map or manual.

He's a fixer.

And now he uses that same self-reliance, ingenuity, and inventiveness to fix messaging problems for organizations whose narratives have been hijacked.

# Break Out of PR Prison

While he prefers to partner with those who are already brave enough to demolish the messaging status quo, he's most proud when given an opportunity to help those clinging to convention find the courage to create and break out.

*The Winkler Group* only partners with those willing to hold it as accountable as it holds itself. Remember, Nick helps entrepreneurs, risk takers, and small businesses create and steer narratives that add value. And he proves that value by measuring what he helps you make.

In a former life, when Nick wasn't fighting the urge to ride the rodeo in Texas, he was one of the better investigative television news reporters in the country. Nick has won a lot of awards you've probably never heard of. His work as an investigative reporter has exposed corruption, illegal activity, and inefficiencies nationwide. His work has sparked legislative hearings, changes to state law, and has sent bad people to prison for years. His work has been featured on ABC, CNN, FOX News and a bunch of network affiliates you probably don't get on your television.

Many of the people featured in his stories don't like him.

Nick is different from the others not because he breaks the rules but because he resets them. If you're still playing by someone else's rules you're at a distinct disadvantage.

Nick can change that.

He's a tenacious preparer and one of the best storytellers around.

Nick bounces all over the country making sure organizations are the primary narrators of the story they want to tell.

He'd be flattered to help create and tell yours.

Nick Winkler

# THE WINKLER GROUP
## STRATEGIC COMMUNICATIONS

**www.thewinklergroup.net**